827-0401

Our Guerrillas, Our Sidewalks

Our Guerrillas, Our Sidewalks
A Journey into the Violence of Colombia

Herbert Braun

UNIVERSITY PRESS OF COLORADO

© 1994 by the University Press of Colorado
P.O. Box 849
Niwot, Colorado 80544

All rights reserved.

Printed in the United States of America.

The University Press of Colorado is a cooperative publishing enterprise
supported, in part, by Adams State College, Colorado State University,
Fort Lewis College, Mesa State College, Metropolitan State College of
Denver, University of Colorado, University of Northern Colorado,
University of Southern Colorado, and Western State College of
Colorado.

Cover photograph by Herbert Braun.

Library of Congress Cataloging in Publication Data

Braun, Herbert, 1948–
    Our guerrillas, our sidewalks : a journey into the violence of
    Colombia / Herbert Braun.
       p.   cm.
    Includes bibliographical references.
    ISBN 0-87081-356-0. — ISBN 0-87081-357-9 (pbk.)
    1. Gambini, Jake, 1932–   —Kidnapping, 1988. 2. Hostage
negotiations—Colombia. 3. Guerrillas—Colombia. 4. Violence—
Colombia. I. Title.
HV6604.C72G363 1994
364.1'54'09861—dc20   94-33877
                                                  CIP

The paper used in this publication meets the minimum requirements
of the American National Standard for Information Sciences—
Permanence of Paper for Printed Library Materials. ANSI Z39.48–1984
∞

10 9 8 7 6 5 4 3 2 1

CONTENTS

This book is based on a number of different sources: (1) taped interviews that I conducted with the protagonists during the week of Thanksgiving 1988, three weeks after the events described herein came to a close; (2) my notes taken during the events, including taped recordings of all but one of the telephone conversations that served as the basis of the negotiations with the Colombian guerrillas; (3) interviews with leaders of the guerrilla movement conducted by journalists and published in Colombia; (4) a Colombian government–sponsored report on contemporary forms of violence intended for wide public distribution; and (5) newspaper reports and magazine articles published in Colombia and in the United States that I read while the events were taking place and shortly thereafter. I am responsible for the translations from Spanish into English. Notations on the sources used appear at the end.

I have changed the names of those who helped us during these events in order to ensure their privacy. I have kept the aliases that the guerrillas used as they negotiated with us. Their anonymity is thereby preserved.

It's been many years now that we've been in this struggle. We've had, I think, one enemy, the worst of all enemies. You know what it is? I'm talking about the isolation of this struggle, which is worse than going hungry for a whole week. Between you, you of the city and us, we who've been out here, there is a huge mountain. It's not a distance of lands and rivers, of natural obstacles. Your voices and ours don't speak to each other. There's little about us that's known among you, and around here there's little of your history that we know.

— "Tirofijo" ("Sureshot"),
Colombia's preeminent guerrilla leader since
1949, currently head of the Revolutionary
Armed Forces of Colombia (FARC), speaking
sometime in the 1960s, somewhere
in the mountains of Colombia

Our Guerrillas, Our Sidewalks

TAKING

TICO

I knew what had happened just outside the village thousands of miles away when the phone rang a few hours later in my home in Charlottesville. It was still dark in Colombia that early in the morning. Most everyone was asleep, even though rural people out there rise early. They surrounded the entire area, gained control of the roads, and made sure that nothing would go wrong. Before anyone but a few of his guards could know what had happened, they were gone.

It felt as though I were out there in the jungle with him. And with them. I could tell you right then what they had done to take him away, even what they had said to him, and also how they would keep him day after day, far away in some isolated camp, always under a heavy cover of trees so that the army helicopters wouldn't detect that they were down there.

It's not that I, too, have been taken away by them or that a friend of mine has. I haven't been close to an experience like this one, at least not in a personal way. I was out there only for a weekend once many years ago. But I knew why they had taken him.

What I couldn't know was that this was the phone call that would bring the news I'd come to expect, that the time had arrived to hear those three dreaded words that had been out there for years, ready to be said, waiting to take us deep into the violence of Colombia.

This was the morning, with the day's third, or maybe even fourth, large mug of coffee already in hand, that I looked down longingly at the empty chair. I wasn't going to be settling down with the morning paper to carefully inspect the tiny box with the results of the latest stage of the bicycle race in Europe that was usually hidden away in the last page or so of the sports section. Cycling was on my mind. I always go for the sports pages first, but there's a special urgency in the summer when the racing season is in full swing. Our cyclists are famous. They're climbers. They ride high above the rolling hills where the coffee grows, scaling the long, steep inclines of three rugged Andes ranges that also isolate many of the nation's lawless regions. I've even told friends, although in jest, that Cecilia and I named our two children after Colombia's most famous cyclist.

I remember taking a small sip because the hot liquid was resting in my mouth when the phone rang in the kitchen. Still perspiring from the bike ride with the neighbors and shivering slightly, bending over in the morning sunshine to leave the mug on the windowsill, I recognized that I needed it next to me. After years of trying all kinds of shortcuts, I had returned to the German-made porcelain Melitta filter that my mother still uses, but only after finally recognizing that the espresso roasted and extra finely ground beans render a dark, clear liquid like no other when it drips slowly through that one tiny hole.

The paper was under my right arm. Holding onto the mug, I had to use my foot to help open the screen door. The phone had already rung at least twice. It was too early for anyone to call. Had somebody maybe dialed the wrong number? If not, it would be bad news about Cecilia and the children in Mexico City or about my aging mother living all alone back in Colombia. Something had happened to one of them. The *Washington Post* fell onto the dining room table as I brushed past it. I carefully sat the mug on the cabinet next to me. My sister was calling from her home in Houston. Her voice wasn't easily recognizable, not at first.

"Tico?"

I must have sounded differently, too. But it was Ulla all right, asking whether it was me. Tico is my nickname, and most everybody, even my undergraduate students, know me by it, and I much prefer it to the Germanic Herbert that my parents loaded on me at birth. And besides, Tico makes me more like a Colombian.

Looking down into the coffee, I was filled with the realization that something had happened to my mother.

"Tico," she said again. "They took Jake."

I could feel my left hand holding onto my head. There they were. The three words.

"Where?"

"In Sabana."

Sabana de Torres. It was the village were Jake worked, where the company had its largest camp. They had got him way out there in the countryside. Jake was gone. It had happened.

Suddenly, strangely, I found that I had a second or two to take a big breath, for this deep feeling of calmness came over me. It wasn't relief that the news wasn't about my mother or about Cecilia and the children. And neither did it come simply from knowing that we were all still alive.

This was a feeling that would become so much a part of our lives. It came immediately. I did know what had happened, and that in itself must have been a relief. But what really must have reassured me at the time was the belief, the conviction actually, that I knew what would happen in the days to come.

Maybe I remember my first reaction so distinctly because I had probably never thought much about how I would feel once the news arrived. Or because my reaction was so at odds with the news. Right at the moment when we were thrust into a situation where others were in total control, not only of Jake and his life but also of all of us, I was feeling that little could go wrong. Maybe the news was just too predictable and not only for us but for others as well. After all, few would be surprised to read in a newspaper that a man by the name of Iacopo "Jake" Gambini, an American oil executive, had been kidnapped by Marxist guerrillas in Colombia.

In any case, it's pretty clear that I didn't invent that feeling, and neither did I have to convince myself that I should have it. It was just there. Or maybe I remember it so well because we've all been trying so hard to hang onto it. When they came for him early that morning three months ago, it did all seem so predictable. Now each day, every hour really, is wearing on us, and we no longer know what's going on. Everybody here is playing it by ear. These are the words we all keep using again and again. Playing it by ear. Going one day at a time.

We've been ready almost from the start to take care of anything that might happen. After those initial hours of confusion following the phone call, we knew what had to be done. We've been prepared. Everyone has worked hard. But it's been of little use.

Now we're waiting, hoping to hear from them. I think we are beginning to wonder whether we will ever see him again. All this feels so much worse now than when Ulla's first phone call came. It's hard to explain, but my optimism is gone. I really don't think this will end well. It just doesn't seem right. Something is wrong. The problem is that I can't put my finger on what that something is. This is a terrible feeling to be living with, especially because I'm the one who is supposed to know. Ulla is counting on me.

But there is no doubt that this kidnapping has a bad smell to it. I think we all know it, but none of us dares to say what is going on in our minds. We don't say anything that might reveal our doubts. We are so careful with each other that it almost hurts to talk. There is a really heavy feeling here.

And then there's him. It's a strange feeling. He's dead to us but alive to others. He's gone from my and Ulla's life, and gone from the children, yet he's alive and suffering. It feels as though his kidnapping is worse than his death. Except that he might still come back to us. But if he does, what will he have gone through? Will he be all right?

But back then when Ulla called, there was that sense that we knew what the guerrillas would do. Everything was going to work itself out. It was supposed to.

So it was that I had taken that long breath, standing there in the kitchen. Jake was gone. It had to be the guerrillas that had him, probably the Army of National Liberation, the ELN, because it's the most powerful guerrilla organization out there.

Tico

For I understood that the guerrillas weren't going to hurt him. Right then I knew that. And I still believe it. For, after all, I do have plenty of good reason to. I know what the guerrillas are up to. But now I can also sense the need to believe in them, and I know that we've all been working hard to keep that feeling because there really isn't any other way to live through this. They have to return him to us.

ULLA

I wasn't at all nervous when Jake told me he was going to spend the night out there. He'd been in Sabana before. Well, not at night, at least not recently. But I knew that if he was thinking of staying overnight, that it was all right. He's no fool. But then I was never told how bad things were down there either. I would've been up here worrying all the time. But that wasn't right either. I should've known more.

I was so scared when I got that call from Vicente. I sat there stunned, thinking about what I had to do. All of a sudden it all happens. Something that was always in the background, all of sudden it's there. You've got to do the best thing. But what? I was scared because Jake wasn't in control. How do you tell your kids that their father's been kidnapped? I mean, all of a sudden you're dealing with outlaws, with guerrillas. How do you deal with a situation when there's guerrillas involved? Guerrillas are bad people.

JAKE

When they came I thought they were workers from a rig who were looking for me so that I could help them out somewhere. Then I saw all the guns and I knew. There were four or five of them. A couple were in green, army-type fatigues, but the others were dressed in civilian clothes with brightly colored shirts. They were heavily armed, all of them. The leader, a bearded man, about, oh, twenty-eight, thirty years old, told me to hurry up. "*Es un secuestro. Rápido. No le va a pasar nada.*" "This is a kidnapping," he said. "Quick. Nothing's gonna happen to you."

As I got up, my dog started to bite at them. I scuffled with them, just sort of pushing them away. I might have hit one. But they said they would shoot the dog. I said "No. Don't shoot him. I'll come along." I was thinking of going off, of running. When we got outside, the watchman told me to go with them, that they wouldn't hurt me.

They grabbed my arms and pushed me out the gate into the truck. We headed out with me in the middle between the driver and the bearded one, and some of the other men in the back. We passed another car or truck, and there were more of them in there, probably about three or four. We went down the road, passed by the landing strip, and started going west. It was about 4:30, somewhere along in there. It was still dark. Very dark.

We must have traveled ten, twelve miles. He was having trouble shifting, and they were having trouble keeping up with each other, one car going way ahead. They would cuss. It was a sandy road. The truck in front of us stopped, and the other one pulled up behind us. They made me get into the other one. Same guys. I got in the middle again. We didn't talk. No conversation. Nothing was said. I tried to see if I could grab the steering wheel and go off into a ditch. Crash. Get away. Escape.

TICO

Jake was gone. There was work to be done. I had to think and get rid of all of my emotions. And they did just seep out quickly. I knew what we were up against, that this was something we could handle.

7:27. Looking at the digital clock on the microwave that had just heated up the coffee, I realized that they must have taken him a few hours ago, really early in the morning. He'd probably already been gone for hours, long before I'd gotten on the bike for that little spin with the neighbors. Maybe they took him while I was writing and waiting for the paper to be delivered. Was there a time difference with Colombia in the summer? After living for almost twenty years in the States, I still could not remember.

Jake always woke up so early, 3:30, 4:00, to work. It's one of the few things he and I have in common. That and coffee. Looking down at the cup again, I wondered whether he had been able to drink his. It was always the first thing he did.

Maybe they wouldn't have taken him if he hadn't been up and about. . . .

"Tico. It's happened! It's happened!"

Ulla was still on the phone. I didn't know what to tell her. The future had caught up with us. Now it was a reality. It was all too obvious, all too knowable.

Why in the hell had he kept insisting on going back out there?

For years I'd made sure that Ulla knew where to reach me should something happen to our mother, but also in case this happened to him out there in the middle of what is called the Magdalena Medio, a huge, rich valley that lies between two of those mountain ranges. The guerrillas have a great deal of power there, and the government and the army only at times make their presence known.

Jake had always said that he had good relationships with all the different groups that operated out there. His company was the major employer in town. He kept saying that his workers respected him and that they knew they were doing better with him than working for anyone else in the region. Nobody had any reason to bear him a grudge.

That's the way he always put it. Bearing a grudge. His words. Not mine. But this had nothing to do with holding grudges. The guerrillas had ample reason to kidnap him. He employed people. He had others work for him, and it was through their labor that he had become rich. Good treatment of workers didn't do anything to change those central facts. That didn't mean anything to the guerrillas. Jake was a capitalist.

"Tico. Tico? I can't believe it. What are we going to do?"

But what could I tell her? I knew she was calling for support, for help. I know all about the guerrillas, for I am not like the other members of the family. My politics don't fit either, and I always used to say that the Americans should get out of Colombia, that the oil ought to belong to the nation. I sympathized with the guerrillas' ideals and kept having this gnawing feeling that I belonged with them. It's not that I'm the black sheep of the family or anything quite like that, but I hadn't gone into the business world or done anything that was really productive. I became a historian.

A few years ago I wrote a book, something like an oral history, about a day in Bogotá in 1948, for which I interviewed all kinds of people. That's what I do. I like to ask people questions about their past and about how they remember it, especially when they all remember it in vastly different ways and have conflicting views about it and about what is right and what is wrong. And that's what I had been doing early that morning before Ulla's call. This time it was about Mexican memories of the student protest movement of 1968.

But right then that day in 1948 was all around me again as I tried to think about Ulla, knowing full well that this was not the time to be roaming around in the past. But it was just over forty years ago, a Friday afternoon in April a few months before I was born, when Jorge Eliécer Gaitán, the rebel leader of the Liberal Party and the country's most popular politician, was assassinated in downtown Bogotá. Angry crowds protested and looted, and they broke into the downtown hardware store where my father worked as the manager. My father always told me that Gaitán was little more than a demagogue who irresponsibly aroused the emotions of the poor, whose emotions, he always added, were all too easy to arouse.

Colombians believe that Gaitán's death and the riot, known as the *bogotazo*, are a major turning point in Colombia, and they trace its descent into violence, into hell, to that day. There was one nation before the *bogotazo* and another one after. After Gaitán came *la Violencia*, a rural war in which as many as two hundred thousand Colombians lost their lives. Poor and middling people who felt they were Conservatives went around killing Liberals. Liberals did the same to Conservatives. The fighting out in the countryside seemed so senseless, so difficult to comprehend, that few Colombians to this day really have a feeling that they know what happened, and historians still don't quite know what to say about it. But most everyone believes that in some crucial way April 9, 1948, split history in two.

The guerrilla movement emerged years later, in the 1960s, out of the bands that had initially fought *la Violencia* in the name of the leaders of the Liberal Party. But when the urban leaders of that party returned to conventional forms of politics with their Conservative counterparts, the rural guerrillas were left out in the cold, struggling to defend themselves against the army. I have long believed that the guerrillas developed because the Liberal Party leaders turned their backs on their peasant followers and kept silent as the Conservatives went about violently dismantling all forms of independent and Liberal rural organization.

Whatever *la Violencia* actually was, I have always known that few, if any, of the leaders suffered from it and that it was regular people, rank-and-file members of the two parties, who lost their lives, their lands, their livelihoods. In Colombia, it's really always the poor who get left behind, holding onto the short end of the stick.

For me, Gaitán represented Colombia's last hope for a society without the most glaring disparities of wealth and power that I'd seen growing up. And right then I couldn't shake the idea that Jake's kidnapping had its roots in Gaitán's assassination. Colombia would have been an entirely different country had that day not happened. Would the guerrilla movement have become so powerful? Would he really have been taken away if there wasn't an "after Gaitán"?

I'd been hoping for years that some kind of a compromise could be found, some sort of an understanding between the government and the guerrillas, something to put a stop to all the years of fighting. At the same time I have always known, of course, that a compromise was impossible. The guerrillas had too many reasons to keep fighting, and the government didn't really feel the need to defeat the guerrillas, assuming that it could if it tried. But I still hoped. It never happened. The guerrillas are still out there.

It was back in 1965 when I was a teenager that Camilo Torres, an upper-class Catholic priest who yearned for justice in Colombia, got into a black taxi just a block from our house and left for the mountains to join the ELN, at the time a pro-Castro group that wanted to bring the Cuban Revolution to Colombia. A few months later Camilo was gone, shot dead by the army. He had turned back in the midst of a hurried retreat to pick up a rifle, to keep it for the revolution. In that instant he had been shot. Camilo had thought the revolution was coming. Nobody back then could possibly have imagined that the guerrillas would still be in the mountains more than twenty years later.

Hundreds, even thousands, of them are still out there fighting. Many are dead. Others come to take their places. And now Jake was with them. Their faces kept staring up at me as I tried to come up with something to tell Ulla.

There was Tirofijo, or "Sureshot," the famous leader of the FARC, the Revolutionary Armed Forces of Colombia. It is the oldest and largest of all the groups. And Manuel Pérez, the former Spanish priest who is the commander of the ELN. He's mysterious. Nobody knows much about him. He doesn't talk to the press. Everybody just keeps talking about a big blue helicopter that transports him all over the country. Alvaro Fayad. Jaime Bateman Cayón. They founded the M-19 guerrilla movement after years of fighting with the FARC. Those two have always had a special sort of appeal for me. And Camilo, of course. And Camilo's friend Jaime Arenas, a university student who followed Camilo into the mountains. Only Tirofijo and Manuel Pérez are still alive.

GUERRILLAS

The first days are too difficult for the man of the city, because the change is just too great. The climate is warm and humid. During the last months of the year there is an unending winter. The period of rains is rigorous in the jungle, and the paths become slippery. There's mud all over the place, and diseases. The rivers overflow, and you can't even find wood to cook with because the trees turn humid to their very heart. . . . There are moments when clouds of mosquitoes make life impossible. No doubt the worst is the *pito* [tick] which rots the flesh where it bites. It produces a sore that just keeps gnawing away, going

Our Guerrillas, Our Sidewalks

deeper and deeper. The skin starts to stick. It doesn't hurt unless you're walking through the jungle, on roots, fallen trees, stones. Then it feels like a hot iron rod is being run through you.

At night, I would fall and roll in the dirt every five minutes, because I wasn't used to walking in the jungle. After four hours of marching my feet would be a wound of open blisters. You come from the city and your skin is real delicate. Two days later, with the humidity and the mud of winter, my feet were a red open sore. We would have to walk more slowly. The *candelillas,* little insects that make the life of the guerrilla impossible in the winter, are the worst. You have to burn them with iodine. The pain is just as bad as if you put your foot on a hot iron.

—Jaime Arenas, a university student
turned guerrilla

But I soon realized that the struggle wasn't going anywhere, not the ways things were. Our little group was always small, because people got bored and left. That was when anyone who wanted to leave could, voluntarily. Many did. In those two years we could've become a large force, of a hundred guerrillas, just with all those who joined. But there was never more than twenty of us because those who came left.

We didn't get into any battles with the enemy—not with the army or the police—and those of us who thirsted for a fight, we were bored to death. Finally we'd try an ambush, but it would fail. We would set up somewhere, lie on our stomachs for eight days, but nothing happened. It wasn't a place where the army would pass by.

In the seven years that I was in the IV Front, we must have had, on average, about one action a year. . . . Sometimes we would do something, anything, like rob some animals, or kill somebody, just so that the army would come around.

—"Antonio," a guerrilla of the FARC

He felt that they wouldn't take him prisoner because he used to say that the oligarchy wouldn't be so stupid. They weren't going to keep him around as a constant banner of agitation . . . Camilo lived a constant obsession with death. For example, he often wrote that the oligarchy always killed the leaders of the *pueblo* [the people]. Like Jorge Eliécer Gaitán. Camilo would always say such things as "Power until death." One of his biggest proclamations was "A people that struggles to its death will be victorious."

Camilo started out with the idea that he'd get killed. He felt that no effort would be wasted to get him. He used to say, "I don't want them to kill me the way they killed Gaitán, on a street in Bogotá. Let them do it while I'm showing the *pueblo* how to struggle. Let them kill me with the guerrillas."

—Jaime Arenas

Since there are so few women, the men get desperate if they don't have a *compañera*. They don't know how to dominate themselves. That's why the *guerrilleros* must have clear ethical norms. Relationships among couples have to be relatively stable and public. Infidelity cannot be permitted. Although I don't pay much attention to these things, I recognize that in the guerrilla they are important. Just like it is very difficult for one of their soldiers to kill one of our guerrillas, it's really easy for a commander to exercise sexual privileges because of his position, and lose his life, or for a *guerrillera* who spends her nights from one hammock to another, to lose hers.

—Jaime Bateman Cayón, M-19 guerrilla
leader

I knew nothing of my wife during all that time, during those two years. When a *compañero* would leave on a mission, I'd ask him to find out for me. But they were all under orders not to tell me anything. I didn't know if she was alive or not, if my child was a boy or a girl. I didn't know where they were. One time a *compañera* who returned from a mission . . . told me that she'd seen them in Pereira, and she described my son to me.

—"Pacho," an FARC guerrilla

Entire months separated the skirmishes, and distanced the moments of *fiesta* of the guerrilla, when you don't feel anguish, but happiness, that tingling inside between fear and joy that tells the guerrilla that he's fighting. Time passes, and the fighting doesn't come. No battles, none of that other dimension that brings you close to life, just like torture brings you next to death.

—Alvaro Fayad, M-19 guerrilla leader

The main characteristic, not only of the FARC, but of the whole Colombian guerrilla movement beginning in the 1960s, was to engage in a few battles here and there, with the belief that the real issue of the guerrillas was political and not military.

—Jaime Bateman Cayón

JAKE

We traveled another two hours at a fairly high rate of speed, as much as could be on those back roads, and then we passed one gate, then another, a cattle gate. When we got inside, away from the road, I knew that my chance of making the truck crack up was gone. I had no chance of getting away.

We went on another half hour or so. They knew exactly where they were going. I mean, they both knew the directions very well. We got to the end of the road, as far as the truck could go. There were three or four more men there with a horse.

I rode the horse for about half an hour, forty-five minutes. Everybody else walked. We went to this one little area on a hilltop. They put the horse off to the side. We all sat down in some trees, and we smoked. I had my own cigarettes. They were looking me up and down, sizing me up. We started talking, of all things, about baseball and football.

They knew I was an American by the way I talked, and everything else, the way I was dressed. They didn't ask me who I was. But they knew. Now, you see, I don't really know if they were just the people that were ordered to go pick me up. None of them called me by my name.

After about an hour and a half the man with the beard comes back, along with another one, who is dressed all in green, with a fatigue cap on. I can see right off the bat that he was the head honcho.

Jake

He comes over and shakes my hand, and I told him, *"Bueno, buenos días, comandante."* He said that no, that he wasn't a commander, not yet. *"Todavía no, comandante,"* he said. He told me to take off my jewelry because it flashes and to give him my wallet. It would all be returned to me at the end.

I felt a little bit of . . . not anxiety, but the final realization that I'd been kidnapped. I had no identification left, my chains, my ring, my wedding ring, my bracelet, my watch, my wallet. I was giving up all my really personal things to them. It was like I was no longer myself.

It rains a couple of times, and they give me some plastic to cover myself. I smoked some more cigarettes, and about four or five o'clock that afternoon, this is a long time later, I took a nap. They sent some food up from somewhere. Rice and beans. They ate theirs out of a canteenlike thing, and they got me a tin plate and a cup of coffee. They asked me if I wanted anything else to drink, or more food, or something, but I didn't eat very much.

They brought the horse back around. It was raining a little bit. They told me to keep that plastic around me, and we started down the hill until we came into a dense area covered by trees. A lot of mosquitoes. We traveled, oh, about five minutes into these trees. Then I smelled smoke, and there was a group of about six or seven more people, both women and men, all dressed in green, they were all in uniform. They said, *"Buenas tardes, tío."* I said, *"Buenas tardes."*

They put me way in the back. I sat down on a log. It was getting dark. They brought me some food, and the bearded one stayed with me. He was in charge. He told them to set up a hammock and a mosquito net so that I could sleep. A girl came, and said, *"Bueno tío, si quiere, puede andar a dormir."* She told me I could go to sleep if I wanted to. The bearded one was there, and I asked him why they were calling me *tío,* "uncle." He said that this was just how they were going to call me.

TICO

Ulla was saying something to me. Slowly I began to make out the words.

"I'm worried about him, about what he'll do. He's not going to let them keep him. He's going to fight them. He always said they'd never take him alive. He's going to do something. Or he'll escape and they'll catch him and beat him up. They'll kill him."

There was a long pause. I'd heard Jake say things like these often enough during the years, but I had never taken his words too seriously. They were just words, bravura words from someone who was sitting right there, bragging in front of me.

But I began to realize what Ulla was saying. There was no way Jake was going to go along with all this. If there was anyone who would try to free himself, who would refuse to cooperate, it would be him.

He wasn't going to subject himself to them. This man had a mind of his own. No. More than that. Worse. He was a self-made man. He had always done things exactly the way he wanted to. He never followed orders and always worked for himself, built his own company. He made sure others didn't have any kind of leverage with him, anything that could influence his decisions. He was an individualist. Freedom, freedom of action, freedom to decide on his own life—that was what Jake had always lived for.

Jake was unlike any other person I had ever met. He commanded attention without really trying. It just happened. Others revolved around him. He was always at the center of what was happening. But he didn't seem to work at it. And he always seemed so carefree and uncomplicated, even happy-go-lucky, as though there weren't a problem in the world, or at least not one that he couldn't solve if he just put his mind to it for a few moments. He always gave the impression that he wasn't thinking, that he left that sort of thing up to other people, to professors like me, or maybe even to those who didn't have anything better to do with their lives. He did things, and he did what he did. What else, after all, was there to do? He lived.

It was as though he felt that other people were the ones who got themselves into difficult situations. And I don't think he bothered himself too much with their problems, mainly because he wasn't really interested in plight or predicament, and also because he didn't much understand how people could possibly get themselves into situations that they couldn't get out of. He expected friends and acquaintances and those who worked for him to go to him for ways to solve their difficulties. He wouldn't do a lot, because he believed that it was basically their responsibility to solve their own problems, but he would at least point them in the right direction, get them going again. Then it was up to them. He expected others to come to him, and I really doubt that he ever went to anyone else for advice. He didn't depend on anyone but himself. Well, he did come to rely on Ulla a great deal for a lot of things. But that's about it. I don't think he had any really close friends, people with whom he could unburden himself. But then I guess he probably never felt that there was much that he needed to get off his chest in the first place. That's why others revolved around him. It was never the other way around.

Tico

When I talked to him about general things, I couldn't quite be certain whether he was listening to me. It usually seemed as if he was not really there, as if what I was saying wasn't really significant, or as if it was all really obvious, so much so that it didn't have to be said. But he gave me the impression, not consciously I don't think, that his mind was also somewhere else, not engaged in anything really deep, but still elsewhere. So I felt that even if he'd listened to me, he would certainly not remember anything I'd said. He was above it all.

But then maybe a week later, or even a year, he'd go back to what I'd said to him, reminding me of my words and reacting to them, asking me something. I know that often enough I was the one who couldn't remember what I'd said to him. So once I got to know him well, I started to realize that he had a phenomenal memory and an uncanny ability to listen and that in fact he was right there most of the time (except, of course, when he fell asleep at the dinner table), soaking it all in, learning, thinking, evaluating. I discovered that, contrary to all appearances, he was always involved in details, in small facts, in figures, maybe even that as he was listening to me, he was also considering the price of pipe, figuring out how much to buy from whom and when. What I came to understand after a while was that he never stopped working, that his business was inside of him, that he was his work.

And some of us, the family and those he worked with, knew that this man who seemingly sauntered through life as though in a semi-state of consciousness kept a detailed diary of events and happenings. I asked him about that more than once, wanting to know whether he wrote down his thoughts and feelings. He always answered quickly. No, he said, he wrote down the things that had happened in the day, and he said it as though that was the only thing worth writing down, as though there were nothing else.

So I guess this is what made Jake different. Most of the people I've known who took life as seriously as he did were also very complicated people, often tortured or, at the very least, quite introspective. But Jake lived life with a rare intensity and at the same time made us feel that all of it just came naturally, that there wasn't much about life that needed to be figured out.

It seems so trite to say this, but he was always looking on the bright side of things. And I think that he was able to do so because he felt that there really was a naturalness to the world, something that allowed each and every one of us to do what we wanted. People, individuals, made their environment, made society. It was not the other way around. The individual was free. All it took was work, discipline, dedication, ambition, and he felt that these were things that everybody easily had or could acquire.

I suppose that he could have looked down on others, simply for not living the way he thought they could. But he didn't. He took people at their best and looked for that in them. Maybe his belief that we are not all the same, that human beings are not equal, that there are important differences among us, allowed him to judge others in a less demanding way than he judged himself. In any case, I can't remember him ever being mean to anybody or saying anything that was critical or hurtful. Although Ulla told us that when Jake had too much to drink, he would start telling people just what he really thought of them, and not nicely, but on a daily basis he never seemed to get angry or hold a grudge. I'm pretty sure that he was incapable of imagining anyone else holding a grudge against him.

I guess the only thing he never managed to do was quit smoking. And now it would be worse. I knew he would be smoking out there all the time, that is, if they gave him any cigarettes. Everything else always seemed pretty manageable. I mean, even though he loved to eat, he could go on these amazing diets and lose a bunch of pounds by the day. His weight could fluctuate wildly from one week to the next. If he had to lose weight, he did. The man had an incredible ability to discipline himself.

Jake was more at ease, more at home, with capitalism, with the free enterprise system, than anyone else I've ever known. Of course, most of the people I know are wary to some extent or critical of what capitalism does or can do to our lives. But still, Jake believed in the market more thoroughly and more wholeheartedly than those who worked with him in the oil business, and more than other capitalists that I've met or read about, because for him the market really was a natural thing. It was an expression of humanity, of human nature. He lived the market and the freedom he was convinced would come to everyone who would just try. Life was a matter of making decisions, having choices.

No. There was just no way that Jake was going to let them keep him. Kidnapping is the worst thing that could happen to a man like him.

He was going to fight. Maybe he would make them so angry that they would shoot him. Or he'd just bug the hell out of them. Refuse to cooperate. Play psychological games with them. They were going to go crazy with him.

That's when the realization came, at least to me, that we no longer really had any influence over him. He was gone. They had him.

I had a sense of what the guerrillas were, of course, and I knew that they would be acting responsibly. But I could get no sense of him out there. I hadn't the slightest idea what Jake would be doing. But it couldn't be good, whatever it was.

Tico

We had to get him back. Quickly. But how? I didn't know. Something had to be done. But there was nothing to do. Absolutely nothing.

We had to do something to make this a short kidnapping. The longer Jake was with them, the worse it would get. I was breathing heavily, feeling suddenly helpless.

So I told Ulla that she shouldn't worry, even though this was a pretty stupid thing to say, for there wasn't much else she could do. Still, the words seemed to make some sense.

They had to. After all, Jake wasn't dumb. He wasn't an idiot. If any American understood what was going on, it had to be him. He knew poor rural people and what the guerrillas were all about. And now that he was in their hands, he'd know that trying to escape was the worst thing he could do. He would be all right. He had to know that.

And kidnappings were nothing new to him. He understood how they worked. Besides, the guerrillas would treat him well and give him everything he needed and wanted. Once they'd received the money that we'd settle on, they would let him go. It was just a matter of time. And he was so physical. Strong. He would manage this. Mental stamina. That's what he had.

"He'll be fine. Don't worry, Sis. Jake will take care of himself. The guerrillas will treat him well. Everything is going to be okay."

But did I sound convincing? I knew that the guerrillas needed Jake alive, that they had to take care of him. That was clear. But was I also trying to prove that to myself? And what was Jake going to do?

And which group had him? Was it different in the way it dealt with kidnappings? I didn't know. There were no answers, for I had never really thought about the guerrillas that way. But they had to know what they were doing. They had to have checked up on Jake before they took him.

I did know that the guerrillas usually did a lot of research on those they were going to take away, if only to find out how much to get from the families or from the companies. Had they found out what Jake was like? I was hoping that they'd looked into his personality. If they had, they would certainly have sent their most professional people out to get him. Levelheaded sorts. Those who had done this many times before. After all, they had plenty of experienced people.

I could sense that what I had to do was to think about all the other times this had happened. To others.

Kidnappings. They occur all the time. They have become so normal that people don't really think much about them anymore. Most victims came back alive. Kidnappings are not really news anymore. Colombians accept them as a fact of life. That's how the guerrillas make their money. They take rich people. And it is hard to feel for the wealthy in Colombia. They have never given a damn for what happens to poor people, so why should anyone care about what happens to them? It's not that I believe that people should get kidnapped. But it happens. And there are reasons for it.

GUERRILLAS

Yes. I've kidnapped. I participated in the taking of the mayor of Simití, another engineer whose name I don't remember, and an *hacendado* [large landowner] from El Banco. Right now Gonzalo has these guys. He's in charge of these operations.

—Manuel Reyes Cárdenas,
chief of finances of the ELN

We utilize the term *retención* [retention] to refer more precisely to the content of our actions. We differentiate them from kidnappings because that's the term that's been used to refer to the actions of the delinquents whose only objective is personal enrichment. In our case, we temporarily deprive people of their freedom for political reasons in the context of a revolutionary war and class conflict. In many cases, the retentions include the payment of a *rescate* [ransom] to ensure the person's freedom as well as an agreement with him concerning his political, economic, and legal relations to others and to society. Moreover, the Camilista Union–Army of National Liberation makes itself responsible for the person retained. That is, society knows who has him.

—Rafael Ortíz, leader of the ELN

Just imagine. We were so poor at the beginning that we personally negotiated the rescue, the payment, with a very well-known man. We got into a car with him and drove around Bogotá. We accepted two million pesos instead of the five million we wanted.

—Iván Marino Ospina, leader of the M-19
guerrilla movement

Kidnappings should be directed against enemies of the people. Otherwise they don't fulfill a political function. What's more, we prefer to detain the representatives of multinational corporations that take out millions of dollars from the country, rather than kidnap a Colombian industrialist, who, even though he has amassed a fortune on the basis of the exploitation of his workers, has done something for the nation.

That's why we kidnapped Donald Cooper, the manager of Sears, and Nicolás Escobar Soto, the manager of Texas Petroleum. Cooper's kidnapping is the one that's netted us the most money, a million dollars. . . . On the other hand, Texas was never willing to come to an economic agreement with us. Maybe the multinational abandoned Escobar Soto because he was a Colombian. The executives of Texas must have cared little for his life when the army discovered the people's jail, and he died alongside our *compañeros*. Hopefully this experience will serve as a lesson to Colombians who sell themselves out to the multinationals: when they need help, the multinationals will certainly abandon them.

Well, yes, making a revolution costs a lot of money. . . . The M-19 manages money just like capitalists do. We have companies, we invest in stocks of important corporations, we do business.

We're not in really good shape at the moment in terms of money. . . . We want to do another kidnapping, only one, but one that would give us three million dollars. . . . That way we would solve all the financial problems of the revolution, once and for all, and at a very low political cost. You figure it out. Three million well-invested dollars give about two and a half million pesos a month. Two million and a half!

—Jaime Bateman Cayón

And since our organization has grown a lot, we've found it necessary to create a national financial commission that controls the accounts of the different groups. . . . If a certain group does not present a detailed cost accounting, it does not receive a budget for the next period.

—Felipe Martínez, of the ELN

We had to take Don Rodrigo Liévano, an *hacendado* who has a farm called "Las Vegas." I took part in the kidnapping and in the negotiations with the family. When we got the money, we gave it to Darío, our commander. And then I said to him, "Help me with my *compañera,* my woman, so that she can work independently and become a dressmaker." He didn't say anything to me, and that is how things stayed. . . .

It's very hard to be involved in work that implies a great deal of money without being able to take advantage of a single peso to help someone.

—"Pacho," a guerrilla of the FARC

TICO

With the receiver still crushing my right ear as I leaned against the dining room table, I turned the *Washington Post* around, not quite knowing why until I saw the date glaring up at me. June 24. Day one.

The thoughts jumping around in my head seemed familiar, old even, although I'd never really had them before. Ransom. That's what the kidnappings are always all about. It couldn't be a question of land because the company owned only a small tract outside the village. The guerrillas come from a long tradition of defensive peasant movements against rich landlords and outsiders bent on taking their lands away from them. Most of those who have been taken are *hacendados,* large landowners. Jake didn't fit that category.

So maybe it had to do with oil. There were three, and maybe even four, different guerrilla groups operating in the middle Magdalena valley, and the ELN had the upper hand right there where Jake worked. The *elenos,* as we familiarly know them, are the most radical, and they had become notorious again after striking a multi-million dollar deal—rumors had it as high as fifty million dollars—with a German engineering company that allowed it to build the nation's longest pipeline. It carries the crude oil north from the valley to the Caribbean coast, where it's shipped to the outside world. Now the guerrillas periodically blow up the pipeline, demanding that the oil industry be nationalized.

It couldn't really be political. But we would be in real trouble if the kidnapping was aimed at forcing the Colombian government to change its oil policies. We might never see him again. Yet the guerrillas had to know that one American hostage, or even many, wouldn't make the Colombian government change its publicly stated policies. And the guerrillas aren't stupid.

No. They had to have taken Jake for ransom. Money. That's indeed the reason most people get kidnapped. That was the only logical possibility. We would get him back.

But the idea kept lurking somewhere in the back of my mind that there was more to Jake's kidnapping. Maybe the kidnappers were a bunch of common criminals. Then we really wouldn't know what we were up against.

The drug cartels? They had recently gotten into some kidnappings, too. But why would they want to take Jake?

I asked Ulla a series of questions about how it had happened, when, where, and who was around to see Jake being taken away. We needed all the information that we could get our hands on. It was also a way of talking to Ulla. Words sounded good. I tried to be calm and professorial.

Ulla answered hurriedly. Vicente had called twenty minutes ago. He was a talented engineer who helped run the company and was Jake's close friend. He was reliable. Responsible.

Vicente had been reached at his home by the supervisor in Sabana. He had lots of information. It seems that he was pretty certain that it was the guerrillas. They came well armed and displayed a sense of discipline. There was clearly a leader in charge of the operation, and they had apparently surrounded the entire town.

All that sounded good. Common criminals wouldn't manage an operation like that. But Jake had put up something of a fight, and it had taken one of his own workers to convince him to go along. There was that horrible thought again. He wasn't going to play along.

"What are we going to do?" she asked.

Not having the slightest idea, I answered with the only words that came out of my mouth:

"Ulla, I'm going to Bogotá."

My country was already back in my gut. During the past few years, I'd tried not to think about it too much. It was too depressing. Perplexing. But I already felt as though I were back in Bogotá, surrounded by six million people, walking the streets of the city I loved and hated, hearing its sound and its music blaring from every corner.

I could smell it: the hustle and bustle of a Latin American city, that happy effervescence and vitality that I missed so much, and even the pervasive sense of conflict and of fear. I knew what it would be like to be back, to sense the peculiar combination of easygoing camaraderie and cold aggression that I breathed every day while I was growing up there.

Jake was gone. I was going home. They had him. Suddenly the violence of the country was no longer something that only touched others.

It was never supposed to reach us. We had always been far removed from the political events of the land, feeling that they had little to do with what went on "out there," outside the house and work. For thirty years out in the countryside, Jake had managed to steer clear of the conflicts that swirled around him.

Now the violence was right there, and in my life, and in the most personal, even intimate ways. And I would be talking to them, dealing with them, to try to save Jake's life.

Needing some more coffee, I tried to collect my thoughts as the black liquid disappeared slowly into the pot below. There was time. I wasn't about to start doing anything without another cup.

But there was nothing to be done. I couldn't sit down, so I paced the small house from side to side instead, the mug always in my hand. I probably kept spilling it as I was reminding myself to breathe deeply, to drink water. That was usually my advice for others, for whatever ailed them, but I didn't always manage to practice it myself. I paced and drank coffee.

The guerrillas? They are professionals. They have to know what they are doing. They did this all the time and had been around forever. They have been fighting for ages. They rarely controlled even small areas of the country on anything like a continual basis, but neither were there many areas in which they didn't have some sort of a significant presence. With sharp inequalities and widespread rural poverty, many Colombians in the countryside have long been relying on them for protection from large landlords, merchants, petty politicians, and even the military and the police, for they know full well that the government will do little for them. I knew that.

In many places the guerrillas are better established than the authorities, the military, the police, or the traditional parties with which they compete for power and influence. They have access to land and food: they direct municipal affairs, provide whatever law and order there are, and control the roads. Landlords have to pay a *vacuna*, a "vaccine," which the guerrillas tell them would keep death and destruction from coming their way. And guerrillas "ticket" people through the *boleteo*, a means of extorting money from them. The guerrillas decide who can and who cannot live and work in areas where they make their presence felt. They keep their followers in line, publicly executing those who attempt to buck orders.

It's not unusual for a soldier and a guerrilla to be walking down the same street of a village somewhere. The soldier might not know who the other man is, or he might suspect that he is a guerrilla. He might know full well.

People know who *ellos*, "they" are, even when they take off their uniforms and leave their gun behind as they go off, say, to pay a young lady an afternoon visit. Since the army and the guerrillas often recruit in the same areas, it is not unusual to find two brothers on either side of the elusive dividing line.

So the guerrillas are something like a semi-clandestine, semi-public form of local government. From their places out in the countryside, they seek to influence national affairs. They cannot be content with local power because their public ideology calls for major transformations, for a revolution. And national demands are also a way of seeking to represent their own local areas in far-off Bogotá, a way of telling local people that the national government is paying attention to them. Other groups, the military, landowners, politicians, all have connections to the capital city. The guerrillas need them also. Without them, the leaders would have a difficult time accounting for their struggle both to their own recruits and to others.

The more I thought about it, the less I worried about the guerrillas. There were just too many things in place that forced them to take good care of Jake, to give him back. But would they be able to deal with him? Jake kept haunting me. And then so many things could go wrong that I tried not to think about them. But Jake was the problem. There was no question about that.

What about the army? It was out there, too, and if Jake's group ran into them, the guerrillas would quickly shoot him. They would rather he die in a skirmish than let the army score a big publicity victory by rescuing an American captive. Maybe Jake would get sick. Did they have medicines?

And all the while I knew that he was out there already planning, scheming his escape, just thinking about it all the time. Or thinking up something that would get the guerrillas to fight one another. Something. Anything.

JAKE

Why had I gone out there to Sabana? A lot of people wouldn't, you know. But I did. I wanted to be able to say that I wasn't afraid to go out there. But I hadn't slept there in quite a bit of time. Six months. A year. You know that it's liable to happen to you. But you always say, no, it's going to happen to somebody else. Why should they kidnap me? They had more tempting targets than me.

We haven't got any labor problems. I felt we had a good organization in which all the workers were happy. The leftist groups had no quarrel with us.

They had no reason to take me or anybody else with the company because of bad treatment of the workers.

I mean, we built up a good thing out there. We worked hard during all those years. I arrived in Colombia almost thirty years ago, after I got out of the University of Texas in July of 1958. And now I was in this situation. I didn't have to have ended this way.

Back then it was pretty hard to get a job in geology. Times were hard in the oil business. I went to work with a geophysical company in Apaloosa, in Louisiana. It was an unpleasant job running jugs, these things that pick up the sound from the explosion on the line. You carry about thirty-six of them; they weigh about three pounds a piece. You walk in rice fields after they've been sprayed and come up with great big old welts all over you from those insecticides. After about a month they had to lay me off. Times were bad.

I went back to Galveston and finally got a job with Core Lab to do mud logging. They are a large outfit, so I told them that I would like to work overseas and that I could speak Spanish, which you know wasn't really true. I mean, I had taken some Spanish at the university.

One day they asked if I wanted to work in Venezuela. I said, yes, sir, I'm ready. I left on December 23. We flew from New Orleans to Havana, Cuba, and on to Caracas. That was just about ten days before Fidel Castro took over. From Caracas I went on over to Maracaibo and started working on the lake. Core Lab was about to send a crew to Colombia. Colombia had always intrigued me because I knew about the gold deposits in the mountains. I always wanted to look for gold, to go prospecting. And I had a lot of books on gold deposits of the world and hardrock mining. I'd written the Colombian consulate before, but they told me I'd have to get a working visa through a company.

This was my opportunity. On October 3 or 4 we went over to Colombia. When I got there, I was very happy. Bogotá was a tremendous town. I was twenty-seven, twenty-eight years old and single. I had the world in my hip pocket.

I went out on the first job, in Playón, in the Aguas Chicas area. Even then it was pretty violent. Not exactly kidnappings, but quite a few of the *finca* (large farm) owners were getting killed and robbed. I guess in the backwoods of Colombia the violence never did really stop.

I worked with them for about two years. They asked me to transfer someplace I didn't want to go, so I just quit. I worked independently for about six or eight months in Tolú and Sincelejo.

I started to look around for a ranch site. I flew out to the Llanos, due south of Neiva, over the *cordillera,* the "mountain range," with another

Jake

American, a young fellow, and we spent about three weeks on horseback and backpack and rode all over. There were several ranches out there for sale, about 20,000 *hectáreas* [1 hectare = 2.47 acres] for almost nothing.

I went back to Bogotá and started thinking about the long periods of time when I'd be out there by myself. It was lonely out there. So I forgot about the Llanos. I still wonder what would've happened to me. By this time I might've built it up. With all the guerrilla activity out there now, I would've had to leave it, walk away from it.

I got a job with Alvaro López, a lawyer who worked for Core Lab, who represented a couple of other companies. He didn't have anyone technical working for him that could go out and sell the products. All this was very interesting work. I gained a lot of experience and met a lot of people. Alvaro López showed me a lot of things about laws and business in Colombia.

In November of that year, 1963, I first met your sister, Ursula, or Ulla, as you all call her. I knew I was going to marry her. We started going out and we got along real well. I was going home on vacation around the fifth of December. I told her I would bring her back an engagement ring. Then when I came back I proposed to her and she accepted me. I talked to your father, and we got married in March. Nineteen sixty-four was a very eventful year for me. It was an excellent year. We got married in March, went on our honeymoon, moved into that nice little apartment. Ursula and I were very happy there, and she got pregnant. Tony was born in December, our first-born child, a boy. Everything was going all right.

But working for Alvaro López wasn't gonna do it. I realized that as long as I was working for somebody else, I wasn't really getting too far ahead. I'm a fairly independent person. I always knew I didn't want to spend my life working for somebody else.

So when I got the chance to buy General Pipe, I went for it. I had a little bit of money in the bank. My father had taught me to be pretty frugal, and I had gotten a few shares of stock from one of my uncles. It just stayed in the bank and kept growing. It's like I tell the kids: somehow or another you've got to try to save something, at least 2 percent or 5 percent. Don't ever, ever start spending more than you're bringing in. Don't ever let that plastic get a hold of you because it'll kill you and keep you broke, and you'll always be a slave. You've got to have the self-discipline.

There was many a time when Ursula and I come up to the States, and we could have bought a lot of things. We didn't have to drive around in that old Chevrolet. We put everything we had right back in. The only luxury I allowed myself was the house, and that was a good investment.

At this time General Pipe had competition in Colombia called AMF Tuboscope, which was one of the biggest inspection companies in the world. I have never been afraid of competition. But I never did like it. I like to try to get rid of it one way or the other. I felt reasonably sure that the way to do it was to do a good job and work hard. Just work harder than they do, and you get more work.

TICO

I called the airlines to book a flight home, and then I called Cecilia in Mexico, paid the bills, canceled the newspapers, placed a hold on the mail, and asked the neighbors to look after the house. I was leaving, I told them. No, I didn't know when I'd be back.

Cecilia had no sense of what had happened. It wasn't fair to expect her to understand. Kidnappings were rare in Mexico.

Then Ulla called again. She was no longer the same person I'd heard on the phone a few hours ago. She was calm, even serene. That at least was how she sounded. A close friend who ran one of the large American oil companies in Colombia had just called her from Bogotá and told her that there wasn't anything to do until the guerrillas got in touch. That could take days, maybe even weeks. I wasn't going to Bogotá.

"Come here," she said. "I need you here. Put the ticket on your credit card, and I'll write you a check."

Now Ulla knew more about the situation than I did.

I quickly recognized what she was saying. Of course, I knew that. We could only wait. Everyone in Colombia knew that. If this had happened to a friend, or to another family, that's just what I would have said, too.

Go to Bogotá! What a stupid idea. What for?

The guerrillas keep families waiting for a long time before getting in touch. It's their way of wearing us down. That's how it's done. Kidnappings in Colombia have clearly defined rules. They go through well-known stages. But this time it was happening to us. I just wasn't thinking straight. But I would. I never doubted that I would start to figure this thing out soon and act like a rational person.

Because kidnappings happen all the time. And Colombia's kidnappings are different and such a basic part of the country's history. People have been kidnapped a long time ago, maybe as many as fifty years, maybe even more. Nobody is quite sure.

Every year during the past decade, the number of kidnappings have increased. In 1987, some nine hundred people were taken away, although the official figures are a bit below that.

I was taking refuge in those numbers, wrapping them around me. It was comforting to know that this had happened to others. Sure, I knew that it was a horrible feeling to have, but it helped.

For a country the size of the United States, that number would mean that about nine thousand people would be taken away each year.

And the statistics are unreliable because many Colombian families never inform the government when one of their loved ones has been taken. They try to keep it quiet.

Nor is it known how many people got killed each year in some violent way. The official statistics said 23,000 in 1987. In the United States, that would come to about 230,000.

We live with the violence.

ULLA

I tried not to think that we wouldn't get him back. I wondered about it, way down in the subconscious maybe. But I knew that other people had gotten back. I was worried that he would do something on his own, something out of our control.

He had always told me that they wouldn't take him alive, that nobody would ever pay for him. I thought he would try to escape. Or that he would get himself into a position where they would be forced to get rid of him, to shoot him. But then I knew that they had to keep him and take care of him. I mean, they couldn't just kill him.

I couldn't imagine him sitting back and letting us take care of things. He was always the one who took care of everything. Suddenly he wasn't there. Jake has always been the one that everyone consults. All of a sudden I had to make the decisions.

I was angry at him . . . for short periods of time. But then I'd think, you can't be angry at Jake. He never willingly does anything bad. Granted, he didn't need to be out there. But that's his work, part of what has made him what he is. I accept him. Way down deep inside, he's just a good person. He has to take care of everybody. He gives up a lot of his time for other people. You can't resent a man if in all the work that he has done he has always included everybody else. Granted, he worked for himself, and he enjoyed it. It's his life, and he couldn't do anything else.

Our Guerrillas, Our Sidewalks

TICO

After mowing the lawn and making a few phone calls, I returned some books to Alderman Library and went by my office in Randall Hall to clear the desk and pick up the mail. Bill Taylor, my colleague and close friend who also teaches Latin American history, was in his office.

"Oh, this happens all the time," I told him. "Don't worry. We'll get him back. It's a normal sort of thing. It happens to practically everybody."

Bill gave me a blank expression. There wasn't anything for him to say. How in the world would anyone be able to respond to what I had just said?

How was an outsider to understand? I was standing in Bill's office thinking how glad I was that this hadn't happened in the States. That would have been too unusual. We would really have been alone. There would have been no rules to guide us, nothing that would have been predictable.

"It's a question of money," I added quickly. "That's all."

"How's your sister?" Bill asked lamely.

"Fine. She's getting things organized. I'm off to Houston to help her."

I walked out of the office. Bill must have wondered whether I'd gone crazy. But I'd said the truth. And I wanted Bill to believe me. We weren't the first, and we were part of an institution that would continue after our part in it had come to an end.

Before heading for the airport, I went back home to pack a suitcase and drink some more coffee. Ulla's was good, too, and strong, but she and Jake used those electrical machines that didn't let the liquid breathe. There would be plenty of it, though. Jake used to bring back a suitcase full of coffee from each of his periodic trips to Colombia.

Even though I suddenly knew that I wouldn't be seeing her tomorrow, it was hard not to think about my mother, for all this would not make sense to her. She would know that there was no way of dealing with the guerrillas. She, too, had a mind of her own. I wasn't going to listen to her. I couldn't. We had to concentrate on the practical and not let ourselves think about all the things that could go wrong. We were going to get him back. Even if Bill believed me, my mother wasn't going to.

But this had to work itself out. The kidnapping was not simply a criminal act. Even if the guerrillas wanted only money, the whole thing was not just a commercial transaction. They had taken Jake to continue their public struggle, not to enrich themselves personally. They were accountable for their actions in ways that only well-known public actors with an ideology and a set of openly expressed beliefs could be. They were bound by rules.

The guerrillas have to know that they can't really maintain their moral voice, call for justice and a more humane society, if they mistreat the people they've taken. They do know that. They have to make sure that they are known for respecting their victims. It gives them a good name and enhances their public image. They keep stating that they treat the people they take away for ransom better than Colombian and foreign capitalists and landowners treat their workers. The guerrillas would also have to treat Jake well if others were going to behave the way they expected us to. If they couldn't build a sense of trust among Colombian families through each kidnapping, it would be a lot harder for them to negotiate successfully with other families later. That was the way it had to be.

I felt that in some strange way our needs and theirs coincided even though we were now on opposite sides, enemies. We both needed him to be well. We had to make a transaction. The guerrillas had to take care of him if they were to get the money. Our task was to convince the guerrillas that we were willing to deal with them. To be successful, we had to trust them and they had to trust us. If the guerrillas felt that we were working with the army or the police, it would be all over. It almost felt as if the government, rather than the guerrillas, was our real enemy.

And him, out there, with a cup of coffee in his hand, his arms resting on his legs. But the image didn't make sense, and I kept shaking it out of my head. I really couldn't get a picture of Jake in my mind. There was no way of imagining him sitting around doing nothing.

I tried to force the thoughts out of my mind. I couldn't think about what Jake was going through. I had to concentrate on the guerrillas instead and on the transaction. We had the money. And the guerrillas were accountable.

JAKE

So here I was. Thirty-two years old. Just bought a small company in Colombia that did pipe inspections for the oil companies.

I guess at that time General Pipe had a secretary, one accountant that worked about a day a month, Reynaldo Olarte, Jimmy Houton, and about three or four other guys that we picked up on a job-to-job basis. The company must have been invoicing about forty thousand dollars a year. I knew that I could cover expenses and get by one way or another, cutting corners here and there and just living trim. It was a busy time. Everything was going just right. I loved it. So did Ursula.

We started picking up some work here and there. When the manager for Tuboscope was sent to Libya, they asked us if we wanted to take over their operations in Colombia. We wrote up a contract, and it never has changed in all this time. We pay them royalties for the use of their equipment. This worked out very well. Got rid of the competition.

During the next years, it really got tough. I didn't really worry too much about the amount of rigs going down. I knew they had to start back up, and they did. In the meantime we had an opportunity to go into Peru. I guess that for a while there that is what kept General Pipe Service going in Colombia.

In 1970 things started picking up. New laws were brought into the Colombian oil code that allowed association contracts. Colombia was having to import a lot of crude oil. With the new laws the oil companies started coming back to Colombia. We were there and we were ready.

I didn't give myself a salary, and sometimes we were way behind on Jimmy, too. Every cent we could get a hold of, why, we put it right back in to buy some more equipment. We took the risk of bringing in tools and equipment without any contracts.

I just had a feeling that it was going to be all right. You say, goddamn, let's go for it. You're thirty-five or forty years old, feeling good. You say, to hell with it; let's make a run for it. We hit it just right.

By 1979 we were doing very, very well. In 1981–82 we started thinking about expanding to the Llanos. We must have had 350 to 400 people working in Sabana de Torres. Eighty-two ended up being one of the best years for us, with the work in the Llanos.

Whatever was happening in the rest of the oil industry worldwide, fortunately for General Pipe, didn't happen in Colombia. It was a period of tremendous wildcat drilling, of companies trying to find out whether there was any oil in Colombia. There was a lot of expensive dry holes over there. They were thinking that in 1990 the price of oil would be about ninety dollars a barrel. This never did materialize, but it was a good time for General Pipe. We were the only people there doing this work.

And everybody said, well, Jake, you have a monopoly. Why sure we had a monopoly. Nobody else wanted to take the risk of putting the money we put into Colombia. And nobody else wanted to work the way we did, 365 days a year, twenty-four hours of the day. The companies were very happy with the service that they were getting in the jungles, having the shops out there and the convenience.

There's a lot of luck, too. Anybody who says that they're in complete control of their destiny is kidding himself. You look at anybody who claims to

Jake

have done it himself, to be a self-made man, and at some point in their lives they had a tremendous stroke of luck.

Mine was when I had the chance to buy the company. The next one was when Colombia decided to start drilling for new oil with the association contracts. If they hadn't decided to start drilling, we wouldn't have made nothing. In fact, we might've gone broke.

But work is the basis of it, you know. You work your ass off and you make it work.

Just like one day (you might remember this): I got a call on a Saturday night, Easter Saturday, and they had a fishing job on one of the rigs that they just didn't know what to do about. I told him I'd take a look. And he said, it's Easter. And we had you all and others coming over. I told Ursula, well, baby, I got to go in the morning. She knew that I wouldn't make the decision to go out there unless it was necessary. And I solved that problem for them. The next day they started drilling again. That was a tremendous sense of elation. Those are great feelings.

You know, during all those years I had a very understanding wife. She never gave me any reason to be jealous, to be dissatisfied with her. We worked together very, very well. In the meantime we had three more children. Ursula did a very good job raising them. My domestic life was as smooth and as happy as you can have.

And believe me, having worked in the oil fields, and knowing some of the problems these other men have with wives and families, I can see how they will never be able to get ahead. And Ursula was also responsible for the growth of General Pipe. Without her I'd never have been able to do it. Whenever I was going to make a major step, she always gave me good advice.

In 1983 the price of crude was down to eight or nine dollars a barrel, and we started getting competition. New types of people started coming into the business, and service didn't hardly mean anything anymore. It was strictly a matter of price. We were still doing well, but it was very hard for me to understand what in the world was going on in this business.

We moved the family up to the States in '83, and I started working about three weeks down there and two weeks up here. I got an apartment in Bogotá. That was all right. I kept myself pretty busy with the work, paperwork, and then going home at night and working on stocks and other things, bringing work home. But I was getting tired of not being home more often.

ULLA

He spent a lot of time with the children when he was home, talking to them. Not activity time. Not like here in the States, where fathers spend a lot of time playing sports with their kids. He was constantly telling them stories.

Oh, Jake's famous for his stories. Well, at least with the children. On Sunday mornings they would all crawl into bed with us, and he would tell the stories. Tony loved them. He would be completely enthralled and take part in the story because Jake always made the children a part of the story. Yes, Tony, Chiara, and Ledette were always characters in those stories. Thomas too. But he was less interested in the stories. When Thomas came around, he would just say, "Oh, Daddy." Thomas enjoyed them, but he would never put himself in the story.

Jake's favorite was the cook of all cooks. He worked for the emperor of all emperors in Russia. He invented Kentucky Fried Chicken, because he met the colonel, and hot dogs and pizza. When the emperor had to go on a diet, the empress would always make sure that the cook of all cooks only fixed small dishes. One day she told the cook that the emperor could have only one egg. So the cook of all cooks, who was Jake, of course, would go out and get an ostrich egg. The emperor was so happy because he had only one egg, but he could eat all he wanted.

Oh, yes, Jake is a good storyteller. One time he made a fabulous dish. Emperors would come from all over and give him all these jewels and riches. One day as he was leaving, he put all his riches in a big treasure chest. As he was stomping through the snow, the big treasure chest was lost, covered by the snow. Of course, Tony was ready to go out and search for it.

Jake liked good food. He was fat at first. It wasn't that important to me. I didn't see that part of him. It got to the point where we had to do something about it. But you see, unless he realizes that he has to do it, he won't because there's no talking him into anything. It's the same with cigarette smoking. He got obese and then decided to go on this diet. He must have weighed 240 pounds and went down to 170, 160, in less than a year. He can't believe it when he sees his big pants from back then. Jake puts on weight so easily.

He learned to cook from his mother. And he was adventuresome in that too. He would throw anything into a pot and see what it would come out like. He loved to cook. It relaxed him. He was always making up new recipes. When he cooked something, it had to be a presentation. It has to make a statement, as Chiara would say.

I'd never met a man who cooked. I mean, he doesn't like to make the daily meals. I do that. But he makes all the special things, all the sauces for the pasta. He makes them in the morning when he gets up, at 3:30. He makes lots of sauces and we freeze them, and he bakes the turkey for Thanksgiving and makes the stuffing. He loves to barbecue. Chicken and spareribs and sausages. The more people he cooks for, the better. He just loves to feed people.

And he's taught the kids. Even Ledette cooks, and she isn't much of an eater. The pig head at New Year's is probably his favorite. Oh, and on the fourth of July he puts out the American flag, and we invite all kinds of people, and he cooks for them all. He'd always be going out to the supermarket to find the best meals and the best deals. He was just different.

We are a very close family. That's unusual nowadays—up here in the States that is, not in Colombia. We're there for one another. We've been lucky that we've had four healthy children and that they've never given us much of a problem, no calamities, nothing major. We have always enjoyed each other's company. The kids have always enjoyed being home. I know that it's odd sometimes, according to Chiara's friends. They're surprised that we all take vacations together. The children like to bring their friends home, which is a good sign. I mean Tony could easily have found an apartment for himself, but he likes it here. The children always call home.

JAKE

We never got involved in politics. Several of our supervisors had relationships with the various politicians out there, with the UP [Patriotic Union] and the liberals. It got pretty violent. In fact, one of the mayors there was a member of UP, and he got assassinated. He had come to see me once or twice. I tried to distance myself from the politicians. It's better not to make friends where politics are so cut and dried. I tried to stay neutral. Being such a big employer in Sabana, I felt that if I gave an opportunity to a political group where they had access to me, they would push that to make themselves look better. I didn't want the company used as a tool. In fact, when one of our men ran for the town council, I was annoyed. I told him, I said, are you running as yourself or as a representative of the company? You see, I didn't want people to think that if they were electing him, they were bringing the company into it.

We always had good relations with everybody. Whenever they needed light posts or a new school, we helped them. Or we would provide a water post or give the children things at Christmas or wire for the electricity. They needed help. They don't have much help from the government there. It's important for any company to have good relations with the community where it's working. Your people are from there, and it would be very diffi- cult for them to do a good job for you if they didn't have a sense that you were also helping them. So besides salary, we felt we owed something to that community also.

We got along fine with all the workers. Except once back in 1981. About twenty or twenty-five employees in Sabana started up a union. We went through three or four months of pretty hard negotiations. It was very unpleasant because a couple of times they almost burned a truck. I was dumbfounded by the whole thing. We had always paid very good salaries. But if they wanted a union, that was their right. We reached an agreement and signed a union contract. About 40 percent of the people wanted to get in. In about a month about 5 or 10 percent wanted to get out. After six or eight months everybody got out except for the three or four leaders. They came to me, and they said, "Well, what is going to happen to us? Are you going to fire us?" "No," I said, "I'm not going to fire you. You all are good employees. You work hard." They are still working with us down there.

We never asked the army to protect us. And we didn't give any guns to the watchmen. We had a gate around the place to keep people out, keep them from roaming around in there. But we could never have kept any group of armed people from coming in. I didn't want anybody killed pro- tecting the property of the company. There was no way that we could have armed the watchmen to make it secure. I felt that the best way to have secu- rity was not to have any guns.

ULLA

He didn't take his hat on that trip. Maybe . . . Well, he didn't wear it any- more; it's just so old now. But if he still had it on, maybe all this wouldn't have happened. Superstitious, I guess. But I kept thinking about all the years out there that he wore the hat. It started out as a very elegant, well- shaped, clean, good hat. I think it was a Stetson. He wore it daily. It has a small rim made out of that suede-felt kind of material, with a band, which it doesn't have anymore. He wore it on all his trips. It became a symbol of him. It was so filthy dirty after a while, so raggedy and torn that I would keep sewing it up with this invisible thread. It had holes in it, and he would make up stories for the kids about Indian arrows going through it. And, of course, they all believed him at the time. It became his good luck hat. He wouldn't go anywhere without it.

Ulla

It got to the point where the pilots in the jungles out there wouldn't want to fly him to the different sites if he didn't have it on. It was just a very well-known hat in the oil business in Colombia. Jake and his hat. And when we moved up here, he put it in the closet, and it became a museum piece. It's unwearable now, so tattered, in pieces. People laughed at his hat. He didn't care. But he sure didn't have it on, you know, not this time when he left.

I don't know what he was proving, but he always wore the worst clothes. Jake loved to put on his cheap shirts. He bought them at Front Row, the discount of discount stores. He never placed much value on clothes. Chiara was always buying him things to wear, and he never did. I guess he just wanted to show that he was a basic, working sort of man; that he wasn't prim and proper; and that even if he had money, he didn't have to show it off.

But maybe, maybe, if he'd had his hat with him . . .

ADAPTING

TICO

The first hours have come and gone. I'm in Houston. I've been here in Ulla's new house before, and I like to visit her, but this is a flat, barren land filled with people who strut instead of walking, and I always feel like I'm on the frontier somewhere, straddling the border between civilization and barbarism. I think I'd rather be in Bogotá. And this is the place that Bush claims as his hometown. The idea of him winning the election in November is enough to make me want to go back and live in Colombia. And there's no way of getting excited about Dukakis or whomever else the Democrats might come up with.

I don't really know if Ulla needs me here or if she is just making sure that I have something to do now that my idea of flying to Bogotá didn't make much sense. In any case, there are all kinds of things that need to be done. I'm starting to write down what has happened, trying to reconstruct what is known about how they took him away and about those first moments of confusion. It's not going very well—the writing, that is—but I feel this compulsion to put ideas and feelings to paper. Maybe it's like a kind of therapy that helps make sense of what's happening. But there's no question that I'm going to keep a record. Taking notes. Maybe I'm just being a historian, trying to be myself, trying to feel a little less disrupted now that I'm in a situation that I can't control.

JAKE

I woke up out there the first morning. There I was. Twenty-four hours. I was out there watching the sun come up. I woke up about five and got up and talked to the guy who was on guard there. Good morning, you know, regular talk. They brought me some water to rinse out my mouth. In about an hour they brought some beans, or peas, and coffee. I asked them if they had any cigarettes, and they brought me one and lit it for me because I didn't have any matches.

That whole day I was thinking what a damn fool I was, and I started walking around that area I had there. Mostly that is all I did. They brought me some lunch, and I ate a little bit.

I heard a motorboat pull up. A couple of guys come in. I wondered if they had made a deal so I could get out. But they were just bringing in the supplies. They brought me some cigarettes, but I had to ask for them one at a time, and they give it to me lit.

The main thing I did was try to protect myself from the mosquitoes. There was just a tremendous amount of mosquitoes. It kept raining off and on, so I stayed under the tarp as much as possible. It was humid. Very, very seldom would the sun get through. My shirt was short sleeve. I still had my red overalls. They had one of these flit guns with Black Flag, and they'd spray me, and that gave some relief.

Why in the world had I gone to Sabana? That feeling was the worst. Why did I put myself in this position to get kidnapped? Why was I so stupid, putting all of you in this situation, my wife, my friends, my children? My foolishness and my hardheadedness. I had a small space to walk around in, about five meters long, one meter wide. All day long back and forth. I must have walked twenty-five miles.

I never did have feelings like that before. It was a completely different kind of feeling that I had in me, where you're almost in despair. Not despair really, but you're berating yourself so much. It's that feeling of saying, Jesus Christ, you dumb ass. What the hell are you doing here? It was all so unnecessary. Why didn't you listen to Ursula?

I was angry at myself. But I was more disgusted with myself for all the pain I was putting everyone else in, for having done something so ridiculous. It was strictly a mental thing. It wasn't healthy. I had to get out of it. Would it have led to mental depression?

I walked all day long back and forth. And all at once I had a sense of peace, a feeling that someone was with me. I prayed. And then I never did ask myself again why I'd gone to Sabana. I just said, it's God's will. And after that everything was fine. There was no more berating myself.

You know, I'm not a terribly religious person. But I had this feeling that God was with me. I still had the anguish for the family, the sense that you all were in a state of turmoil. But there was a connection between me and my family. From one minute to the next my self-suffering ended.

I said, now, let's see what we can do to get out. What do I have to do? What do you have to do when they start questioning you?

TICO

SUNDAY, JUNE 26

Through the oil companies in Bogotá Ulla has learned about organizations that make a living out of negotiating with guerrillas and terrorists. They're located in Miami, and another one is in England. Ulla has wanted to get their help from the beginning, and I haven't tried to argue against her. On what grounds? I can't, after all, let my own political views into any of this.

So I told Ulla to go ahead and choose one of those companies, using her friends in Bogotá to help her make up her mind on which one was the best, because I couldn't do much for her there, and then, of course, I don't want to either. And I really doubt whether they could do anything, if they would be useful in any way. These companies are probably filled with a bunch of old right-wing CIA and FBI types who know next to nothing about Colombia and who think that the guerrillas are nothing more than a pack of criminals.

In any case, Ulla has already come to an arrangement with one of those companies, and they're going to be working on the case. They have been asking questions, trying to reconstruct the kidnapping. But all that's already been done. I can't imagine that these guys will come up with anything new.

One thing is clear: the kidnapping has got to be kept quiet. Fortunately, Ulla has already told me that she isn't going to talk to anyone. She's one who keeps things to herself.

It's a good thing that the Colombian government doesn't get much involved if asked to stay away. The Americans have always stated publicly that they don't negotiate with people whom they so easily refer to as terrorists. And if the army gets the foolish idea of going off looking for him, trying to free him from his captors, the guerrillas will kill Jake rather than let the army score a victory.

Hopefully the news won't hit the papers because if it becomes a public thing and others get involved, if his nationality becomes an issue, or if this gets tied to the oil question, there will be nothing left to do. This has to be kept within the family. It's a private matter, a financial transaction.

And also, few things in Colombia are worse than the newspapers. Forty years ago they were among the world's best. Now they are merely crass commercial enterprises with huge color pictures and hardly any information.

Colombia's dailies have always been owned by important political families and have been the mouthpieces of the traditional parties, with a dim sense of what objectivity is about, but in the last years they have exhibited little, if any, regard for the facts. It's almost as though writers and editors don't double-check anything. We never know what we'll find in them. Fortunately, kidnappings are rarely a big story. There won't be journalists from the major papers coming around asking questions.

NEWS

The Army of National Liberation—ELN—kidnapped the manager of the Paiper transnational petroleum company in the Department of Santander. According to the authorities, the army and the police are carrying out intense operations throughout the entire region of Sabanalarga de Torres in an attempt to find the commando of the ELN that kidnapped the Italian Jacobo Gambiny, manager of Paiper, a transnational petroleum company. According to what could be determined, Jacobo Gambiny, the manager of the American transnational, was kidnapped by the subversives at the moment that he was inspecting various camps in the rural zones of Sabana de Torres. The authorities reported that *el señor* Gambiny arrived in the zone in a helicopter from Barrancabermeja, where the principal offices of Paiper, a petroleum company that is a concessionary of Ecopetrol and that searches for oil in the Magdalena Medio, are located. The authorities have revealed that the kidnapping took place at three in the afternoon while Gambiny was with various other executives, although it is not known if others were kidnapped along with the Italian.

—*El Siglo* (Bogotá)

The authorities have no leads on the whereabouts of the American executive Coope Gambini, 60, kidnapped on Saturday. The executive was kidnapped when he was at the company, which he owns and which operates in the municipality of Sabana de Torres, Santander. The Camilista Union, of the Army of National Liberation, has claimed responsibility for the kidnapping. It demands a high sum of money in exchange for the liberation of its victim.

—*El Tiempo* (Bogotá)

Venezuelan military units have been moved to the northeastern border with Colombia after it became known that a kidnapped entrepreneur in that country was going to be sent over into Venezuelan territory, according to police sources. These sources would neither confirm nor deny an account published by a Caracas newspaper that a secret meeting had taken place on Tuesday at the border between the police forces of both countries. According to the daily *El Nacional,* this has been the second meeting between the chiefs of the security forces of both countries in the past month. According to the newspaper account, the meeting is tied to the intense military mobilization on the border after it was learned that the Army of National Liberation had kidnapped the Italian Giacomo Gambini. Gambini is an executive with the Piper petroleum company, and according to versions circulating in Venezuela, he was to be taken by his captors to a zone of difficult access in the Sierra de Perijá, on the Venezuelan side of the border. Last year nine Venezuelan soldiers lost their lives in battles with bands of *narcotraficantes* [drug lords] in the above mentioned zone. It is known for its high degree of danger and is permanently patrolled by the police and the military of Venezuela, in search of armed Colombian groups.

—*El Espectador* (Bogotá)

The general headquarters of Manuel Pérez, the Spanish priest who is the commander of the Army of National Liberation (ELN), was dismantled yesterday by troops of the Fifth and Eighth Army Brigades. The camp, known as the Government of the New Colombia, was located on the border of the Departments of Santander, César, and Norte de Santander, in the jurisdiction of San Alberto, in an area known as El Playón. The entire area was being controlled last night by the army. . . . According to extra-official sources, the overall leader of the ELN managed to escape thanks to a modern system of radio communications. According to General Farouk Yanine Díaz, Commander of the Second Division, this is the largest guerrilla camp that has been destroyed thus far. "No one was captured, but there was an intense battle. . . . Our purpose is to exterminate the scoundrels that cause so much damage to Colombia." The army is in control of a very wide area around Catatumbo. If necessary, the army will use helicopters to determine the location of new camps.

—El Tiempo

(Bogotá, Colombia [Associated Press])—Police were still searching for the manager of a U.S. oil company who was kidnapped by leftist guerrillas this week for a $2 million ransom.

Giacomo (Jake) Gambini, 42, an Italian-born U.S. citizen, was abducted by leftist guerrillas Monday as he left his office in Sabana de Torres, 200 miles north of Bogotá, police in the Department of Santander said.

They said the rebels belonged to the pro-Cuban National Liberation Army and were demanding a $2 million dollar ransom.

Gambini's hometown in the United States was not immediately available.

Police said that Gambini worked for the Piper Co., which according to industry sources provides technical advice to companies searching for oil in northeast Colombia.

—Daily Progress (Charlottesville, Virginia)

State Department officials said Saturday they will not negotiate a release of Galveston oil company executive Jake Gambini, kidnapped by leftist guerrillas trying to nationalize Colombia's petroleum industry. State Department spokesman Dennis Harter said the department will only condemn the actions of 20 pro-Cuban National Liberation Army (ELN) commandos who abducted Gambini June 24 as he was about to board a helicopter in the town of Sabana de Torres, 200 miles northeast of Bogotá. "In these situations, we let the local government handle it," Harter said Saturday from State Department headquarters in Washington, D.C. "We do not get involved."

—Houston Chronicle

Gambini is the first American executive kidnapped in more than two years. Two engineers working for the U.S. engineering giant,

Bechtel Corp., which built a portion of the pipeline, were abducted by the ELN December 10, 1985, from an oil pumping station near the village of Uru, 280 miles north of Bogotá. One of the engineers, Edward Stohl, 62, of Santa Rosa, California, died of an apparent heart attack while a captive. The other was released after payment of an undisclosed ransom. A high ranking Texaco executive in Colombia, Kenneth Bishop, was kidnapped by a rebel group and freed after 38 days for a reported $1 million ransom in 1983.

—Houston Chronicle

Members of Gambini's family could not be reached Monday by the Associated Press to discuss the kidnapping.

—AP, in Houston Chronicle

"Why did they kidnap him? That's exactly the question we have been asking ourselves since it happened," said a Gambini family spokesman who asked not to be identified. "Who was it, and why would they want him?" Though family members— including two brothers who live in Galveston, a Colombian wife and several children—are concerned, they are also confident Gambini is physically and mentally tough enough to survive the ordeal. "He's a very physical man. He'll probably do better than the people who have him. He's got tremendous mental stamina," the spokesman said.

—Ken Lanterman, Houston Post

JAKE

It looked to me like they were an organized group. They had the uniforms, the discipline.

You could see that the bearded one was in charge and that he was responding completely to the other one, who took my papers and everything else. They had grenades; they had army belts on. Even the bearded one changed out of his civilian clothes when he got back and got into his uniform.

Jake

They were not just a bunch of bandits that decided to pick me up to see what they could get for me. But I didn't know who they were. I didn't ask them. I thought it wouldn't do much good. They were going to tell me exactly what they wanted to anyhow. Why put myself in a position to ask something that might, you know . . . I mean, they could tell me anything. They were in control.

They were still trying to size me up, trying to figure out how I would react to things, keeping a very close eye on me, making sure that I wouldn't try to run away. But they didn't put any rope on me or handcuff me or hobble my legs or nothing. There was no need for it. They knew it. I couldn't get away.

They had brought some sort of a mattress, a small pallet really. They made a bed on boards with some limbs and put the mattress on it and the mosquito netting over it and the tarp over that. They brought me a thermos bottle full of coffee.

At first I was a little suspicious of the coffee, thinking maybe it was drugged. So I drank a few sips, waited five or ten minutes to see if it had any effect on me, and I drank about a quarter cup and stopped. Then I felt at ease that there wasn't anything there.

I drank very little in the way of liquids to their standards. The only thing I really needed was coffee to quench my thirst. I was very careful about food and drink to see if I could detect a strange taste or if it would have an effect on me. I liked to eat something that they ate also.

I urinated a few times on the first day. But the next morning I had to take a shit. I knew I couldn't just move about, go off in the shrubs or anything like that. They made a hole for me, about a foot and a half wide, off to one side about forty feet or so.

It's a terrible feeling. You tried to pick your time when there wasn't that many people around or there wasn't a girl on guard. If you knew that the guard would be a girl during the next four hours, you would try to see if you could go before it was her time to come on. You'd go with a man. It was a silly thing in a situation like that, but you still have certain. . . . One time that I really had to go they switched guards on me, and there was this girl. I waited around a while, but they didn't change her. Finally I told her, I said, "Hey, I have got to go to the bathroom." She called one of the men. They were considerate; they respected.

Walking down there, with a guard behind you, you have a man that is standing guard over you. It's terrible. Just having this man there with a gun, it was the most demeaning thing of all. It made me feel angry that I was in a situation like that, that a situation like that existed. Even the prisoners in the hardest jails here in the States have a toilet right there. At least they don't have to ask anybody. It's a natural function. There shouldn't be any situation in this world where a man has to ask if he can go do a natural function. I think that is a basic right. But I had to wait for them to say okay.

I've always had good bowel movements. I like to read, take my time, smoke a cigarette. That was another thing. You can't really smoke a cigarette. It's hard to squat and smoke.

A man that doesn't have trouble defecating has a halfway chance of getting through the day in a good mood. A man who's constipated is going to be grouchy and is going to be hard to get along with. I never did have any problem.

They gave me some toilet paper, a bar of soap, and asked me if I wanted to bathe. I felt very dirty. We went out to the river. They had a log out there where they bathed, too.

When they saw that I was bitten by mosquitoes, they put some cream on my back, on my arms. They helped me bathe, to make sure that I wouldn't fall, because apparently there was a bunch of thorns and stickly things in the water, and you could get them through your foot. They were very careful. I could see right off the bat that they didn't want me getting hurt. The *comandante* told me that they were going to get me something clean to wear and some shoes.

When it was time for dinner that night, the young girl that brought it to me, she said, *"Tío, tengo algo muy especial para usted. Pero tómala, no pide que es."* What she said was that she had something real special for me to drink, but that I shouldn't ask what it was. Boy, I said, here it comes. I put it to my lips and it was some kind of bubbly wine. It was bad. I made a big thing of tasting it. Then I told her, no, I don't drink. I have an ulcer.

I lied, you know, I just told them that. If I start drinking, I'm afraid it might start bleeding. I guess the girl said this to the guy with the beard, and he came over and asked me if I was in need of any medicines or anything. I was asked that the first day also.

They gave me the playing cards. But instead of being a deck of fifty-two, it was the European type of forty cards, so I had to redesign a solitaire game to make it fit that deck. The other was seven across. With that one I had only six. It took about a day to redesign it to see if it wouldn't be too easy or too hard to win.

Playing solitaire. The first of my thousand and one games of solitaire. There were days that I must have played a hundred games. I had never played much. Only in the army, where you have a lot of time to kill. They would all watch me. I showed one or two of them how to play.

Jake

They called it the *juego solitario*. *"Está jugando solitario,"* they would say. How proper and fitting. That was the pastime. I had that deck of cards with me all the way through to the end. The solitary game. How fitting.

TICO

THURSDAY, JUNE 30

We are all together. The children have gathered around. Tony has come back from Ecuador, where he has just started working for the company after graduating from the University of Tulsa in May. He passed through Bogotá, but quickly, mainly I guess because Ulla was afraid that he would be kidnapped as well. It's a stupid fear, but it's there nonetheless. He talked to our mother, who seems to be bearing up well and getting lots of visitors.

Chiara returned from her vacation in Greece, and Ledette is here from her summer job at Vanderbilt. No words, just a few hugs, with everyone trying to keep the tears back. Fortunately Thomas has plenty of good friends in the neighborhood, and he's able to stay out of the house for hours on end. Our sister Ditha will be coming from Guatemala to stay with Ulla. The two sisters are close.

Ulla is quilting, especially at night. That's when there isn't anything that can happen and the dark hours just stare back, when the guerrillas are not going to call. Each morning brings a little bit of hope. But hour after hour, once dinner is over, Ulla sits at the table with a beam of light shining down on her, quilting. Little strips of cloth, all perfectly coordinated, placed into an intricate pattern. Tiny decisions with immediate results. Ulla concentrates so much that I wonder whether she hears the conversations. Her fingers are always moving. Besides her concentration, there's little to indicate how she's feeling or what's going on in her head.

We are all busy, but there are just too many hours in each day. There is total silence. All that we know is what the newspapers are saying. There is no news from the guerrillas. The hours drag, and each day seems longer than the next. There is nothing left to do but plan and wait.

SATURDAY, JULY 2

I haven't had a drink since I got here. Maybe I just want to be as sharp as can be, to keep the mind alert. There's no way of knowing when important decisions will have to be made. And I've been on Jake's bike, but it's pretty heavy and rusted out. Besides, there are no hills. It's all flat here and pretty ugly, too, not like the wonderful hills and the scenery around Charlottes-ville, up to Monticello, and around the Blue Ridge Mountains.

But I've got to keep in shape. I may have to go out there into the jungle to negotiate with them. I've got to be ready. And I really want to go out there and face them. I can talk to them, reason with them. I understand them.

SUNDAY, JULY 3

We know it's going to take time. By now we all know that. But how long? How will they get in touch? A letter? A telephone call? Will Vicente or someone else in Bogotá bump "accidentally" into one of them on the street? Who is it going to be? Which one of them took him? The ELN? The FARC? The EPL (Popular Army of Liberation)?

We sit around and talk about them all. Nothing about the way in which Jake was taken offers any idea of who they might be. Time and again we go over all the details of what happened that early morning. There is nothing there. But there's little doubt that it was the guerrillas. They were so well organized.

The newspapers claim it was the ELN, but how do they know? We have called friends. They say that the guerrillas don't identify themselves to some journalist or take responsibility for kidnappings, at least not until they are over. The professionals from Miami agree. If they know what they are talk-ing about, it must be because they've been hired so many times before.

We are beginning to learn about the clearly defined steps and stages that families go through. What stands ahead is predictable. Little can go wrong. They will probably tell him to name someone to do the negotiating, or he might even do it himself.

Everybody says that this would be highly unusual, that it hardly ever hap-pens that way. But Ulla knows that's exactly what Jake will do. One day there will be a letter or a phone call, he'll tell her how much to pay, and that will be the end of it all.

If not, we'll be in for a long give-and-take. They'll ask for an astronomi-cal sum of money, we'll make a counteroffer, and so it will go. That's the way it works. It turns out that families apparently end up paying around 10 percent of the guerrillas' initial demand. Once a sum is settled on and the guerrillas have their money, they return the person they've been holding.

But that's the scary part. They always demand the money up front. Fami-lies have to wait for hours or maybe even days. It might even take a week before the release happens. We can only rely on them to honor their part of the deal.

The two million dollars mentioned by the newspapers has settled in our minds. That's probably what they'll start out with, and then the negotiating will begin.

MONDAY, JULY 4

There is usually a huge celebration in Jake's house on this day. After all, he's a man who has a huge American flag blowing in the wind from a high pole outside his home.

But at least the long wait is turning out to be strangely comforting. It's proof that the guerrillas have him and that he has gone along without doing something to free himself. He's going along with this because if something out of the normal has happened, we would've heard. Ulla seems to be worrying less about what he might do. They have him. There can be no question about that. Ulla is calm, at least outwardly. There's never a sign of any tension about her. We all keep looking at each other for any signs that the pressure is getting the better of us. By all appearances, we seem to be doing well.

We're not thinking any longer about how he scuffled against them and about all the footprints that were found on the road next to the company truck that they left behind on the road outside of Sabana. But Ulla still wonders about his glasses. He was always losing them, leaving them wherever. So he had a steady supply. One was left behind in his office in Sabana. Would he be able to read?

We're on the phone almost all the time. Even though we already know most everything that we're hearing now, old knowledge does seem kind of new, unexpected even. More than that, though, it is important to confirm what we know.

Almost everybody we talk to wants to know whether Jake has kidnapping insurance. No, we answer. There's a slight pause at the other end of the phone line, then some reassuring words. The insurance policy would have paid for everything, including the ransom payment, all our expenses, and even these professionals whom Ulla is paying. It seems that Jake had concluded that the insurance policy was too expensive, something like a hundred thousand dollars per person per year. According to Tony, Jake figured he'd have to pay the guerrillas less for the ransom.

We are shutting up. We stop calling friends. We do what we can to make the issue disappear. We are shunning the press as though it were the plague.

The local papers keep calling. All news that does not come from them, from the guerrillas, is bad news. We don't want to know about it.

JAKE

After about the sixth day, we heard some helicopters go over a couple of times. The seventh day they came over again. Everybody hid. On Sunday afternoon they told me we were moving out. They busted up the camp.

After a while two motorboats came up, and one of them was driven by this *comandante*. We took off. Me in the front, one on each side. It was night. I didn't have any idea where we were going. We traveled about two or three hours and crossed what I thought was the Magdalena River, then went up to some *ciénaga*, a "marsh."

We landed and went uphill. There was a little clearing there. They made a place to lay my pallet, fixed the mosquito netting, and I went to sleep. It was real late by then.

This place was a little bit better. We were up on a hill. The mosquitoes weren't as bad. Once the sun came up, they'd all go away. I felt better.

I started to identify them. The girl Sonia had no other duties but to cook for me and give me water, wash my clothes, give me cigarettes. After three days there she let me have my own pack. The bearded one brought me a radio. Music. I never did try to change the dial. I didn't touch it. Played solitaire. Listened to music.

The bearded one told me that the family had been notified that I'd been kidnapped, that I was doing all right. He told me they were a political group, and kidnapping was their only way of raising money for the movement. And he told me that I would have to write a letter to let my people know that I was all right.

TICO

WEDNESDAY, JULY 6

The days are filled with seemingly endless details. We are always doing something, planning, organizing, imagining, thinking up what we call contingency plans. We do so many things that the next day we hardly remember what they were. We put the answering machine on the phone and buy a fax machine. We're ready. We hope to get a letter. Or if they call the office in Bogotá, Vicente knows what to say. The professionals have talked to him at length about what he is supposed to say. I don't see why they bother with all these details. How can Vicente make any mistakes? How can anybody make any mistakes at this?

We're ready. We have done our job. We aren't going to make any mistakes.

THURSDAY, JULY 7

The Italian ambassador in Bogotá was relieved to hear that Jake was not an Italian citizen. The Colombian military asked if they could be of any assistance. They wanted to know whether the family was going to negotiate. What kind of a question was that?

But I know why they asked. What else can they do but ask? Yet it still seems like a stupid question. What else is a family to do? Tell the army to get a battalion out there and bomb their loved one to freedom? I really do worry about the government. Only the guerrillas can help.

Just as I expected, the professionals don't think very much about the guerrillas. To their mind, this is just a financial transaction.

But I can't keep my mind away from the guerrillas. Isn't that what I'm supposed to be thinking about, anyhow? That's how I'm supposed to help.

I'm starting to think about them in new way, seeing them from the inside. There must be abiding internal reasons that oblige the guerrilla leaders to deal honorably with their captives, and these are ultimately what count for us. It's not just a matter of goodwill.

If young members of the guerrilla movement start to feel that kidnapping and the money obtained from it are ends in themselves, rather than necessary and justifiable means toward greater social and political goals, how will the leaders manage to keep the movement together? There will be little to keep individual guerrillas, or bands of them, from going off on their own once they get some experience and learn how easy it is to kidnap someone. Rather than build guerrilla unity, the kidnappings would make the guerrilla movement fall apart, splinter into bands of petty criminals.

Important leaders can't be the ones who keep the kidnap victims in some camp somewhere, week after week, months at a time. They have more important things to do. Small specialized groups of guerrillas are probably charged with these menial, yet critical tasks. Each one of these groups lives with its captive in considerable isolation, far from the leaders and far from families. Each one of these groups might make the captive its own. The temptation must be huge. As soon as a group of guerrillas begins to treat a captive in even slightly different ways from the instructions it has received, that group could begin to establish an informal level of independence.

There must be practical safeguards in place to prevent this from happening. But an abiding sense of political and ideological commitment has to be one of the strongest. By obliging guerrillas to treat their captives well for the good of the revolution, the leadership manages to exert daily, even intimate control over far-flung followers. All this is good, for it tends to ensure Jake's fair treatment.

Now I'm even glad the common criminals are around for they might just make the guerrillas more responsible. The criminals are a threat to the guerrillas, not just because they lay claim to some of their victims, but because they don't have to behave as public actors. They can kill and torture their captives or agree on a sum of money and then not deliver. Criminals undermine the relationship with the families of captives that the guerrillas work so hard to establish. The more criminals there are in the kidnapping business, the more honorably the guerrillas will deal with Jake and with us.

The guerrillas have to go out of their way to demonstrate that they're not common criminals. This is good for us, but I also know that the criminals will soon get the upper hand. Their task is easier. They have no responsibilities. There is nothing to stop more and more people from getting into the business for private reasons. It's a form of Colombian capitalism, trading in human beings. History is on their side.

There used to be a code of honor in the kidnapping business. You could be pretty sure that if you or a member of your family had been taken once, you'd be safe from then on. The guerrillas even told that to their captives. It was part of their goodwill. It was also a tangible sign of their power and influence in society.

But the system seems to have broken down. Some Colombians have been taken more than once, as have various members of one family. Perhaps there are too many guerrilla groups struggling over a limited number of possible victims. More likely, it's the common criminals who have done the most to undermine the old honor system.

Still, the guerrillas are remarkably successful in maintaining their reputation. When a kidnapping goes wrong, Colombians think that common criminals are involved. They tend to reach the same conclusion when a person is taken twice or when more than one member of a given family is abducted. That's a problem. It lets the guerrillas off the hook should something go wrong.

Tico

NEWS

Please, have mercy, give Alfonso back to us or tell us the truth.
Tell us if you've killed him.

> —Bernardo Herrera, father of Alfonso
> Herrera, a geologist kidnapped presumably
> by the guerrillas, 890 days before

I was having dinner a few days ago with a group of friends from
the coast. Of the twelve people at our table, three had recently
suffered the experience of having close members of their families kidnapped by the guerrillas. . . . The most incredible case
took place in Córdoba. The uncle of one of our fellow diners
had been paying a *vacuna* to the EPL for many years. When he
refused to continue doing so, they decided to kidnap him, with
the help of the administrator of his farm, who got cold feet at
the last moment and told his employer. The next day the administrator was shot to death in front of his wife and children. A little later, the EPL burned down the farm and assassinated the
uncle's driver.

> —Enrique Santos Calderón, journalist.
> Santos comes from one of the most
> prominent political families in Colombia.
> The Santos family own *El Tiempo,*
> Colombia's major daily newspaper

Giancarlo Ventolini, the Italian entrepreneur who'd been kidnapped by the FARC on August 8, was freed outside of Cali. Ventolini, 65 years of age, suffers from serious health complications
that forced the guerrillas to let him go.

> —*La Prensa*

The Army of National Liberation let it be known that the freedom
of the five geologists it kidnapped fifteen days ago in the province
of García Rovira is still far off. It also urged the government to

respond to a recent proposal. . . . A short while ago, the organization had announced that it would suspend its attacks against the
oil pipelines if the government accepted two conditions. First,
that it freeze the price of gasoline for an entire year, beginning
August 18th. And second, that it indemnify the families of the
campesinos [rural people] who had lost their lives in the peasant
marches this past May.

In addition, the ELN plans to establish some sort of a dialogue
with the executives of Carbones de Oriente, the company for
which the kidnap victims work. It wishes to determine how the
company plans to exploit the coal resources of the area,
especially in Cerrito.

—*El Tiempo*

The former mayor of Simití, Luis Napoleón Barba López,
returned to his home safe and sound. He was kept for five
months by a unit of the Army of National Liberation (ELN).
Barba López, 70, was kidnapped for some time along with his
brother Marcelino, who was conducting the negotiations for
his rescue.

—*El Tiempo*

Today the kidnapping phenomenon has spread like wildfire. The
target can just as easily be a rich *hacendado* as a humble man of
the city. A few months ago some common delinquents kidnapped
a little girl from the Bello Horizonte sector of Bogotá. She was
the daughter of the neighborhood shoe repairman.

—*El Tiempo*

Jan Meertens, the Dutch national who was kidnapped by the M-19
eight months ago, was liberated safe and sound by the Tarqui
Artillery Battalion. The Dutch professional said that his kidnappers kept him in a small room of four square meters, with no sun-
light or fresh air. The room didn't have any sanitary facilities. "I

didn't see the sun for six months, but when they realized that I was getting sick, they let me out in the sun for a few minutes each day."

—La Prensa

The Tribunal of Public Order has determined that kidnapping is not an act of terrorism but a form of rebellion. Magistrate Ernesto de Francisco affirmed that they are a means of destabilizing the constituted democratic political system. Kidnappings carried out by the guerrillas, according to the Tribunal, seek to affect public opinion, and to obtain moneys from individuals or the State in order to strengthen the forces of subversion.

—La Prensa

And he said to me, *"Tío,* the problem is that we have to survive and don't have other ways of financing our campaigns. To maintain people in arms costs a great deal of money. The kidnappings will not come to an end."

I remained in that camp from March 29 until May 13, the day they let me go. Life was completely routine. They woke up and did their "drills," and their exercises. A commission would go out to get the firewood; others would just sit around cleaning their guns. They took turns taking up guard positions. And they did nothing else. For about an hour at night they'd have their conferences, but I'm unaware of their content.

—Roberto Mutis, cattle rancher
taken by the FARC

TICO

FRIDAY, JULY 8

It's been about two weeks now. We're trying not to count the days, but when this first started we thought that it would last just a few days. Now we've been in this for half a month. And we know that it's going to take a lot longer. But how much longer?

Our Guerrillas, Our Sidewalks

We're doing what we can not to think about him. It's almost like a dam that we are building. Keeping everything back. Holding it in. We seem to feel that if one of us just mentions him, then all our thoughts and feelings, our fears really, will come pouring out.

We are all afraid of what he's going through, of how he will react, of what he is going to do. Two weeks! He's been there all these days. Every day. Every morning. What in the world has he been doing all this time? We just can't imagine.

What's it like out there? Hot? Cold? Where is he sleeping? My God, what is he doing?

We know that this is something unimaginable for all families, but this is different because of him.

There are all these rumors around about how kidnap victims have just the grandest of times out there with the guerrillas, eating and drinking and resting. But that's not going to work with Jake. He's not going to take anything from them. Will he even talk to them? How is he going to survive?

It's the strangest feeling. It's like he's dead, gone, and at the same time more alive, more part of our thoughts than when he was with us. We're thinking about how he's living, even though we never mention the subject. The most we can dare talk about is his glasses.

You can't worry about someone who is dead because there's nothing you can do. But we can do nothing but worry about him, and we can do nothing, absolutely nothing, to help him. It's horrible. It's like the worst of all situations.

We don't want him to be dead, but then neither do we want him to be living through this. Not him.

But we are going to get him back. We know that.

And he's stronger than most anybody else they've ever taken. We've got to keep all that in our minds, too.

JAKE

I heard some people come in on a motorboat as I was trying to go to sleep. It must have been about day sixteen or seventeen. The next morning the bearded one was gone, and there was this new man who had taken his place.

Ricardo. He didn't say much to me the first day. Sized me up and down, looking at me. He was always cleaning his gun, reading his manuals.

Three days after that the *comandante* came back again with another man. They asked me who I wanted to do the negotiating, and I told them Vicente Ortega. They brought a tape recorder and had me write a letter and make a tape. I said I was fine. But they didn't want me to put any date on the letter or in the tape.

That was strange. They said that they would put the dates on. I knew that any letter that you all got without a date would not reassure anyone. There was not going to be any liberation until I wrote or said some things with a date on it because you all wouldn't pay out without a certainty that I'd been alive, say, thirty-six hours earlier.

I thought, why, hell, you're not getting out now.

One day just goes into the next. When I was taken, I never thought that it would last that long. I tried to figure out how long Ken Bishop and Mike Stewart were taken. I remembered that Ken was probably gone forty, or fifty, days.

I couldn't figure how I was going to exist thirty or forty days like that. I said, boy, it's going to be tough. It's an awful feeling, thinking that you are going to have all those days like this.

At one point, on about day fourteen or fifteen, the bearded one shattered my hopes. We were talking about the countryside, and he said, "Well, before you get out, you'll be staying at some little hut someplace and looking out over a hill in the evening, and it will be beautiful," he said, "with the sun going down, cattle around." He made it sound like it might be a while. That depressed me. But then I said, well, he's just talking. I put the thought out of my head and got back to thinking that it was going to be a short stay.

When the supplies started running low, I thought it was because I was getting out. Whenever they started bringing in the supplies, there went my hopes. I'd look to see how many sacks of potatoes they'd bring in, and when it was two or three big sacks, I knew it was going to be a long time. Ten or twelve days. Goddamn. Another ten or twelve days.

When Friday came I would think, well, it didn't happen this week. I don't know why I was thinking that everything would take place during business days, as if it were an office. Sundays and holidays. For me those were the longest days. And when Monday was a holiday, I knew I was in for a long weekend.

It was a thing of ups and downs mentally. And seeing butterflies. If a butterfly landed on my head, you know, that was a good sign. Boy! You were going to get out. That ol' butterfly landed on your head, picked you out. Any little sign.

TICO

MONDAY, JULY 11

I'm back in Charlottesville with Cecilia and the children, who have come home from Mexico. I just keep telling her that there is little to worry about. But Cecilia hasn't really understood. I tell everyone that these things take time. Everything always turns out well. It's a business. We're in the dead period. The guerrillas are keeping us waiting. They're trying to wear us down. But we're strong. That's what I keep saying.

GUERRILLAS

The guerrillas are well established throughout the Magdalena Medio. They count with self-defense groups among major sectors of the population. The majority of the *campesinos* . . . support the guerrillas.

—*La Prensa*

A recent study of the Magdalena Medio explains how this area, just like others that are similar to it, has undergone a transition from small and medium agriculture to extensive cattle-raising. This is typical of our areas of *colonización* [spontaneous frontier settlement]. This area has witnessed a profound decomposition of middle level and small *colonos* [frontier settlers] creating an impoverished population that has little chance of moving elsewhere to initiate a new series of *colonizaciones* And they cannot work off the land due to the expansion of cattle-raising.

. . . A recent study of the National Federation of Cattlemen (FEDEGAN) points out the following: "If we take a panoramic view of the geography of the rural guerrilla, and superimpose upon it the geography of cattle lands, we can rapidly reach the conclusion that the two coincide, are closely related." But more than a mere cartographic association, this phenomenon clearly demonstrates the existence of enormous social conflict.

—Report of the Commission for the
Study of the Violence

The zones where the ELN begins to work are zones of colonización. In our first period, or first stage, we lived practically on the
limits between the jungle and the new areas of colonización.
Due to the voraciousness of the landlords and the violence of
the 1950s, many colonos had no choice but to leave their lands
behind, and they went off into the jungle . . . and started to cut
trees, to plant, and to establish their little holdings.

—Rafael Ortíz, leader of the ELN

The government is currently unable to stop the violence in frontier zones of recent *colonización,* in Urabá, the Magdalena Medio,
Arauca, and Caquetá.

—César Gaviria,
Minister of the Interior

JAKE

I tried to figure out what the company was worth. They said they usually
took 50 percent of a family's net worth. The guy with the beard told me that
right from the start.

I made no comment. I told them, "I have no control over what my people
give, what you will receive for me." I said, "I'm here; all I can do is wait."
That was my story from the start.

I wrote a note authorizing Vicente to do the negotiating. I thought
things would start clicking real fast. I said, hell, they will get hold of Vicente
tomorrow, and I should be out of here in four or five days. I thought about
you at the time and about César. I said, well, Tico is up there at the university, he's going to be busy, and this will go real fast.

But they wanted somebody from the family. I said, "Well, there's nobody
from my family here. My wife lives in the States, and right now I'm sure
she's under a doctor's care. She goes to pieces." You know, I lied.

And I told them that my son is a young boy who just got out of the university, and he wouldn't be able to handle anything like this neither. And they
said, "Well, do you have any American friends here?" I said, "No, I have very
few friends."

They kept telling me that they were a political group and that they were
doing this for their movement. I said to myself, well, no matter what their

political ideas are, no matter how they dress it up, it's still wrong to use this type of extortion to raise money.

I felt like my body was being used as a bargaining point. They've got you, and you want him back, you've got to give us money. Whenever I thought about it this way, I felt very dirty. I felt violated. It's wrong. I mean, you're starting off on a rotten basis. These people who were ordered to get me, were they going to be running the country or parts of the country? I can't see how they'll ever be good for the country.

In some ways I might see that they have certain reasons. We all know the social injustices in Colombia. But I cannot condone a social group coming to power if they have used kidnapping as a means because I could never have faith in that group.

It's the same way with a military commander, a lieutenant, or whatever who has used torture to get information from these leftist groups. He advances to major and controls more people; then he becomes a general and minister of defense. And then in a revolution he comes to power. What's he going to do with his opponents? He's going to torture them, eliminate them. It's the same with kidnapping.

They told me many times that they were sorry they got me. I felt like telling them, you all are talking about being just to everyone and about human rights, but what has happened to my human rights? If you take my human rights and justify it, you can take the rights of ten million people and justify it. Human rights are human rights.

If a man is starving on the street, and he is completely poor, at least he's free. He might have economic problems and sick children, but at least he's free. He is not having somebody telling him when he can go take a shit. It's worse than being in a concentration camp. There you might have a hundred prisoners and ten guards. But one man and twelve guards? That's tough. You have no rights. You have no freedom. Only your mind. Fortunately.

I couldn't decide how they could get away with it. I'd say that about 99 percent of the Colombian people are against kidnapping.

No matter how much you might dislike a person or what he's doing, I don't think you can take pleasure in his being kidnapped, having his body held for ransom. If they have something against someone, don't kidnap him, goddamnit; kill the son of a bitch right there. Assassinate him, but don't kidnap him.

It's an extraction. The next time you're going to ask for more. You start feeling, hey, I can do anything I want because I can kidnap. It must be like a terrorist on an airplane with a bomb, and he says, hey, I'm going to kill

Jake

everyone unless I get what I want. And then they get bolder as they go along. Where will it end?

If everybody has that feeling, that your ideals are so pure, so good, that you can do anything, bring any government or family to its knees . . . then it's all over.

I can't imagine anybody, the first time they kidnap somebody, not having qualms deep down inside. I can't imagine anybody enjoying the suffering of another human being. They knew they were causing the family to suffer. I mean, if the family didn't suffer pain and anguish, the whole thing wouldn't work. It's part of their thing.

It's worse than death. Your body has been completely taken away. You're subject to their will. Your family is subjected to their will. This is against everything I have ever lived for.

It's a completely wrong thing to handle you like a horse, or a dog, that they are going to barter and negotiate over. It makes you feel like you're a pound of meat. That's a bad feeling. They're holding all the aces. They've got your body.

I'd rather have died in the kidnapping attempt and be left there like a dog in the ditch.

Death is no problem. In certain situations it is better for a man to be dead. It's a natural thing, you know, like being born. I am not going to say that we are going to go up to heaven and live in a golden palace. Maybe death will be the last few seconds of one's life, and you say to yourself, it's all right. And that's it. Maybe there will be nothing more. And that's your heaven.

Or death can be a fight, not wanting to die. And you die unhappy. Or you say, what have I done with my life? You have regrets. Maybe that is hell. But death to me is not something to be afraid of. I certainly was ready to die out there. And if you all had taken that money and given it to a charitable hospital, fine.

Yes, indeed. Vicente and César and the others had orders. I told them. I told them I was against paying.

ULLA

He was fun and kind and thoughtful, even though he did fall asleep that first time we went out. He made me look at things differently. I had gone through life accepting things. All of a sudden there were other things to see and do. Everything was fun. Spontaneous. Easier than with Mom and Dad. When I went on a trip with Jake (this was after we were married, obviously), there was no worry. We would go rent a car and drive to wherever, and we stopped somewhere to eat. No problem. Remember Dad always used to say that about Jake? No problem. That was Jake's life. He found a solution to everything.

I learned a lot from him. If I hadn't married him, I would be a very different person. It's not that I have challenged myself to become somebody great or anything like that. But I'm very happy with who I am and what I've done. And it's because of him.

I have not led a dull life. Kind of lonely at times, when he would be gone for many days. We were always in this together, but Jake was always the strong one. It has always been the two of us, too. He wouldn't go out and do something on his own without taking all of us into consideration. Talking to us. Consulting. But he is the initiator.

He was just different. I never worried about whether he was going to be successful. I guess it didn't matter that much to me, you know, the money. But I just took it for granted. Maybe because he did. He was always working to be successful.

I guess he wanted to be a rich man, but not to the point that he would be sacrificing everything. He just worked his butt off, as he says. He worked harder than others. Others in the oil business always admired the way he worked. Everything was done correctly, and he would go wherever, morning, noon, and night. Very few others would do that. He was a worker. That is all there is to it.

He was proud of himself, you know, for what he managed to do. But yet he didn't boast. Maybe inside, maybe to himself.

TICO

TUESDAY, JULY 12

The days are dragging. There are really low points where nothing makes any sense. Won't the guerrillas just give up their fight and go away?

No. I know that's not going to happen. We will have to deal with them no matter how long this thing lasts and no matter how much they talk about laying down their guns. The government and the guerrillas are always talking about peace and about entering into a series of dialogues. Every time I read about another initiative in the papers, I hope beyond hope that something will come of it. I spend hours scouring *El Tiempo* in Alderman Library, reading one back issue after another, looking for clues.

Clues? But what kind of clues am I looking for? I don't exactly want the guerrillas to give up. I do want some kind of resolution to the conflict, and to this kidnapping, but I know that if the guerrillas give themselves up, they will all just be killed on the streets of the city. I don't want that to happen.

In any case, only one or two of the guerrilla groups, mainly the M-19, is likely to return to civilian life any time soon. The M-19 doesn't have him. They kidnap in urban areas, in Bogotá. The guerrillas know that with peace, they will no longer exist. Without guns, they will not be able to compete against others who seek power and influence in hundreds of little hamlets throughout Colombia.

And it's pretty clear to me that the guerrillas can't exactly extoll their violent struggle, especially because they stand no chance of winning. They have to proclaim that they're fighting to bring peace to the nation. Talking of peace gives them a measure of popularity and an image of statesmanship.

The civilian rulers in Bogotá are not losing much sleep on account of the guerrillas. The leaders of the Liberal and Conservative Parties don't feel greatly threatened by them. They know that the guerrillas cannot come to national power, for they won't be able to take over the cities. Bogotá is beyond their reach. I've long believed that the politicians don't really want to get rid of the guerrillas because this way they can always ask the people whether they prefer the current system or a nation ruled by the guerrillas, knowing full well that the most Colombians will take the politicians as the better of the two alternatives. The vague possibility of a guerrilla takeover actually serves to bolster the politicians.

The vast majority of city dwellers don't support an armed insurrection, while many in the countryside fear the guerrillas. People certainly don't want a bunch of gun-toting, bearded rural men galloping through the streets of their capital city, taking over the National Palace and sitting in Congress. The prospect is simply preposterous. Colombians of all walks of life easily understand that their country isn't anything like Cuba or Nicaragua.

Liberals and Conservatives can lose followers to the guerrillas in many local areas without fearing for their power. The government and the military can be ineffective and weak in rural areas, and be seen as interlopers there, and yet not lose a passive sort of legitimacy elsewhere, principally in the cities, where more than half of the population lives.

If the government isn't much to be proud of, many people clearly believe that the guerrillas are a far worse alternative, even though they have some good ideas and at times their hearts are in the right place. The traditional leaders know that they will continue winning elections every two and four years. They compete against themselves, not with the guerrillas, for whatever popularity they can get.

The politicians don't need to compromise with the guerrillas' demands for the social distribution of wealth, an agrarian reform, the nationalization of oil, or the opening up of the political system. But neither can they simply pretend that the guerrillas don't exist. As elected leaders they need to propose solutions. The guerrillas give them something to talk about, something to be politicians with. They also compete against one another with plans, programs, and ideas of what to do. Thus, one president after another calls upon the guerrillas to enter into a dialogue, to do what the guerrillas themselves state they want to do.

Politics in Colombia is the fine art of shadowboxing.

The most public and potentially far-reaching peace initiative in recent history was the brainchild of Belisario Betancur shortly after he became president in 1982. Although formally a member of the minority Conservative Party, he had long sought some measure of independence from it in an effort to build a movement that would transcend the two traditional parties. Betancur wanted new bipartisan commitments that would make government more effective, and he had long understood that he would make it into the presidency only with a significant Liberal vote.

Belisario, as he was popularly known, brought a sincere style and a personal conviction to his effort to end the rural violence, and he caught the imagination of millions of Colombians. But the maverick president had little actual power. He was opposed by economic elites, the military, wide sectors of his own party, and, more often than not, by the Liberals as well. His opponents worried about the reach of his amnesties, while the guerrillas never came to trust him, fearing that he did indeed lack the power to make his promises count.

The guerrillas had experienced the deaths of many of their number who had turned themselves over during prior amnesties. They were most often shot dead while walking the streets of the city. Since 1985 more than seven hundred leaders of the new leftist movement, the Patriotic Union, a moderate offshoot of the Communist Party and of the FARC that had arisen to take advantage of the president's peace proposals, have been carefully murdered. One of the main purposes of the various amnesties over the years has been to get the guerrillas out of the mountains and into the city, where they are easy prey.

Belisario's presidency ended in a debacle when the M-19 took over the Palace of Justice in the central plaza of Bogotá in November 1985, allegedly to demonstrate that the president was betraying them by not following up on his agreement to enforce the amnesty. The M-19 wanted to reinitiate the dialogue.

The military, clearly fearing for the integrity of Colombia's national institutions and perhaps seizing the opportunity to inflict a mortal wound against the guerrillas, quickly attacked the building before the president had a chance to give his authorization. The army didn't trust him.

The scene of tanks and heavily armed soldiers destroying the burning building were seen on television screens across the world. The result was the death of eleven justices of our Supreme Court and of an unknown number of civilians working in the building, as well as of all the guerrillas inside.

Colombians felt a deep sense of loss. The army violated the civilian traditions of the land by acting in total disregard for human life. The president lost his remaining power and credibility. The M-19 had crossed the lines of acceptable warfare.

Out in the countryside, the guerrillas had used the respite of the amnesties to emerge stronger than ever. If the government gained in anything, it was in further puncturing whatever heroic aura the guerrillas still had, as many Colombians came to feel that the guerrillas spoke of peace only to further their efforts to wage war.

Virgilio Barco was voted into the presidency by a landslide in 1986. A laconic man and longtime politician, scion of a family that once privately owned some of the nation's oil deposits, Barco clearly felt that his predecessor had gambled and lost but that the guerrillas were politically weakened no matter how many guns and men and women they now had. He was determined to deal with them from a position of strength. The new president seemed to feel that the majority of Colombians were behind him.

Barco has worked cautiously, slowly. Bits of his peace plan have been dribbling out. I can't help but hope. Maybe something will come of his efforts. I hope against everything that the past has taught me.

But there's no way that the guerrillas are going to be defeated militarily. The army finds itself in a really difficult situation, for it is not exactly in a state of war against the guerrillas. But neither can it provide the nation with peace. Leading military men clearly understand that they don't have the means to bring the guerrillas to their knees.

If guerrilla warfare is an irregular war, it's even more so in Colombia. The guerrillas control only the few areas where they have their headquarters, and these are so heavily guarded that any attack will signify substantially greater losses for the army than for the guerrillas, without even a military victory undermining the local power of the many fronts into which the insurgent movement is divided throughout the country.

THURSDAY, JULY 14

I can hear Cecilia on the phone now talking pretty much the way I do. She is trying to explain all this to friends who keep asking. She tells them that these things take time. These kidnappings happen all the time. Everybody in Colombia has gone through them, she says. She's becoming Colombian.

It's comforting to listen to her, and now I don't have to keep convincing her that nothing is going wrong.

It can only take time. I try to keep writing, to figure it out.

The guerrillas are too entwined in local life to be rooted out. The only way to weaken their power is to intimidate their followers, common folk, *campesinos,* men, women, and children. But such actions will inevitably lead the army to be seen as an oppressive, occupying force by many rural Colombians and lead them perhaps more thoroughly into the arms of the guerrillas. The army is neither willing nor prepared for such a battle.

And neither are the politicians, for a massive onslaught against the guerrillas in which many thousands of innocent Colombians would inevitably lose their lives would lead to a considerable loss of legitimacy for the government and the traditional parties. And such an onslaught will once again provide the guerrillas with the sense of national heroism that they had in the late 1970s, when President Julio César Turbay attempted to defeat them.

Unable and unwilling to overcome the guerrillas, both the army and the politicians state that Colombia's democratic values and civilian institutions do not permit them to defeat the guerrillas. Some generals assert that the laws of the land won't allow them to attack the guerrillas unless they attack first. The army also blames the politicians for not allowing it to fight the real fight, while the politicians often accuse the army of being incompetent and corrupt.

Now the guerrillas are busier than ever. Things have gotten much worse in many parts of the countryside. The guerrillas have a new and formidable opponent: the drug lords. Colombia is an ideal place for processing and distributing cocaine, if only because of its weak government and tortured geography.

The new cocaine elite is finding its place in rural areas by buying up land that the older landowners sell off when they find that they can no longer do battle against either the guerrillas of the left or the right-wing armies of the drug lords. Land is changing hands in the Magdalena Medio at unheard-of rates.

The "drug lords," the *narcos*, are more interested in land as a means toward political power and as a form of prestige than as actual wealth. That obviously comes from elsewhere. So they rarely make their lands produce. As they bring in cattle and get rid of rural labor, Colombia witnesses a new concentration of land in the hands of the few. Impoverished rural people are being forced to flee in search of land and work elsewhere. The guerrillas are finding that the age-old rural conditions that they have been fighting against are getting worse.

What the army cannot do, right-wing death squads often bankrolled and organized by the *narcos* do with relish. These paramilitary groups are blaming the state of rural violence on a weak-kneed government and a spineless military, on institutions they claim are more interested in their own well-being than in that of the nation. These groups inform Colombians that they are fighting against a communist menace that threatens the very essence of the nation, and they proclaim the defense of property, religion, the family, and tradition. They band together with the discreet help of the police and the military to try to dislodge the guerrillas.

But they rarely confront them directly. The death squads go after small landowners and rural workers who are known or presumed to be local supporters of the guerrillas. The newspapers are full of information about one early morning massacre after another of defenseless men, women, and children. In small towns throughout Colombia, young boys are looking up at men with machine guns slung over their shoulders who tell them to run and find another place to live. They flee, leaving a father or a mother, perhaps a sister, lying dead on the ground in front of a tiny shack.

It just keeps getting worse. It's come down to a struggle between the guerrillas and the *narcos*, and I'm back to where I was when the army killed Camilo. The guerrillas are the only ones left who can protect the *campesinos*.

NEWS

By midnight it was still not known why a group of thirty armed men, apparently members of the Popular Army of Liberation (EPL), arrived in the hamlet of Santa Lucia, in the jurisdiction of El Tomate, in the department of Córdoba, killing fifteen people in cold blood, burning down the twenty-four homes of the town. It is the fourth massacre in Córdoba this year. Nobody could understand what was happening. Nobody in the town had been threatened. The so-called Army of National Liberation (ELN) operates in this region. Therefore, it is assumed that this is the group responsible for the massacre.

—La Prensa

According to various sources, the inhabitants of what was once El Tomate had been threatened a few days previously. A group of men arrived in the hamlet and told the people that they had a few days to get up and leave. This is happening all over Córdoba.

Campesinos who sympathize with one or another of the guerrilla groups are marked as being members of that group. According to the Popular Army of Liberation (EPL), many of those who died in El Tomate were part of the EPL. The same group also stated that they had nothing to do with the massacre, and claimed that paramilitary groups were responsible. The other guerrilla group that has been blamed for the massacre has also stated that it was not involved. In a message to the media, the Army of National Liberation stated that the guilty ones are the landowners of the region.

—La Prensa

The current Colombian justice minister kept flying into a temper about the dastardliness of the guerrillas. But he had difficulty expressing indignation about the mafiosi until he was prodded. On some level, I felt, he was grateful to have *los mágicos* [the drug lords] on the government's side of the civil war—especially since for most of the decade they have either been neutral or pro-guerrilla, sometimes paying taxes to the rebels.

—Howard Kohn, writer

What is happening in Córdoba—where kidnappings are multiplying—is symptomatic. The guerrillas arrive in Saiza with a list of members of the self-defense groups, whom they execute. This action then prompts a military retaliation against El Tomate, whose inhabitants are presumed to be sympathetic to the EPL. And so it goes on, a chain of massacres and countermassacres, in the midst of the total impotence of the government.

—Enrique Santos Calderón

Shaken by the Segovia horror, I asked a landowner in Cartagena what he made of it. He shrugged. "They are all Communists there." Was that grounds for killing them? "Look," he said, "this is a rich country run by brilliant intellectuals. But there's no communication between them and the poor. The government promises roads, clinics, electricity, drinkable water, and then never delivers. In Mexico they subsidize the tortilla, and the people don't become Communists. We don't."

Virtually everyone here, regardless of political stripe, agrees that the majority is miserably impoverished and that the government has been either inept or uncaring. Yet, many imply that the situation can't be solved. "Isn't that the real source of the violence?" I would ask. "Doesn't chronic misery breed potential assassins-for-hire and *narcotraficantes?*" More shrugs. It was a subject that clearly made many people uncomfortable.

—Alan Weisman, Fulbright scholar

It's just that a lot of things happen here that the rest of the country does not find out about. There are people here who have been kidnapped three times. There are families that have had to pay a *rescate* to the FARC, another one to the EPL, and are now being forced to pay a war tax to the ELN. A situation like this cannot go on forever. People are getting tired of it. We have only begun to count the dead here.

—Anonymous landowner

STAYING

JAKE

We moved to the third camp. I'd gotten to know Ricardo and the other ones a little bit. We were not friendly, but at least we were getting to know each other.

Jesus, you live with somebody for twenty days, you know, you're able to identify everyone, and you start picking out their daily habits. I felt comfortable with them. And they were getting used to me, too.

I thought to myself, how long is this group going to stay with me? Will I have to get used to some new people, or will they send another bunch that will specialize in giving me the drugs or torturing me? Each time a boat came up, I'd be wondering if they were bringing in the person who would administer the drugs. One day Ricardo said, "*Tío,* all the other people that we've had, they've formed a much closer relationship with us. They want a certain beer, and we get it for them, and they relax and take it easy."

I explained to him that there was a lot of difference between me and a man who has a ranch out here, a *ganadero* [large cattle owner] in Sabana or in San Alberto. His cows, his land, and his ranch are his whole life. His is a slow-paced life. I'm used to doing engineering work, talking to people, making decisions. I was always moving, from morning until night, from one place to another, getting calls, making decisions. All of a sudden I was taken from making decisions to nothing.

I told him. I said, "I don't have anything to do here. This is becoming an unbearable situation."

I don't think it was very smart of him to compare my situation with a rancher. The families felt the same anguish. But he was implying that these *ganaderos* sort of enjoyed it. I can't really understand that. How can you enjoy a situation like that, with the family going through all that stress?

I wanted no special favors from them. I think they respected that. I think that deep down they were the same way. I told them I didn't need any special food. I didn't want tuna fish or sardines. I ate their corn and their peas and rice.

I was no trouble to them. They told me that many times. I made up my own bed. The only thing they'd do for me is cook and wash my clothes. They wouldn't let me wash them. I never asked them anything.

It puts you in a bad position. I don't care who it is, but people will respect you more if you show some kind of a moral standard. Don't show weakness. I guess I also did it for my own self-respect, so later on I could say that I didn't let them get me down. I was still me.

They told me I could have whatever I wanted, *aguardiente* [anise-flavored sugar cane liquor] or wine. I always refused. That's the last thing I wanted: to have my mental capacity influenced by alcohol. If I had started drinking with them, it would have placed us in a different kind of a situation. When a man drinks, conversation always starts. You let yourself go. I didn't want to feel like they were my drinking buddies. No way at all. These people were holding me prisoner.

Ricardo told me about some of them who would ask for women. And they got them women. Why, hell, I could have no more gotten a hard-on out there than the man on the moon. If they had gotten me a woman as beautiful as Raquel Welch, I could have done nothing sexually. That was the last thing on my mind.

The sex drive was gone, completely. The situation that I was in didn't warrant me thinking about sex. I didn't think about women. And that is very unusual for me. In fact, when he told me about them requesting women out there, I couldn't quite believe it. I mean, here's a man who is kidnapped, his family is trying to negotiate his release, and he's thinking about getting sex. Those two things don't make sense to me.

TICO

WEDNESDAY, JULY 20

I keep on postponing my trip to Bogotá. But if I don't go, it means we aren't doing anything to get things moving. We need to do something, at least to feel that we are taking some kind of initiative. But what if I go, and then we don't hear anything, and I return to Charlottesville empty-handed? That will be worse. The last thing I want to do is sit around waiting in Bogotá.

But I have no choice. A one-week round-trip flight will have to do. Maybe we'll hear from them.

I'm taking along a book for Jake. It's just the right one, a travel account of a hundred Italian cities. It's not about the United States, and there's nothing political about it. He'll enjoy reading it, remembering his last trip to the home country, and it will focus his mind on the future. Once he's free, he'll be able to go to all those places. It's an easy read. He's a voracious reader, but I don't know whether he'll be up to something more difficult. Does he have his glasses?

I want Jake to know that I'm sending it, so he'll think about me and name me as the negotiator. I'm ready. I'll go into the mountains and sit around a table with these guys.

But since I can't write anything in the book for fear that the guerrillas will think it's some kind of a code, I asked the manager of the university's Newcomb Hall Bookstore if he had a rubber stamp identifying the store and the city. After a short search, he came back with one. I can't imagine what was going through his mind as he watched me carefully stamp the title page.

I'm off tomorrow morning. First to Washington, then Miami and Bogotá. The flights out of Charlottesville to Miami are more expensive.

THURSDAY, JULY 21

The news reaches me at the Miami airport during the long layover, as I am reading the book I got for Jake, waiting for the man from this company that Ulla contracted to show up. The man, whom I will call Nelson, introduces himself to me. I wasn't looking forward to the encounter, but he looks okay.

He tells me what has happened. The clipping from the paper has been faxed up to him.

> The president for Latin America of the petroleum company General American Pipe, Jacobo Gambini, and the company's president for Colombia, Fidel Lillo Shifihnno, were assassinated by members of the Army of National Liberation (ELN). The bodies of the Italians, who had been kidnapped July 3, were found in a grave in Las Palmeras, a farm in the vicinity of Sabana de Torres, Norte de Santander. Both bodies exhibited horrendous signs of torture. Police reported that Lillo's head had been practically mauled to bits, apparently with a sledgehammer. His body also showed various knife wounds and had been incinerated. Thanks to the investigative work performed by the CIAES, the Intelligence, Anti-Extortion and Kidnapping Command of the Fifth Army Brigade, most of the gangsters who committed this crime are in the hands of the authorities.

Ulla already knows. I am the only one who doesn't. I call her.

The story got on the wire in minutes. Apparently the AP stringer in Bogotá picked it up. The journalist from one of Houston's papers called me in Charlottesville early in the morning to check on the story, to see what I, as the spokesperson for the family, knew about it. We've established this system where the press can talk only to me.

But I was gone. Cecilia didn't know what to tell him, so he called the house in Houston. Thomas answered.

The journalist wanted to know if the boy had any information about his father's death in Colombia.

My nephew had no answer.

Ulla realized that something was wrong and yanked the receiver from his hand. She listened briefly, blurted something, and hung up.

Fortunately, Ulla had already found out what had happened. Vicente had called early in the morning to say that the reporters had probably gotten cadavers mixed up. Or they just thought it was Jake and put the news in the paper.

> The army, meanwhile, said that neither of the bodies found in a shallow grave outside the town of Sabana de Torres Wednesday was that of American oilman Jacobo "Jake" Gambini, who was abducted by leftist rebels June 24. Army Col. Eduardo Arévalo said, "At first we presumed that one of the bodies corresponded to Gambini, but today the colonel identified one as a kidnapped Italian citizen, Fidel Angel Lillo, and the other as Colombian Miguel Henao. We have no evidence that Gambini might be dead," said Arévalo, commander of the Fifth Army Brigade in the city of Bucaramanga, 195 miles northwest of Bogotá.
>
> —United Press International (UPI) wire
> from Tom Quinn in Bogotá

ULLA

We were thrown into a completely uncontrollable situation. You don't know how to handle it. That was the worst of it. What are you up against? You don't know how to do things. It's not like you're sick, and you go to the doctor, and he tells you what's wrong. He knows exactly what to do. We had no idea.

I tried to use my head more than my feelings. To cope better. I didn't want to be Jake's wife and not deal with this well. I wanted to have learned that from him. People wondered if I had any feelings. I know Mami did. But if I let too many feelings out, or let myself feel too many things, I would have managed for about a month, but not four or five. You let your feelings out and get exhausted. Then what? It was more of an action thing for me, of doing things outwardly.

At times I was in charge. Sometimes I didn't want to be. At other times I didn't think that I had to be. But then I should. For me. For Jake. And I don't know if I was really in charge. It was such a group effort. I was also being protected. I hate that. I didn't want to be kept from knowing what was going on. If I let too many feelings out, you would all be overprotecting me. I cried. At night. Alone.

I didn't talk much to people. I didn't need to. I just don't know who I would have talked to. They would listen because they felt sorry for me. I didn't want that. No. Because I still have more than many other people. I've been very fortunate. I mean, I have everything. Well, if he didn't come back, I would have had everything for a shorter period of time. I don't really have a right to talk to people about my troubles.

TICO

THURSDAY, JULY 21

It is already dark when I arrive. The flights from the States always get here at night. As far back as I can remember, there were no flights coming in from the States in daylight. But I was on one once, when we had to stay overnight in Panama because of mechanical failure and flew into Bogotá on the morning of December 23. I was coming back from college to spend the holidays.

With only a small suitcase in hand, I am one of the first ones out of customs. Five or six men surround me immediately in the darkness outside. In English and in Spanish, with corresponding intonations, they ask if I want a taxi.

They compete with one another for the ride, even though the cabs are lined up on a first come, first served basis, some waiting hours in line to get a trip into the city. It's worth it. The cabbies rest while they wait; they converse, read the paper, and don't use up any gasoline. And there is always a hefty surcharge between the airport and the city, especially at night.

My cab is not the next in line. Somebody struck a deal. Traffic policemen usually make sure that the rules are being followed and the correct surcharge is paid, but they do so only during daylight hours, not at night. Nothing changes in Colombia.

I make out the familiar lights of the city off in the distance, all lined up along the side of the mountain. I wait for the feel of the road under us, clunk, clunk, clunk, each time we drive over the thick connecting ridges between concrete slabs. The driver swerves from side to side, avoiding the potholes.

Back when I was a student in Pittsburgh, there was nothing I could say to convince my friends that Bogotá had many more potholes than their city did. It has rained, and the taxi has to slow to a snail's pace more than once where the water covers the highway, reaching almost as high as the doors.

I tell the driver to take the long way around, through the outskirts of downtown, for I want to get an initial feel for the city again. I open the window to let the cold night air in, to breathe deeply and gather my thoughts.

My mother will be waiting at the top of the stairwell. It must have been a bad day for her. I am sure that she is still halfway convinced that Jake is dead. She isn't going to be able to shake her conviction that for once the papers are telling the truth. Why else would I be arriving on this very day?

I look out the window.

"How's the president doing," I ask nonchalantly, after a few words about the weather, the rains. Everybody in Bogotá is always talking about the weather. There are no seasons, but it changes daily, by the hour.

"Ahí está." "He's there."

"And the guerrillas?" I ask. He mutters something to the effect that they are there, too.

"Popular?"

"No," he answers. Then he thinks about it again. "Well, sometimes. With some people, you know."

"They still kidnapping people?"

"Oh, yes. You read about it in the paper. And they took Gómez."

Alvaro Gómez is the leader of the Conservative Party, the son of a much-hated president back in the early 1950s, and himself a perennial candidate for the presidency. He was taken away three weeks before Jake, as he was making his way to hear mass on a Sunday morning in a church just around the corner from his apartment. It was the M-19.

I ask about the peace.

"Ah, it's there. There's peace, in most places, most of the time."

"What about the dialogue?" I want to know.

"No. Not much of that. This president doesn't talk much with them. He's not like the other one."

I don't pry any further. He wants to know where I am from, what part of the States, and what life is like there, and whether it's easy to get in and to get a job, and what salaries are like. He tells me he has a brother in New York, who left fifteen years ago and works as a mechanic. He is doing all right, sending some money back to their mother, and visiting every so often.

My mother is waiting on the stairwell on the second floor. We talk about other things, but she is tired, so she goes to sleep quickly.

I'm back in my old room, up on the third floor. It's cold. I can't sleep.

FRIDAY, JULY 22

I go to Jake's office this morning to talk with Vicente, César, and Jimmy. But there's not much to say.

In the afternoon my mother and I do what I knew we would. We go for a walk, a short stroll around the block.

She walks slowly and as straight as ever, but with the help of a cane now, looking down at the sidewalk in front of her, measuring each step.

I offer her my arm. I enjoy walking, especially in big cities on pavement and even more so in Bogotá and when the weather is good.

We are silent for a while.

"He used to jog past here early in the mornings," she says, "when I was still asleep. Right here."

She stops and is pointing out into the street with her cane, leaving it in the air for a while.

"But I never saw him."

She doesn't say anything else. There are tears in her eyes.

I know now that she's been worrying about him over the years, fearing that he'd be kidnapped on the empty morning streets.

We walk on, but we can't make it around our block. She told me we wouldn't, that we would have to turn around.

She points to it with her cane.

"See," she says, "there it is," a mixture of anger and righteousness in her voice.

There has never been any resignation to her. All her views, everything she has always told me about Colombia, are being confirmed right before our eyes.

The sidewalk in front of us is barely passable.

Somebody in the building next to us has done some remodeling, leaving stone, brick, dirt, and sand in a heap on the sidewalk. People have trampled

Tico

a narrow pathway along one side, but there is no way my mother can make it across.

"It's been there for months," she says. "They don't care. And it's right there in front of their door. *Siehst du? Siehst du?*" "You see? You see?"

The sun is beginning to go down. It gets cold quickly in Bogotá, and windy, so we start back. My mother has always been deathly afraid of the wind, just like all the other Germans I know.

When we get back, we find that a letter with a black rim around it has arrived. An old acquaintance is expressing his condolences. He read the newspaper. We go inside for biscuits and coffee. She drinks tea because it's better for her heart. And she has a thyroid condition.

All day long I have been remembering what it was like when my father was alive. They used to go for walks all the time. It was probably their favorite pastime. They didn't venture far from the house, no more than ten blocks or so in any one direction. They would meet friends, to walk together. *Spazierengehen.* I heard the word all the time as I was growing up.

My parents are German. My father came over in 1920 as an apprentice to a hardware store. He met my mother at a town party in the Ratzkeller in Bremen while on vacation in 1932. They got married, and he brought her back.

For me, Germans are walkers. It's like a vocation for them. It's healthy, good for circulation, my father used to say. My mother knew that it was something that was done. Good for the digestion, too. It was best to walk after meals, after dinner, before retiring for the night.

When we went to Germany in the summers, it was largely so that they could go for long walks, either in Bremen's stately Bürger Park or through pathways in the Black Forest. We would walk to cafés and have "coffee and cake," *Kaffee und Kuchen.* I was bored to tears.

Now I am beginning to understand.

Each time we returned from Germany, my parents bemoaned the state of Bogotá's sidewalks. It would be days before they'd venture out of the house for an afternoon walk. The sidewalks, they said, were not made for walking. I criticized them for being so fussy. They were prejudiced, I said.

Now I'm suddenly aware of the sidewalks, too.

I've only thought about them in the abstract before, as a sign of urbanity and perhaps even more as an expression of the ideals of the modern, liberal world we inhabit. I've always remembered that great German saying, *Die Stadtluft macht frei.* "City air makes us free." The city against the countryside, the new ideas of the Enlightenment, of individualism and citizenship, against the inherited worlds of serfdom and the feudal past. Many major European thinkers, such as Marx and Weber, have placed the origins of the modern world in the growth of the city. And my father always talked about the fact that he grew up in Hamburg and Bremen, two of the first free cities of Europe.

Bürgersteig. The word for "sidewalk" in German. *Steig.* A step up from the road, from the mud, carefully constructed, even, and predictable. Built to be walked on. *Bürger.* The "citizen." The freedom of citizenry, all of us citizens, equal before the law, walking together, fluidly past one another on our sidewalks. Sidewalks join us together. They are a sign of nationhood, of civilization even.

JAKE

The light of the fire. The aroma of burning wood. That's what would wake me up. It smelled so good. They were heating up the water for coffee and getting ready to make breakfast. I'd lie there five or ten minutes, quietly, without making any movement.

I had this idea that I'd pick up some information by listening to them while they thought I was asleep. But I only got to hear what they wanted me to hear. I'd stay under my blanket.

It was pretty cool up there in the mornings in the mountains.

TICO

SATURDAY, JULY 23

All around me is a new country. Somewhere in the back of my mind I've known that it exists. I could sense it reading the newspapers in Charlottesville. And friends and colleagues had made references to it. You'll never recognize it, they would say. Everything has changed, others would add. You won't be able to find your way around Bogotá anymore. It's grown so much.

But these are isolated statements. And actually, the newspapers painted a more familiar picture than the one I'm seeing. They were full of war, of guerrillas, of battles, of kidnappings. And that's what I expected to find. That's my Colombia.

But I don't see anything that might look like war as I walk the streets of Bogotá. If death is stalking this country, I can't really tell. I see a nation full of energy, of vitality. I sense that one person after another is racing ahead confidently and with gusto. I'm out of touch. Others feel safe. I don't.

Most everything really has changed. There is hope, rather than fear, on the streets. The pervasive aversion for the poor that for me had always been the very essence of Bogotá is gone. Women are dressing up again, walking around with their jewelry on.

There was a time in the early 1970s when affluent and even middle-class people kept their finery at home, for they could be sure that a street urchin or some criminal would assault them, to rob them of what they had. Earrings kept being ripped off women's earlobes. The pain, men were told, was intense, and we could see that it was always accompanied by profuse bleeding.

My father had his hat taken quietly from his bald head on a cold morning as he walked out of the hardware store on what was then Bogotá's main thoroughfare. The thief came up to him, greeted him respectfully, tipped the hat from his head to a man standing behind him, who in turn put it on and walked away. My father was then informed that he no longer had to worry about what might happen to him on that stretch of sidewalk, for he'd made his contribution. And he did feel safe in front of the store after that.

Back then we wore our watches on the right arm so that someone couldn't just walk by the car and snatch it away as we waited for the green light. But then thieves took to burning the left arm of the drivers with a cigarette. As they reached out in pain with their right hand, they found that their watch was being quickly taken from them. If they ran after the thief and left their car alone, they could be pretty certain that it would be gone when they got back.

As a youth I marveled at the sophistication of these forms of robbery and, only half in jest, referred to them as a daily form of class warfare. If that's what it was, then the rich have won. There are more Mercedes Benzes, almost all brand new, on the streets than I'd seen during all my years growing up in Bogotá. And BMWs. If there was ever a time when people tried not to show what they had, that time is gone.

Now all I see is a feverish conspicuous consumption, almost as though something isn't worth having unless someone else knows about it. Bogotá has become a city of elegant people. It's surprisingly difficult to figure out who has real money and who is middle class. There used to be a real difference between my clothes and that of a taxi driver. No longer. I find that many of them, as well as many others who clearly work for a living and work for others, have adopted the quiet, calm, self-assured, and at times even arrogant public demeanor of the upper classes.

Our Guerrillas, Our Sidewalks

Women are walking all over the place, even alone and at night. The streets all the way from downtown to the north of the city, where the more affluent areas are located, appear to be safe and in ways that the streets of major American cities are not. The fear is no longer there.

Neither are there street urchins. Those who do beg on the streets don't look anything like they did just ten or fifteen years ago. They're clean and pretty well dressed and plump even, and if they don't happen to be begging, I wouldn't know they're beggars. It feels strange to be giving money to somebody who isn't all that different from me.

People tell me that Bogotá no longer has an urchin problem. The life of the poor is improving. I'm also told that charity is in decline. People no longer give as easily to the poor, a few cents here and there, as they walk around, sit on a bus, or lounge in a café.

Increasingly, the idea is taking hold that poverty is the poor person's own fault. But I still see a lot of people reaching into their pockets at the sight of tiny outstretched arms. Other *Bogotanos* inform me that the urchins, the *gamines*, as they've always been referred to, have gone underground into the city's sewerage system. Life on the street is too difficult. They are being severely repressed by the police, even killed by roaming groups of vigilantes.

The fear that the propertied people once felt is being replaced by defiance. Their lives are no longer threatened by petty thievery. Life itself is at stake. Men and women boast of the number of bodyguards they employ to protect them. Others claim that the minister of defense has given them his official authorization to bulletproof their car. A full-page advertisement in a weekly magazine informs readers that they're the lucky ones, for they are still able to see the ad. If they're alive, it's only because they've turned to the most professional people in the business to have their car protected from flying bullets. With that kind of an expensive ad in a magazine, I'm sure that there is more competition for the business than the minister of defense knows about.

The danger that comes with all this is too obvious. Fear of what the poor might do has been a main incentive behind what little social reform there has been in Colombia. It was what motivated Gaitán as well. If the elites feel that they can't be touched, they will stomp on anyone who might get in their way, and they'll do so with relish. Elites see others in Colombia as so thoroughly inferior to them, so different, that fear is really the only thing that might tie them to the poor.

Tico

SUNDAY, JULY 24

People aren't thinking the way they used to. The economy just keeps growing. Colombia is an economic success story. A new ideology states that the market is responsible for equilibrium and harmony, that government intervention can only be disruptive. Protective tariffs are being progressively eliminated and the economy more thoroughly integrated into the outside world market. Imports are up. I can find practically anything I might want in stores. The president's economic advisers speak about liberation and *apertura*, about the freeing of the economy, about the restructuring of it in terms of the international market. The age of protectionism is over.

Foreign capital is rising in mining, in coal, and in petroleum. More and more consumer and capital goods are being acquired from abroad. As the industrial sector weakens, so does the organized working class. And the tax structure has been reformed to benefit the affluent, for more of state revenues are coming from sales taxes rather than from income and wealth. Consumer goods are taxed at an average of 11 percent, one of the highest rates in the world. Speculation and financial capital, rather than production, are where the big money is. Narco-dollars greatly contribute to this process. The idea is to make a quick buck.

Still, 40 percent of the population, about twelve million people, are living in what the president calls "absolute poverty." Weak and disorganized, they're the least able to protest the new thinking. But I wonder where they are. Like in other modern countries, the poor are there, but they're increasingly less visible. And all those who are doing better, those whose lives are improving, if ever so slightly, are everywhere around me, making themselves as visible as they can. An expanding middle class is joining the ranks of property.

In the 1960s and 1970s, many of the intellectuals were leftists. Indeed, a person couldn't be much of a thinker, a theorist truly engaged in the problems of the country, without being a Marxist. Capitalism was understood to be the cause of all the nation's major problems. It was a dead end. It was incompatible with the nation and the interests of the people. The guerrillas were widely seen as a viable option, perhaps the only one, especially when Camilo Torres joined the Army of National Liberation in 1965.

There are only a few leftist or Marxist thinkers left. And they no longer feel that the guerrillas have much to offer either, and fewer still endorse their tactics. Nobody is in favor of dynamiting the oil pipeline or kidnapping people or forcing landowners to pay the *vacuna*. At most, I'm told the guerrillas have become somewhat of a pressure group that might force the government into some much-needed reforms. But capitalism and inequality, for good and ill, are in the future.

Our Guerrillas, Our Sidewalks

MONDAY, JULY 25

Music blares from every street corner. Bodies sway, even when the melody drifts softly down a long street, barely audible. Sidewalks and streets swarm with buyers and sellers. They're dealing.

The cafés are full of men drinking *tinto*, small cups of black, yet mild coffee. Each one of them comes in with a newspaper under his arm. They sit closely together around tiny tables, talking, always talking. Conversations are subdued and quiet, but all of them together make the cafés hum. Conversations are invariably interrupted by loud laughter.

The men are not huddled together. They aren't whispering. They're not talking about conspiracies. Nor are they afraid of being overheard. There is democracy in Colombia. And they aren't saying anything that is subversive. Even if they are, it doesn't much matter.

Newspapers, magazines, and television screens tell the story of *campesinos*, of rural men, women, and children massacred in their villages at daybreak, of the extermination in large cities of street urchins, vagrants, delinquents, poor folks, homosexuals, and street sweepers.

But few people want to read the newspapers anymore, especially not for news. Another massacre gives way to yet another massacre. Everyone is shocked. Government officials and newspaper editorials condemn the latest action and in the strongest terms. Then there is another. Repetition. Who killed whom? Only the victims become known. Who's responsible? Everyone knows that nobody will ever know. Few people seem to want to read the newspapers anymore.

I can sense that people around me are siding with the new killers, not openly but privately. They understand that right-wing death squads are responsible for most of the deaths and that these roving bands are funded and organized by *narcos* and landowners and even at times assisted by retired military officers with plenty of connections to the army.

What everyone knows, and often seems to condone, the government fails to recognize. According to the leaders of the country, all these deaths are a huge mystery. Public officials aren't even admitting to the existence of the death squads. As many as 140 such groups are roaming the countryside. They all have names. All, or at least as many as can, seek out one word: Rambo. Rambo I. Rambo II. The Revenge of Rambo. The Avengers of Rambo.

It seems that the government and the newspapers are at least publicly at odds with what is on the minds of city people. While many *Bogotanos* regard the guerrillas as part of an increasingly irrelevant past, public officials talk about little else. For them the guerrillas are the main problem of the nation. And as the Colombians I encounter talk openly about the *narcos*, the government and the media try to hush the subject up.

The government knows how to deal with the guerrillas and does not fear them. Politicians turn them into a major issue. But the government does not know what to with the *narcos*, with a rival capitalist elite, and thus tries to forget that they exist. Or some leaders of the government understand that maybe the *narcos* will quietly get rid of the guerrillas and their anonymous peasant supporters.

The press and the law are precise in their use of language. The guerrillas are guerrillas. They're subversives and rebels, not criminals. They engage in criminal and terrorist acts, but rarely if ever are they referred to as terrorists. The government goes out of its way to state that the guerrillas at least have high ideals and political ideologies and principles. They, too, are part of the public, political forces of the land. They don't act for private gain. Only if they are also public figures can the government speak with them, come to political agreements, talk about amnesties.

But many of the people I talk to increasingly refer to them as simple criminals, destroyers of private property, and rarely do I find anyone who thinks that peace agreements with them are in any way possible. Nor do many people think that the kidnappings will ever stop. They're just too lucrative a business.

TUESDAY, JULY 26

The drug lords are new. They're more novel to me than anything else I see. They were not around in 1979, when I'd last lived in Colombia for an extended period. Colombians talk about them with relish, almost with a sense of relief. While few people appear to be interested in the guerrillas and in the massacre of *campesinos*, all have a tale to tell about the *narcos*. They don't seem to be a problem. Drugs are simple, classifiable, identifiable.

The idea that the nation suffers principally from a violence of drugs is comforting, for that is a new form of violence, different from those of the past, less messy, less at the heart of Colombian history. It has nothing to do with Liberals and Conservatives, with the political passions that tore the nation apart just a generation ago. Were it not for all those insatiable appetites in the States, all that craving for immediate satisfaction, all those piggish noses up north, the problem would not have started in the first place. And the *narcos* are only violent against those who get in their way, especially against those bent on extraditing them to the United States. Besides, I'm told time and again, they mostly kill each other off, the Medellín cartel fighting against the Cali cartel.

The drug lords are seen as an economic elite, different but not that different from previous elites, like the tobacco kings and the coffee barons, who made their money through the export of primary goods, products of the land. That's the way everyone gets rich in Colombia.

Early one morning about a year or so ago, when a high-rise building was virtually destroyed by a powerful bomb in Medellín, journalists rushed up to the top two floors to see what they were like on the inside, for Pablo Escobar, one of the three biggest *narcos,* lived there with his wife. The journalists came out astounded by what they'd seen. This was the apartment of a man of sophisticated tastes, a man of culture, even of learning. There was nothing gaudy or overdone about the apartment, nothing nouveau riche about the place. The drug lords are no different from other elites. They're part of the economic patterns of the past. They're everything that the guerrillas are not and cannot be.

A best-selling book describes the drug lords as men of honor, men who never go back on a deal and who don't forget a debt. They're imbued with a precapitalist mentality and are well on their way to becoming established. Comfortable and easygoing in public and overwhelmingly generous, they engage in conspicuous consumption but are cautious in private, for their fortune did not come easily. They accumulate wealth with the constant fear that they might lose it.

Many *Bogotanos* feel comforted because the drug lords represent property and the market. They're testimony to the ideal that small people can make it, can rise up the ladder. Many feel that only the armies of the *narcos* will be able to destroy the guerrillas since those armies are far more technologically advanced, more modern, than even the army. At least they have the will to get rid of their enemies.

People from all social classes keep telling me that the guerrillas have been killing and destroying at will for decades, kidnapping and robbing with impunity. Now the *narcos* are fighting them. They're the only hope the nation has left. Few object when I tell them that the *narcos* are building alliances with other property holders, landowners, to form self-defense groups.

I'm told that because the government does not protect landowners from the guerrillas, the former have no other choice but to take justice into their own hands. Only the *narcos* have the balls to get rid of the guerrillas. The drug lords stand behind their words. They can win the war.

Colombians seem to understand, to know, that "wars" can't be waged against market forces. Capitalism is stronger. Maybe this is one of the reasons,

Tico

beyond nationalism, for which so many are opposed to the extradition of the *narcos* to the United States. They know that getting rid of individuals, no matter how important they may be, can't put a dent in the cocaine traffic. There will be someone else there to take the place of those who are gone. Or maybe two or three will step into the void.

Bogotanos don't want to talk about wars, whether they're against the guerrillas or the *narcos*. Maybe there isn't a war going on, but there are certainly warlike things happening. The situation is all so ill-defined that Colombians don't quite know what to make of it or what to call it. There are different kinds of war, or fragments, in so many different parts of the country, filled with such diverse actors, that it's next to impossible to classify them together as something coherent that can be dealt with or solved through some systematic action.

At the same time, there are plenty of Colombians who are left untouched by the wars or are touched by them only occasionally, or by chance, or for only days or months, that it's hard to feel that the nation itself is at war. If it is, Colombians appear to feel that they can live with this war. It brushes past them, flows through them, comes and goes.

Time and again, no matter where I go or what I read, I come across the same phrases. "We're doing all right; it's the country that's all screwed up." "Colombians have a great ability to get used to anything." "Nothing seems to astonish Colombians anymore." "The economy is going up." "As long as they leave me in peace . . ."

If there is war, many Colombians say, there is also much else. Why don't I ask about that? I'm told not to pay too much attention to the politicians. They're after only their own interests. And the newspapers? They want only to sell newspapers. Time after time, I'm told to listen to the man on the street.

Bogotanos are working and working hard. And studying and learning. Getting ahead. Moving up the social ladder. They're struggling to make a better life for themselves, to buy a better home, to be somebody. They're buying and selling, dealing. There are other things to talk about. Work, for example.

WEDNESDAY, JULY 27

If anything holds this nation together, or at least the nation that I come into contact with, it's a new belief. It's new to me at least, although I now recognize that it's had a long life in the country's history. The people are hardworking. That's what Colombians are saying about Colombians. This is a nation of entrepreneurs, of wheelers and dealers. People here know how to make a buck. As they talk to me, I can see the glimmer in their eyes.

While few completely endorse the new cocaine elite, there is a back-handed admiration for them everywhere. For the *narcos* are a clear demonstration that Colombian capitalists can beat capitalists of other nations at their own game. They make money and just like that. Puff! At the snap of their fingers. In an amorphous, general sort of way, the *mágicos* represent the new nation that I see around me.

Few people want to talk to me about what I want to talk about. There is much else besides war. What about kidnappings? I ask. Yes. It's terrible, I'm told. Everybody agrees. And everybody tells me not to worry. These things happen. They happen all the time. Don't worry. It's just a business. All they want is money. They will take good care of him. Don't worry; he's fine. All you have to do is wait. They will get in touch with you. This happens all the time.

Colombians want to talk about other things. Progress, for example. Life in the United States. Economic growth. Peace. Clothing. Movies. Rock bands. Rock music covers all the social classes of the nation, maybe even poor *campesinos* with small transistor radios. But I don't know. I'm in the city, and there is no way of knowing what life is like in the countryside. But here it's especially poor young kids who are taking to rock. Barrio bands are cropping up all over the place, with electric guitars and all.

A sense of purpose fills the air. Individuals have a direction. The optimism feels genuine. It's not the sort of reverie that haunts cities during an economic depression or before a war. There is no army at the gates. The economy is well on its way to becoming modern, ruled by the objective criteria of the market, by efficiency. The mild forms of state intervention in the economy before 1974 have come to an end. Subsidies of mass urban transportation, food, and education have virtually ceased. Social expenditures are down. The much heralded agrarian reform that came with the Alliance for Progress has come and gone without having had much of an impact on land tenure.

I see a sprightliness to many a step. People glance at one another, then look again, the trace of a smile on their lips, a sparkle in their eyes. Men, women, and children are seemingly ever busy at something.

At night downtown Bogotá swarms with people carrying books beneath their arms. The night belongs to learning. It's the time to take an extra class. English perhaps. Sewing. Business Administration. The night is also for dancing, joking, and drinking. We can drink long into the morning, confident that a friend will be there to straighten out our path, guide us through the difficult sidewalks, see to it that no harm comes our way.

I've got a day left. Tomorrow. Then it's back to Charlottesville. There's been nothing. We haven't heard a thing.

NEWS

Enamórate y sobrevivirás. [Fall in love, and you will survive.]

—Bogotá street graffiti

The most violent country in the world? The international center of drugs? Maybe. But the rock concert in El Campín demonstrated how hollow those clichés about the nation can sometimes be. Those sixty thousand happy, irreverent, tranquil youths, who came from all over, who packed together for more than ten hours in perfect harmony, are communicating something deep. In the midst of all the death that bleeds us, of the *narcotráfico* that gnaws away at us, the spectacle in El Campín was an epic poem to life and peace.

—Enrique Santos Calderón

The shoe phenomenon as a symbol of social and cultural acceptance explodes in our midst. Reeboks appear, and they are used as much in aerobics classes as in the university. Executives use them the most. Walking around with their black Reeboks, this generation has lost all sense of politics, at least for the moment.

The key to identifying fake Reeboks from the real, imported kind lies in the odor. The impostors are known as *chandas* because they smell of cheap glue. The legitimate ones, however, exude the discreet enchantment of silicone.

"Reeboks are not a fashion; they're a style of life, almost a philosophy," a young coed told us.

Never before have our youth thought so much about their feet as today. Generally, they thought with them. Never before have our streets smelled so of imported leather. "Reebok or no Reebok. That is the question."

—*La Prensa*

They dance from the ground upwards. Their feet softly paddle and their hips begin to sway. It's the release of a communal rhythm. Children wriggle like elvers in the spring tide. The old yield to it gravely, like trees to the wind. And the young dance as angels might make love, their hips close, fluent, inexhaustible, their feet hardly touching the ground.

—Roger Garfitt, poet

El país se derrumba, y nosotros de rumba. [We dance as the nation tumbles.]

—Bogotá street graffiti

JAKE

The creeks are always nice. Clear running water. Sometimes there would be a break in the trees, and I would be out there in the middle of the creek. The sun shining down. Very quiet. Very restful.

Taking a bath was a luxury. Beautiful water. They'd give me a pan, the same one they had for me in the mornings to brush my teeth and wash my face. I'd soak myself real good and take that pan and throw water on me. That first pan of cold water. It never ceased to shock me how cold it was. It felt very relaxing, refreshing.

The irony of it. Here I was in the middle of a creek washing myself, cold water, with a guard standing over me. I'd wonder, what in the hell are you doing here? You think to yourself, Jesus Christ, how many more days am I going to be out here? During the whole day, always in the back of my mind is one thought: is someone going to come today? Am I going to get out?

NEGOTIATING

TICO

THURSDAY, JULY 28

The phone in the office rang at 2:50 in the afternoon. We can't be sure, but maybe our wait is over.

A man called, asking for Mr. Vicente Ortega. Vicente was out of the office. The secretary transferred the call to César. That's how it was always done. And that was the way we had planned it, too. I was here at home.

CÉSAR: Hello.

THEM: Vicente Ortega?

CÉSAR: No. Vicente Ortega is not here. Who's calling, please?

THEM: Vicente Ortega?

CÉSAR: No. My name is César Ramos. I work here. What can I do for you?

THEM: Vicente Ortega is not there?

CÉSAR: No.

THEM: Look. Listen. If Vicente Ortega is not there, tell him I'll call him later.

CÉSAR: Who's calling him, please?

THEM: No. Who are you?

CÉSAR: I'm César Ramos.

The caller hung up.
I'm canceling my flight. I'm staying, of course.

FRIDAY, JULY 29

I went to the National University early, hoping to be back in the office quickly in case another call came in. It did, when I was out.

Vicente answered at 9:40. The call lasted five minutes and forty-five seconds. We're all surprised at how long it was.

THEM: Okay. Look, it's that . . . on behalf of a friend of, of Iacopo Gambini.

VICENTE: Yes, sir.

THEM: Needs to speak with you.

VICENTE: Aha. Aha.

THEM: As quickly as possible.

VICENTE: Aha. Aha.

THEM: It's urgent.

VICENTE: Yes, sir. Aha.

THEM: Listen. To tell me when you can come. To give you directions.

VICENTE: Yes, sir. When? How about next Monday?

THEM: Monday?

VICENTE: Yes, next week.

THEM: Look. Can't you come today or tomorrow?

VICENTE: Where?

There's almost two minutes of directions. It's out in that part of the country where Jake is.

THEM: Look. It's so that you can come with one other person.

VICENTE: I can come with someone else?

THEM: Yes. But only one other.

The directions are complicated. And Vicente has to get there at exactly the right time.

They went over the directions again. Vicente will have to fly to Bucaramanga early the next morning. From there he has to drive some hours along a good, paved road. Then it's off a small side road, up a ways, and from there, once the road ends, a brief walk.

VICENTE: Okay. I'll try to be there tomorrow. Anything else? Hello. Hello?

The caller had hung up.

SATURDAY, JULY 30, A.M.

César has gone instead of Vicente, and he will go with Norberto, one of the company's most trusted workers. They are to meet up in Bucaramanga. Both of them are from around there and know the area well. They are risking their lives.

The meeting is out in the middle of nowhere. We're really nervous. Everything is beginning. Nelson has told us that the phone calls appear to be legitimate. It looks like we're dealing with the guerrillas.

We're beginning to move. Soon we will know so much more. But now things can start going wrong.

The guerrillas might not accept the substitution and refuse to speak with César. We don't think it's likely, but they can be kidnapped as well for a short time, to see him or something, or for long, for ransom, too.

We were up for hours last night, planning, thinking of all the possibilities. César is to make it clear he is only an intermediary. He has no authorization to offer anything, to negotiate. He will go to listen and report back.

We practiced all kinds of responses with him. We have things we feel need to be said. But he knows what to do, what to say. I've gotten to know him well. The man's got cold water running through his veins. Nothing rattles him. Vicente is different. Emotional. High-strung. Nervous. César took a pair of glasses in case Jake didn't have any with him.

César wore a white shirt, blue jeans, and blue Reeboks. He's gone.

SATURDAY, JULY 30, P.M.

We waited hours. The minutes just sat there. It seemed like ages. I tried not to look at the clock on the wall. César wouldn't call until early afternoon at best unless something had gone wrong. I tried to keep my eyes from the black phone on the desk.

We got hungry at around noon. Jimmy and Vicente suggested that we go out for lunch because César wasn't going to be able to call until later, but at the last moment I insisted we stay and have the food brought in. Something might happen and he would call earlier. Maybe it would turn out to be a short meeting.

We were just starting to eat when his call came in. 12:45. I looked at the big clock on the wall. It had to be bad news.

César was at a roadside telephone. He had just left them.

"*Todo bien.*" The words we had decided on. "All is well." Contact.

We are in communication with the guerrillas. We are talking to the guys who have him.

It's over. Finally. The wait is over. Now it's just a matter of negotiating. The end is in sight. Everything is fine. We are in control.

It wasn't such a long wait. It wasn't long at all. We've done well. If they had intended to wear us down, they should have made us wait a lot longer. We're in business.

He's alive! I know that is what all of us are thinking. We don't say it. But that has been our biggest fear. He didn't do anything. They wouldn't have gotten in touch with us unless he was alive.

Now it seems to me that during all these days that have passed, we actually did think that he was dead. He's so alive now that I feel completely differently. Now I know that I had pretty well decided weeks ago that the reason they were not getting in touch with us had nothing to do with the rules that everybody kept telling us about. It was because he was dead. He had told them to fuck off, and they had decided to cut their losses and gotten rid of him, buried him somewhere, and we would never know.

It's strange how you become aware of the thoughts and feelings that you have been carrying around with you when you no longer have them, when they are lifted from you.

He's alive. I can't believe it. It's actually true.

I am off to call Ulla. "Sis, we have contact." That's pretty much the only thing I told her. We each are left with our own feelings, feelings we can't express, feelings we can't acknowledge having had.

CÉSAR

After Norberto and I got there at the airport, we rented a car and drove up the highway for about two hours until we started seeing the signs they had told us about. Twenty minutes later we saw the road. We were almost certain that it was the one they had told us to take. We drove on a bit more, just to make sure, another three or four minutes, and turned back.

The road was really bad, just like they had told Vicente it would be. We took it for a mile or so until we could go no farther, and then we started to walk. We crossed the river. Fortunately, it wasn't that deep. We walked for a few more minutes when I started to get the feeling that we were not alone.

Suddenly, they were all around us.

The men in front of us were heavily armed. There were many of them. They had combed the area. We looked at them and they at us for the longest time. Slowly one of them started to walk over to us. He was clearly in charge and the only one who spoke. It was the guerrillas all right.

"*Buenas tardes*," he said, speaking very slowly, softly. "Which one of you is Vicente Ortega?"

"No," I answered, presenting ourselves. "Don Vicente could not come." I told him who we were and all that. And that Vicente was sick and couldn't make it.

He waited for the longest time, just looking at us.

"Okay. We know what we've come for," he said finally, speaking very slowly, softly. "I have been assigned to negotiate this matter. Don't worry. Tell them that this is purely an economic thing. We're a group that has suffered a lot, and this is a struggle that we must continue."

"Yes, sir," I heard myself answering quickly. "We understand your position and we know that this is a business. How is he?"

"He's very well. He's behaved very well. The first week he was real bored, but that's normal. We gave him music and news. Don't worry. We often give him the newspaper to read."

"Does he have his glasses?"

"Huh? What?"

"His glasses? Does he have his glasses with him."

I gave him the glasses, and he took them.

"I don't know. I don't remember if he has his glasses or not, but I'll take them to him. Don't worry."

"Fine, *señor.* Why don't you let us take something of his back so they'll know that I've talked with you, to calm them down a bit. You know."

He showed me two pictures. *La señora* Ulla and *la señorita* Chiara. He had more pictures that he did not show me. They were in his pocket.

"Don't try to do anything strange. We're very serious. We want to bring this thing to an end quickly."

"No. Don't worry. We also want to solve this quickly and in the best way possible. Please keep in mind that the company is not a multinational, as the newspapers reported. It's a small company. And it's feeding quite a few of us."

"Yes, I understand all that. We know all about that. We know. I've talked with *el señor* Gambini, and he's told me everything. We know that what the newspapers say is false."

"Imagine our reaction when we read in the paper that he had been killed."

The *guerrillero* took out a piece of paper, with *señor* Gambini's handwriting on it and all kinds of personal information: birthdays of the family, his

César

address in Bogotá, the car he drives. I read it, but he didn't allow me to keep it.

"We want proof from today."

"What would that be?"

"Tell *señor* Gambini to inform Vicente through you what the name of the dog is, the one they have in the house.

Then he said with a straight face, "Okay. So what is the name of the dog?"

Norberto told him real quickly. "That's it. That's what we want you to tell us."

I almost started to laugh, but I knew I couldn't.

"Fine. But today's impossible. He's a little bit far away from here. And don't ask me where or who we are. In time you'll know."

"By the way, Vicente says that if you want to talk with him, he will be at this telephone number from three to six this afternoon. It's a direct line."

"I'll call. I don't know if today or tomorrow. We can't be going out all the time. We have very strict security. When I call I'll identify myself as 'Eulises.'"

I felt that we were about to say good-bye.

"How is he? What vices does he have? Does he chew gum?"

"That man smokes all the time. And he drinks one cup of coffee after another. He doesn't eat much. But he's fine. When we have a case like this, we give him anything he wants. We give him all the cigarettes he asks for."

I knew it was him. Finally I felt that the man was leveling with me. We had the proof that we were looking for. The coffee and the cigarettes.

"Listen. The next time give us more time to get here. It's complicated. We don't want to arrive late. Next time do you want us to bring you anything? Booze? Cigarettes?"

"No. No. We will leave that for later."

Norberto wanted to get involved. I could tell. He really wanted to talk to this man.

"Listen," he blurted out, "what's your military name? Tell us."

"In time you'll know. For now call me Eulises."

"If we run into the others, what do we do?"

"Who are the others?"

"The army."

"Give them a good excuse. Tell them you are buying cattle."

"I don't know anything about cows. But Norberto does. Okay. Eulises. Thank you. Good-bye."

"Thank you for coming. Have a good trip back."

JAKE

Every night they gathered around far enough away so I couldn't hear them real well. Each night one of them had to prepare a lecture on some subject that Ricardo had assigned. The labor movement. The role of women in the guerrilla organizations. They talked about the political system of Colombia. The history of the Communist Party. The Bolshevik Revolution. The guerrillas in El Salvador. All kinds of subjects. During the day they took out their manuals and studied.

TICO

SATURDAY, JULY 30, LATE NIGHT

César is back. He has accomplished everything and more. We have the real proof we're looking for. It's him!

Now we really know that they didn't kill him in the first days. He's been with them all this time. Smoking and drinking coffee. It's him all right. He probably hasn't tried to escape again. We're in business. Contact has been made. We're on our way. The long silence is over. It has to be over.

The letter. There's a letter from him in his handwriting, and he has authorized us to negotiate. He's playing along. He's cooperating.

I am realizing that this has been my biggest fear. For years he has always said how he was opposed to the kidnappings, how he wouldn't allow anybody to pay a cent for him, how they could just shove it up their ass. Now I can even remember him saying those exact words.

I guess I had forgotten all about that, but now I know that it has been on my mind all the time. He wasn't going to go along, and we would have no way of forcing him. He would refuse to be bartered for. That's what he was opposed to. That's exactly what he was so opposed to. Paying money for a person.

Has this been Ulla's fear all this time, too? Of course, it has. How can I think it hasn't been.

But he's cooperating. He actually wrote a letter. We've got it made.

But we still don't know how much they want.

It doesn't matter. Now it's just a matter of settling on a sum.

SUNDAY, JULY 31

I can understand why they didn't call yesterday, even though we waited around just in case they took César up on the suggestion we had told him to make; to call Vicente. Of course, that was obvious. Why bother calling before César can get back to report to us?

But there was no call today either. We tried to joke around. They keep to normal working hours, we kept saying. These guys are businessmen. Maybe there are too many people in the towns on Sunday, and it's too dangerous for them to call.

But this silence is bad. My mood swings are amazing. I've never gone up and down so violently in such a short period of time.

Eulises had said he would call. Did César hear right? Has something gone wrong? Has Eulises been caught by the army? Had Jake been at the camp that the army overran?

Maybe he's dead, and it's all over because they can't get the name of the dog, and they know it's no use trying to talk to us without it. Or are they going to ask for a lot more money than we'd imagined and feel like they need to make us more desperate?

Dead time. Nothing to do. I've always hated Sundays anyhow. There was never anything to do.

NEWS

Only after an election on Sunday can one see in Bogotá—and I imagine throughout the rest of the nation—such a sudden and intense social life. So many diplomatic cocktails, elegant dinners, and small proletarian parties at the beginning of the week can be explained only by the morbid democratic greed to comment on what has taken place at the ballot box. Everyone has to try to be in everything. Because you can hear anything at all, and all is possible. And because it is true that each one talks according to how he did in the elections, we have to conclude that no one did poorly. After hearing one version after another, only one conclusion is possible: this past Sunday produced lots of victors and no losers. Everybody hit the jackpot; nobody did badly. What a wonderful way of dressing up reality!

—Enrique Santos Calderón

Our Guerrillas, Our Sidewalks

I earnestly beseech you to punctually attend the plenary sessions of the House of Representatives. It is with a sense of preoccupation that I have noticed that during the last sessions we have not been able to reach the necessary quorum to carry through the important bills that stand before this body. Conscious of the immense responsibility that we have as members of the party of government in the success of this legislation, I come to you to solicit your decisive presence so as to ensure the success of the task that has been bestowed upon us.

—José Francisco Jattín, president of the
House of Representatives

When the secretary of the House of Representatives, following the orders of its president, called the roll, he obtained the response of only 95 members. It was concluded that 104 were absent. They will not receive their salary for that day.

—*La Prensa*

More than four hundred thousand candidates ran for a total of 9,733 elected positions in the congressional elections of 1986. This is not a step toward the impersonal rule of English-style democracy, as the idealists would have it. It thoroughly demonstrates the total loss of power of the two traditional parties and the rise of personal ambition.

—María Teresa Herrán, journalist

TICO

MONDAY, AUGUST 1

They call late in the morning. Sunday is gone, almost as though those long hours never happened. It's the same man who called the first two times. It isn't Eulises. César can tell.

We want to talk money. How much? Can they tell us? Now. Over the phone. No. He says no. Damn!

Tico

It's going to be another meeting close to where the first one was. But we don't want to meet with them again and try to keep the negotiations to the phone. Vicente tries and tries, but they won't budge. And they want him to go. Vicente. But we need our proof to continue negotiating. Those are the rules. We need the name of the dog

THEM: What?

VICENTE: Do you have the name of the dog?

THEM: You killed the dog?

VICENTE: What?

THEM: We have to order a dog?

VICENTE: No. We have to know the name of the dog.

The caller is desperate. Things are not going as he wants them to. He is nervous, breathing heavily. We figure he doesn't know anything about the dog. He only has instructions to get Vicente into the mountains. He knows nothing else.

But at least there's no question that we're dealing with the guerrillas. They don't tell their people more than each one needs to know. We have to continue. It's not the caller's fault.

But why can't they give us the name of the damn dog? Why aren't they making it easy? What's all the mystery about?

Maybe Jake is too far away, and the caller hasn't been told yet. Jake wouldn't refuse to give the name. Or would he? No. After all, he's already authorized the negotiations. But maybe he'd been forced to write that letter.

Maybe . . . no. They have to know by now that they won't be able to negotiate with us unless they can give us constant proof that he's alive. After all, the guerrillas are not dealing with idiots. We know the rules.

But that dog. Why did we even bother to ask? Maybe the guerrillas are angry that we didn't trust them.

It turns into a ten-and-a-half-minute phone call. The connection is bad, and Vicente is never quite sure what he is hearing.

Once again, the instructions are complicated, and we can't afford to get them wrong. Again, we make all the arrangements. Vicente and César are to go tomorrow morning. They'll take Ulla's letter to Jake and the book I've brought with me from Charlottesville.

I quickly make a hotel reservation and give Vicente the number where he can reach me as soon as they can after the meeting is over.

I don't want to wait around in the office to get the news. There are too many people around, and since both Vicente and César are going to be out, everybody will figure out that some sort of negotiation is taking place.

Even though I know that the office discipline will be there, that the culture of kidnapping will not be broken, that everyone knows not to talk or ask questions, I still feel uncomfortable. Neither can I wait at home with my mother right there. No phone calls to the house. She doesn't know that we've established contact. I can't afford to have the guerrillas stringing her along from one day to the next. I can't have her asking me what's happening each day.

TUESDAY, AUGUST 2

Nelson flew in from Miami last night. The professionals want to be closer at hand, and Ulla has agreed. Jimmy, Vicente, and César have come to trust Nelson.

Calculating that the meeting will last about an hour, Nelson and I go to the hotel room at two in the afternoon. That is the earliest they can call from some roadside phone.

I insist that we enter the hotel separately. I know that they have been following me from the beginning, and I sure don't want them seeing me walk into a hotel with some gringo. Nelson goes first, and I come about twenty minutes later.

I can't read or write, just can't concentrate on anything.

Nothing. Nothing happens. The phone doesn't ring. I look out at downtown from my room on the twentieth floor. Four hours. Something has gone wrong. There is no other explanation.

Now I can understand what Nelson said about what a bad idea it is to be in the room alone, just waiting for the phone to ring. I am even glad that he is around.

It is beginning to get dark. The sun is going down. Vicente and César have been taken. I am convinced of it. We won't hear from them until at least tomorrow. Maybe the army has got hold of them.

We have to call their homes. What am I going to tell their wives?

The phone rings. It is Vicente.

"Five," he says. He says nothing else.

"Five what?" I want to know. I slowly recognize what we are up against.

"Five big ones," he says.

Five million dollars.

Tico

I sit there on the bed with the receiver in my hand. It is like I can't move. I am really paralyzed. How in the world have they come up with that sum? Now what are we going to do?

I guess Nelson has heard me say it is five million.

"Don't worry," he says, almost nonchalantly. "It's only their opening gambit."

I could wring his neck right then and there.

But Ulla is waiting. I have the hotel operator place the international call. I can hear myself saying it. "Don't worry, Sis. It's only their opening gambit. They can't be serious."

Then I call Vicente's wife. "*Todo bien*," I tell her. "Everything is fine. They're coming back." She must be wondering whether she will ever see her husband again.

I can't believe it. Five million dollars? It's absurd. How long will it take us to reach a settlement? What in the world are the guerrillas thinking? Jake's going to be gone a long time. This is ridiculous. As far as I know, we're facing one of the highest demands ever made for anyone in Colombia. This is ridiculous.

VICENTE AND CÉSAR

THEM: We've set a sum of five million dollars.

THEM: Look. We have a fixed sum in mind, and from it we're not going to go down. Tell the family that they shouldn't start out too far down and from there go up slowly, step by step. We'll just lose a lot of time.

TICO

TUESDAY, AUGUST 2, EVENING

Categories. I keep thinking about categories of people. What kind of a category have the guerrillas put him into? What in the world are they thinking? If they usually take 50 percent of what a person is worth, do they really think my brother-in-law has ten million dollars? They have to be crazy.

Jake has done very well. I know that. But ten million? Is he worth that much? It's not something we talk about. Only once many years ago when he was driving me to the airport, he told me that if I was ever in need of anything, let him know. He could help. He let me know that he could really help. That it would come pretty easily. He wanted to be there for me.

But do the guerrillas know something that I don't? If it's their opening gambit, how far down will they go? How much money do they think Jake has? How much do they *know* he has?

Do they expect Ulla to sell the company? That will take months, if not years. What's it worth? Jake tried to sell it a few years ago, and there was only one buyer. The deal fell through for some reason I never really found out about. Nobody would buy the company now unless they thought that they could really get it on the cheap. And the oil business is in a slump.

I keep coming back to the same question: what category have they put him into? Maybe he's in one all his own. After all, there aren't too many foreigners in the oil business who are majority owners of their own company. But the company doesn't do any drilling. It's not one of those big ones. The newspapers never even got the name right. Nobody outside the oil business has ever heard of the damn company. And we told them it was not a multinational. And Eulises had said that he knew that. What the hell is going on? Are they confusing General Pipe with American Pipe or General Tire or General Electric?

I'm angry. My brother-in-law built the company up almost by himself. What in hell are they thinking? He's a moral man. He's treated his workers better than anybody else. What right do they have to do this? I walk. I swallow hard and breathe deeply, rhythmically. I've got to keep the anger down, got to get rid of it.

Categories. Colombia. Categories of people. How can people simply be placed in categories like this? I hate it. If Jake has all that money, I can really understand why the guerrillas kidnapped him. They would think nothing of it. It would be their right. Millions of dollars, and all around them the guerrillas see people eking out a miserable existence. They, too, are poor. If someone has ten million, and he gets to keep half of it, he's still in pretty good shape. They are only depriving a person of a few days of his life. And they give him back. They use the money to bring change to Colombia. It all makes too much damned sense.

JAKE

I didn't allow myself to take a nap in the daytime. It was tempting. It would have been a way of killing time. And they told me, "*Tío*, why don't you take a *siesta*?" But I knew I didn't want to do that. If I took a nap, I wouldn't sleep at night.

Night was the best time of the day. I'd lay there under the mosquito netting. With darkness coming in I had my privacy. They couldn't observe my face or see my eyes. I never could figure out how long I stayed awake. One hour. Three hours. Once I fell asleep it would be a good, solid sleep. Every once in a while I'd wake up because they would be constantly putting their flashlight on me. I guess it was for security. I got to know who was on guard by the number of times they flashed on me because some did it constantly and others did it very few times. It would wake me up a little bit. I'd turn over so the flashlight couldn't hit my eyes and go back to sleep.

TICO

TUESDAY, AUGUST 2, LATE NIGHT

It's been a long day and an even longer night. My bones hurt. Vicente and César got back two and a half hours after they called. We go over all the details of the meeting. They have brought back the documents César was shown the first time, a letter from Jake authorizing Vicente to do the negotiating, the pictures of Ulla and Chiara, and the note with all the personal information on it. Eulises only released them to Vicente. The note is more in Italian than Spanish, and that worries me. I didn't know Jake's Spanish was that bad. Ulla reassures me that it is.

After quickly faxing everything up to Houston, we go through each piece of paper as though we are in the presence of long-lost historical documents. It's comforting to know they're his. But I feel goose bumps all over me and slight shivers.

It feels eerie to see pictures of Ulla and Chiara, smudged and bent at the edges, to know that they've made the trip to the mountains, been taken away from him, been in their hands, and been brought back to us. I don't think I would feel the same sort of uneasiness had the pictures been of Tony and Thomas. Where all have they been? What have they been through? It's almost as though my sister and my niece have also been kidnapped. Raped.

The note with the personal information is dated July 25. Our relief at hearing from him a whole month after he was taken away ends moments later when Ulla calls to say the date is a fake. It's not in Jake's handwriting.

There it is at the top of the note for all of us to see. Of course, it looks different. Why hadn't we noticed? Why did they do that? They used the same pen and obviously tried to imitate his handwriting. But the difference is there, glaring out at us. Why? Why bother?

We pore over the documents again, looking to see if there is some kind of a code in what he's written. There has to be. Why did he pick those precise dates and facts? Is there some kind of meaning in the order of things?

But there isn't anything there. We aren't getting any directions from him. He's not doing the negotiating. It's up to us. Jimmy still thinks that Jake will take over the negotiations.

The next steps will be the most difficult, and we don't know how much time we'll have to make them. What are we going to offer them? We need to decide on our opening gambit, and they've thrown us completely off balance.

We are up until almost midnight. It's been an exhausting day, especially for Vicente and César. My bones hurt from the tension of those hours in the hotel room, from the walk, and my anger. I can't imagine how Vicente and César are feeling. We know what the rules are, but now that we have to use them they don't help much.

WEDNESDAY, AUGUST 3

We are having a terrible time coming up with the right figure. We thought about it all day yesterday. Are these really the rules? Has everyone given us the right advice?

Nelson keeps telling us to stop thinking about the five million dollars, that we have to be rational. He says that we can think only about what we can pay and not what the guerrillas say they want. We have to think about what is realistically possible, create our plan, and stick to it.

We've got to think both about our first offer and about the long run in order to create a situation where we can be consistent, where the guerrillas can figure out what we are doing, how we are negotiating, so that they can come close to predicting our moves. They have to see our rationality, to know from our first offer pretty much what they can expect to get in the end.

The rules, and common sense, dictate a sum that will be sufficient in their eyes to let them know that the kidnapping was worth it. They were going to make a bundle. Otherwise they might just decide that it's been a bad move and even kill him. Maybe.

And I know that the guerrillas can't afford to let families get away with paying too little, for then their business would enter into something like a depression. Our need is to protect his life. We have to come up with a figure that is less than what we are willing to offer, so we can move up, but not a lot less, so they won't be able to string us along for weeks and weeks.

The rules are there, but we don't know what's going to happen next. Are they playing by the rules? Not if they want five million dollars. I keep having to tell Nelson that I am indeed trying to be rational about all this.

Half a million. That's the sum that I kept hearing. It's what Ulla said from the start. That was Jimmy's sum too. I didn't ask questions then, and I'm not doing so now. But a half-million is what we have been aiming for. Maybe it's what Jake thought it would take. I think it's also a sum that Ulla can get a hold of pretty quickly.

We come up with different figures and rationales. Nelson consistently suggests the lowest. He knows more than the rest of us and is less involved. He can't know what it's like.

But we can't agree. So it's up to Ulla to decide. We each put our views in writing and fax them up to Houston. Jimmy, Vicente, and César are higher.

It doesn't take Ulla long. She goes along with my suggestion, which is slightly higher than Nelson's. He suggested a quarter of a million dollars. I wanted something more manageable in pesos and something that would indicate that we hadn't just picked an easy sum, like a quarter-million.

Ulla tells us to offer them 80 million pesos. At the current exchange rate, that's 266,000 dollars.

Right then and there we also decide what our increment or increments will be. The five million are not playing a role in our decision. At least I don't think they are. We're still angling for that half-million.

But what if he knows? Does he know? Do they talk to him about all this? Did they tell him what they were asking? Then it's all over. I mean, if he finds out that they are asking for five million, that's it. He'll stop. I mean, he won't cooperate anymore. There won't be anything we can do.

But why does he still have to cooperate? Can't they now go ahead even if he opposes the process? He's done the authorizing. We have the letter. How can he stop this? I don't think he can. Not anymore. There is nothing that he can do. It's out of his hands. We make the decisions now.

But I hope he doesn't know. It will just kill him. Nelson says the guerrillas never tell their victims anything about the negotiations. They are kept in the dark. I hope he's right. He's got to be. I mean, he's been involved in dozens of cases. He knows a lot of things that I have no idea about.

THURSDAY, AUGUST 4

The call comes in at 2:35. It is short.

There is going to be another meeting. Another day. Another time. Another place.

But the process is moving along. Suddenly it seems that it's moving quickly. We're making progress. The negotiations are about to begin. Got to forget about the five million.

CÉSAR

"Is it safe?"

"What do you mean?"

"They're all over the place. We saw them just down the road."

"Who?"

"Them. The military. There are trucks all the way up and down the highway."

"No. Don't worry. They're over the hill there. We have everything under control here. What are your people offering?"

"Eighty million pesos."

He became very serious, and he kept looking at me physically, in the face. I felt like I was no longer me. Eulises brushed his hand against his forehead slowly, and slowly he shook his head.

"No. That's very little. That's why I told you not to start so far down."

This man is a professional. I can tell he has done this many times before. And he's just a kid. Not more than twenty-five. Here he is. We are talking about millions of pesos, and he doesn't bat an eye. He has me cornered.

I didn't know what to tell him. Norberto was standing behind me. I knew he was going to say something.

"Look, Eulises, tell us who you are."

"It's not convenient to tell you."

"It's just that there are so many groups that one doesn't know who's who anymore."

"All the guerrilla groups are the same. Our goals are all the same. It's only important that the family knows that we are a serious organization."

He paused. He was looking at me directly again. He hardly moved an inch.

"We made our demand because we know his economic capacity, and we know what he has and where it is. We studied this case well, and we know that he is a powerful man. We take those that make their money off the labor of others, taking away their salary, their fringe benefits, and anything else they can. That is why our working class is so poor. Look, we are a serious organization. We have our *estado mayor*, our general staff, and all those things that an organization needs. This has been studied well. Our new petition is three million dollars. *Verdes.* Greenbacks."

TICO

FRIDAY, AUGUST 5

I'm ecstatic. It's the best phone call to Houston.

"Hi, Sis. . . ."

We picked the right sum to get things going. I feel as though we've made two million dollars and in just a matter of hours.

But best of all, they have accepted our offer. We're dealing. The process is on. They're willing to negotiate. The rules are working. Everything is predictable.

Of course, they came down. And they will do so again. Things are moving. Maybe we can have him back in about ten days. In the next conversation they'll say two million, maybe less. I'll get back to Charlottesville in time to prepare my fall classes.

I sit alone in my room and work on charts. Our increments, their offers. At the rate we're going, it's a matter of two, maybe three more meetings. Maybe we can do it over the phone. It's what we really want. It's quicker, safer. César has worked out a code to use on the phone in case the police have our phones tapped.

But we don't know whether they will actually go along. Isn't the phone safer for them, too? I'm keenly interested in their safety. If the army gets to Eulises, we're in trouble. They might even think that we are behind the action.

SATURDAY, AUGUST 6

We've had a great eight days. A week before we had heard nothing. Now, suddenly, we're closing in on a deal. Even Nelson is surprised at how well things are going. We're ready for the next phone call. More than ready. Anxious. My heart is pumping. I've known how to deal with this from the start.

TUESDAY, AUGUST 9

The phone doesn't ring. Nothing. Emptiness. Silence. Dead days. It's so bad that I can't sit down to write. I can't read anything. Can't concentrate. The first two days we could sort of understand. That was Saturday and Sunday. But Monday and Tuesday? The dark thoughts return. Something has happened. Maybe they are arguing about how much to come down.

WEDNESDAY, AUGUST 10

It's a bad connection. And there is a new voice on the other end.

THEM: Hello?

CÉSAR: Hello.

THEM: This is Eulises.

CÉSAR: Ah. Yes, sir. How are you?

THEM: Very well, thank you.

CÉSAR: What's new?

THEM: What?

CÉSAR: What's new? What's up?

THEM: No, nothing. It's just to find out if you're going to pay the money for this job, at nine hundred a meter.

We are a little confused at first. He is using the code that César settled on with them. And he is talking in Colombian pesos. He wants to know if we are going to pay the three million.

CÉSAR: Look. One little thing. Tell me, do you have the name we asked for?

THEM: Eulises Two.

CÉSAR: No. But don't you have the name? The name of the dog? The name of the dog?

THEM: Look, brother, we've sent for it. But, unfortunately, the name hasn't arrived.

CÉSAR: Look, let me tell you something. Tell Eulises, Eulises One, that the family has to know the name of the dog before it can start talking about salaries.

I don't think the code that Eulises suggested is all that great. If Maza Márquez, the head of the secret police, or one of his lieutenants is listening in, he'll catch on to what is going on pretty fast. But then he already knows. He knows we will be negotiating. Why are we bothering with all these codes? Why have they insisted? What makes them so nervous on the phone?

THEM: Ah. Okay. Fine. Then. Look. When the kid arrives with the name, then we'll talk again.

CÉSAR: When? When? When will he arrive with the message?

THEM: Tomorrow. *Mañana.*

CÉSAR: When will you call me?

THEM: Maybe tomorrow. If the kid arrives with the name.

We're getting nowhere. That damn dog. I'm getting ready to wring its neck. But at least they know we're serious.

And César manages to ask Eulises Two if they have a new offer. At least they know we are fully expecting them to come down.

But the caller hangs up quickly when César asks the question. He isn't about to negotiate. He has no idea what the sums involved are.

FRIDAY, AUGUST 12

Apparently the kid didn't arrive with the name of the dog, for we waited all day yesterday, and the phone didn't ring.

But today it has. Friday is turning out to be our big day.

Yes, he has the name of the dog. The man on the other side of the line is nervous. He can't get it quite right. It sounds close, but we have our doubts.

Can he spell it, please?

He gulps. F-A-I-S-E-R.

No. That is wrong. But it's close. The caller is trying to keep his composure. What will happen to him if he gets it wrong? What will his superiors say if we don't accept the name?

César asks him to pronounce it again. It seems all right. But we want to make sure, feel comfortable.

Piper. That's the dog's name. From General Pipe. The other dog's name is General. Not terribly original, but that's it. They may even have guessed it right.

But when we first came up with this question, after discarding about ten or fifteen others, I never for a moment thought it would turn out to be difficult for them. My bicultural background serves me little. Should I have known not to ask them to pronounce something that sounds different, especially over the phone? I mean, these are rural people with little or no education, and they feel uncomfortable enough dealing with us to begin with. And then we give them something in English.

César tells him he is going to verify with the family. Can he call back, in an hour or so? Sure, the caller answers, much relieved.

I am willing to go along with the name. So is Jimmy. It is close enough. I mean, they can't have come up with something like that on their own. They can't risk it. Vicente and César don't take a position. Nelson wants no mistakes. He wants to make sure that Ulla is in on the decision.

We listen to the tape of the conversation. We put the tape recorder next to the phone so Ulla can record the words in Houston on the answering machine.

It is good enough for her.

We are ready to move. No call. We're looking at the weekend.

FAISER? The guerrilla came up with his own spelling. There's no note. Jake told them the name, but he didn't write it down. Or if he did, something happened to the note. No. Jake's far away, far away from where the calls are being made. They telephoned the name to the caller. Maybe they have radio communication. But he's far away. These guys know what they're doing.

SATURDAY, AUGUST 13

The call comes in at 2:20. The name of the dog is fine, we tell them.

Do they have a new salary? No.

We go up ten million pesos, to three-hundred thousand dollars. The caller has what he wants. He hangs up.

Tico

TERRORIZING

JAKE

It all started on August 13 when the leader comes to the camp. It's the first time I see him. He comes about three or four in the afternoon, with the second in command, the one that I gave my jewelry and everything to on the first day. He told me they were having trouble in the negotiations with Vicente, and they'd like to know who else I could name as negotiator. I said, "No, it has to be Vicente. I don't know anybody else." He wanted me to give a description of César. Then he asked his second man, "Well, is that it?" He said, "Yeah, it sounds like him." They were afraid that Vicente might have brought a military man with him.

He asked me to write a letter so they could also negotiate with César. He told me that he'd heard that we had a very big company in Sabana. He asked me where else we had operations. So then he goes back and gets everyone together, quite a long distance away, and talks to them all.

In the morning he comes to me and he says, "When you're released, when you go to the airport, we'll give you back all your belongings." He told me not to give anything to the man who was going to give me my things, no money, no nothing. With that he shook my hand and left. He left me with an impression that things were going to start happening.

There was a buzz in the camp. Something was going on. That afternoon I went to take a bath. The cook shack was about twenty feet away. Sonia said, "Boy, *el tío está acabado; está muy acabado*," that I was looking tired, wasted. And Juan said, "Yeah, but as soon as he gets out, he'll have a real long vacation, and he'll be all right in a short time." He said it loud enough for me to hear. Well, that naturally excited me. That night as I go to bed, little Juan and another one who had just come in are talking. "Say," he said, "the news has just come in. They asked four thousand million for him, and apparently they offered to give two thousand million, and we haven't heard yet whether they're going to accept." I heard this. They were about fifteen feet away. Nice round figures. Twelve million dollars. Six million, six million. The next morning one of the girls asked Ricardo for some cigarettes. He came over to where they kept my cigarettes, and he said, "Oh, yes, he's got more than enough to last him until this is over now." He left me four packs of cigarettes and gave the rest to her and the others. And he said, "Since you all are staying here when we leave, we'll give you all but the one or two packages that *el tío va a necesitar*," that I would need.

They started preparations to go. They brought my boots so that I could make it up the hill. It was raining and muddy. Then Ricardo said to one of the other ones, "Go cut some vines, so that when it's time to get out of here, we can tie them to the *tío* and pull him up if we have to." They laid them under my bed. This was Tuesday morning. At noon Ricardo said, "No, don't fix dinner today. I don't think we'll be here for dinner." But that evening nothing happened.

The next morning there was quite a bit of excitement. They were all talking to me about how things were in the States and what I would do there. Ricardo said, "Well, when you get out, what are you going to tell the reporters?" And I said, "What reporters? I don't think nobody is interested in me." "Oh, yes," he said, "everybody will be interested. People will ask you how you were treated. What are you going to tell them?" "I still don't think they will interview me," I said, "but I'll tell them you all treated me very well, you all are well disciplined, you all didn't mistreat me, and I had everything I needed." "That's fine," he said. "We don't like it for people to get the wrong impression of us."

That night they were talking again, and this little one named Juan said again, "Looks like they accepted the two hundred thousand, and tomorrow they're going to pay, and we'll be leaving here for Sabana." I was getting very excited. The next day was Wednesday. And again no meals. They were waiting to see what was going to happen. They had everything packed.

When the guard on top of the hill would knock real hard on a tree, they would know that they had a message or that somebody was coming in. At about three o'clock, one of them says, "*Ricardo, hay alguien; hay un mensaje.*" "Ricardo, somebody is here; there's a message." So he went up there, and then he came down pretty fast. He said that Vicente had brought a military man along, so they took the money and were not going to let me go. They were going to ask for all twelve million dollars. The plane was going to leave Sabana without me, and they could have their big party in Bogotá without the *tío*.

After a while then he was talking to Mónica, and he told her that Ursula was in Bogotá and that she was going to get together tomorrow morning with a woman commander. I tried not to react to none of this. They cooked something and I went to bed. I was pretty down in the dumps. And I said, goddamn, Vicente, how dumb can you be? The sum of six million dollars never entered my mind. Then that night I started thinking about it. Where in the hell did they get that money? And how did they get it so damned fast? I thought maybe the government, something, I don't know. Sold the company somehow and equipment, the house, and your mother's money, sold shares, my brothers, my mother, friends, Ursula's jewelry, maybe the oil companies were helping out. But that didn't make much sense neither. I kept wondering if Ursula had sold the house with all the furniture in it.

Where were they living? Anyway, I felt disappointment and anger, and I was little bit pissed off at Vicente.

That night Juan said, "Well, looks like we're going to move to a new location in the next few days, and there we're going to start treating *el tío* a little different." He said, "We're going to learn everything that he has, and then we might just kill him." That didn't make much sense to me. I could see the sense of trying to find out everything I had, but why kill me?

The next morning about noon, Ricardo comes back down from the hill, and he tells Mónica that Ursula had gotten together with the woman commander, *la señora se encontró con la comandante, y hablaron, y después de un rato la señora la llamó una ladrona, una puta, y se puso furiosa la señora, y la llamó todos los nombres que usted se puede imaginar.* That didn't sound right to me neither. The first thing I thought was how in the hell did they let Ursula come down there to Bogotá, and why would they have let her meet with this lady commander? And I couldn't think that Ursula would call her a whore and use all that bad language. I mean, no way.

Then Ricardo says, "Now we're going to get all the money we asked for and more. Now we've got it. We're going to hold off if we have to for years, but we're going to get what we want. *Años, si es necesario.*" I didn't react. And they told me that Ursula had came down in a private jet to make me believe that Ursula is beginning to show money. I couldn't quite believe that.

The next morning it's raining, and Mónica gets under the tarp. She says, "Why don't you write a letter saying that you want to get out and that they should pay a certain sum of money?" She felt sure that I'd heard the sum of two thousand million. So what did she want me to do—ask her, "What do you want, two thousand million?" And she would have said, "No, four thousand." And I would have said, "No, we don't have it," and start negotiating between two and four thousand million. You see, she was thinking that I knew that they already had two thousand million and they wanted more. She was trying to get me to admit that we had two thousand million.

I said, "Look, Mónica, if you want me to I can say pay two hundred million dollars, but that doesn't matter because there are no two hundred million. It is all whatever they want to pay and what is available. I have no control over that. I'm just here. I'm one of the central actors in this play, but I'm not the director." So she told me that they had one man that was held for five months until he wrote the letter, and then he was out in five days. I said, "Well, I can't do anything about that."

They started talking about moving. Ricardo and Mónica got to the end of my bed. I had gone to urinate, and when I'm coming back, they're talking about the move and starting the *terapia física,* this "physical therapy" thing.

Jake

Man, that sounded bad. The next morning two or three of them left, apparently to fix up the new location, and two days later we left. In the meantime there was some talk of Ursula and that now they were going to check on us.

You could see everybody's mood toward me had changed. Sly remarks— that two of them would hold me down and beat me up. But they said these things off to the side where I could just barely hear them. They whispered to themselves, but always so I could hear them. I just played like I didn't hear anything they said.

TICO

TUESDAY, AUGUST 16

Nothing. No call. I've got all this time on my hands. I pore over the newspapers. Looking. I come across a story in *La Prensa,* a new Conservative Party newspaper. I rip the words from the bottom half of the page and put them into my shirt pocket so that I can read them to Cecilia over the phone in the evening.

> The exchange of human beings has been converted into a new aspect of kidnapping in Colombia. The criminals have dedicated themselves to exploiting it without a second thought. If the victim gets sick or is too exhausted by the long captivity, it doesn't matter. He's simply exchanged. And family members, anguished at his illness, resort to the exchange as the only means of salvation.
>
> In Cali, a man who had been kidnapped was released when the criminals realized that he was the only one who could provide them with the money they wanted. The details of the transaction were kept secret, at the insistence of the authorities, until the *hacendado* and political leader Rogelio Rodríguez García, who had been taken more than a month ago, decided to talk to the press about the operation that took place last Thursday, in which his nephew was obliged to replace him.
>
> According to the police, a priest served as intermediary in the negotiations between the family and the kidnappers, who apparently belong to the so-called Army of National Liberation (ELN), which operates in northern Valle.

The authorities disclosed that after making a payment of ten million pesos, the guerrillas agreed to liberate the *hacendado* and Conservative politician as long as his nephew Ovidio Antonio Maldonado Rodríguez would take his place. The family was given another twenty days, at most, to pay another twenty million.

Cecilia doesn't have much to say about it. But somehow I feel differently now. I don't feel that silence that's been separating me from everyone. This silence is ours. It seems as though we have communicated something to each other. The words convey something about Colombia that I haven't been able to find the words for.

I carefully fold the uneven piece of paper into a little square and put it in my wallet. I know I'm going to start reading the newspapers even more carefully from now on. And I'll keep all those voices that are in those pages. They're ours, too. All of them.

ULLA

I wish I could have hated the guerrillas more. But I don't hate them. I don't understand them. I mean, I realize that they're wrong. Everything they are doing is wrong. Maybe I hate them as a group, but I can't hate individual people. There are so convinced in their own beliefs, so convinced that what they are doing is right. It's their way of seeing things. They feel that they are being oppressed and that they have reasons for acting as they do. They feel they have a right. I can't judge that. We are wrong for them. The way we live is wrong.

TICO

SUNDAY, AUGUST 21

Nothing. Still silence. We wait day after day, but the phone doesn't ring. They've just disappeared. They're gone. Every afternoon I call Houston. "No, Sis. Nothing today."

What's going on? They accepted our offer. They negotiated. They came down 2 million dollars. Everything was fine. And we did our part. Everything was going by the rules. Are they going to make us wait again? Maybe they don't like our increment. That's what tells them how we are going to be negotiating. Had they expected us to go from 80 to 160 million? Have we made a mistake?

MONDAY, AUGUST 22

I look out the window of his fourth floor office. His desk is just as he left it. We use the office but try not to reshuffle too many things. The last notes he made for himself, a few names and telephone numbers, remain on his desk, although never in the same place. His shortwave radio is there. It's the best that Sony has to offer, bringing in BBC, Voice of America, Radio Havana Cuba, whatever, as clearly as FM.

And we keep his creaky, dilapidated chair that leans to one side. It's really in bad shape. I couldn't have gotten anything done on it, but I'm sure he never thought about what he was sitting on as he worked. I make my daily afternoon call to Ulla from his desk. The pictures of the family stay where they are.

I look out from the office and from César's, too. The two windows face two different streets. I go from one to the other. On my way between them I walk through Vicente's office to a small refrigerator they have there to get bottles of cold mineral water or Coke. Liquids. Lots of liquids. And coffee. Cup after cup. They make good coffee in Jake's office. He made sure of that. And lots of it.

Everyone in the office keeps right on working.

Newspapers and magazines are everywhere. *El Tiempo* and *El Espectador*, the main Liberal Party newspapers, and *La Prensa*, a new daily newspaper that started publishing on August 1. It's owned by a family that controls one wing of the Conservative Party, and it's by far the best of the lot, maybe because it's new, maybe because it's of the opposition party. There are also occasional copies of *El Siglo*, a long-standing Conservative paper, owned by Alvaro Gómez, who'd been kidnapped by the M-19, and sometimes I bring *Voz*, the paper of the Communist Party. Vicente sometimes brings *Vanguardia Liberal*, the paper from Bucaramanga, from that part of the country where Jake is almost certainly being held. And *Semana, Cromos, Hoy X Hoy*.

I take them all home with me at night to clip the stories I've marked during the day. And the *New York Times*, the *Wall Street Journal*, the *Economist*, *Business Week*, *U.S. News and World Report*, and *Newsweek* are also there. Jake and Vicente have subscriptions to them all. But the secretary makes sure I return each copy of the *New York Times* after I'm done with it. "*El señor* Gambini will want to read them when he gets back," she tells me.

Our Guerrillas, Our Sidewalks

We wait for something to happen, for the phone to ring. Sooner or later it has to. I set up camp in César's office. He doesn't allow anyone to smoke in there, his desk is always clean and orderly, and that's where the phone call will come in, either through the direct line or through the secretary.

Standing in front of the window, I get a sense for the street below, its pace, its rhythms. It's a narrow, one-way street with traffic going west. It seems like it's hardly wide enough for the buses. When it was built, nobody thought it would become a major thoroughfare. It's a busy place, full of retail shops, mainly shoe stores, which is what the street is known for. But there are also parking lots, some restaurants, clothing stores, an appliance store, and a bakery or two.

I can't see the street vendors from the window, for they stand mainly on my side of the street and also farther down, but I know they're there. They each have small stalls on their own place on the sidewalk, where they sell shoes, purses, cigarettes, bubble gum, and toys, a little bit of everything, most of it obtained on the black market by contraband. Most of the vendors have a license, and the police are always coming around to see if all their papers are in order, hoping they aren't so they can see the fear in the vendor's eyes, or the hatred, so the police can impound the stalls or make a little money on the side with bribes. The vendors cover almost the entirety of the sidewalk, making it almost impossible to pass.

Directly across the street there are two shoe stores, divided by a narrow glass and metal door that leads to the second floor of the building, where one or two families live. One man owns or operates both stores. He arrives each morning except Sundays at a few minutes before ten, jumps out of his car, unlocks the doors, and quickly leaves just as traffic begins to move again because the light has changed. I watch the four young saleswomen standing before the stores waiting for the owner to arrive. I'm sure he comes back in the evenings at around seven to close up, but by then I'm at home with my mother.

Once the stores have been opened, the saleswomen wash the sidewalk. It's always the same two who wash the little piece of territory in front of each store. They're probably the assistants. The young ladies inside are in charge. They take care of the cash register. Those who wash scrub away with great energy, strength even, getting at the dirt in the crevices. Each has a pail of water and a strong broom and plenty of soap. They know what they're doing, no doubt having done it for years, if not here, then elsewhere or in their homes.

I can see how they each carefully do their little section and nothing more, leaving the narrow passageway between the stores dry. It looks a bit dirtier at first, but as the day wears on I can't really tell the difference anymore, especially if it rains. The job's done when the large rubber mat that covers the entrance to each store has been washed. And they also wash the windows, but not every day. There are no street vendors on their section of the sidewalk, and I keep wondering whether they would do their daily washing if a vendor set up shop shortly after.

It feels as though I'm looking into the past. The maid in our house used to wash our sidewalk. I don't think she does that anymore. But now Carmen sweeps it. The lady of the house in front of us when we lived in Mexico washed hers about two or three times a week. Cecilia's sister has the maid do the same once a week. And Cecilia told our maid to sweep ours each morning. I saw it in many Latin American cities as I walked around in the early mornings, in La Paz, in Lima, and in Santiago. And there are lots of drawings of women washing sidewalks in urban centers in the nineteenth century. People have taken care of their sidewalks in Latin America or have had others take care of the sidewalks for them.

I don't know what the laws are like throughout Latin America, but in Bogotá nobody is quite sure whether the sidewalks are public or private. We do not own the sidewalks in front of our homes or our stores, for they belong to the government or to the nation. But we are responsible for taking care of them. And if the government does not build them, we do. It seems as if we see our sidewalks as an extension of our home and as a reflection of who we are.

Now that I think of it, this is why the sidewalks in Bogotá are not made for walking. This, at least, is a reasoning far different from the one my parents used to use. The sidewalks are not uniform. On a block every little section before each little house or store is different. The materials vary. So do the colors. The elevation can change. And often there is a gap between one and the other. Some sidewalks are in great shape, and others are in disrepair. Perhaps some homes are owned and others are rented, or some owners are having a tough time making ends meet. Others maybe don't care. Or standards can vary from one person to another.

The sidewalks are in particularly bad shape for our part of the city in the blocks around our house. The government was going to build a huge highway real close by and started to buy up all the land. The houses came tumbling down, and then the government decided not to build. There are many empty lots now, and the sidewalks are overgrown with grass and have become places where people leave their garbage. Dogs mill around, and rats are all over the place. That's what the sidewalk looks like that's on the other side of the street from where my mother's heap of construction material has been left. Maybe the owners who kept angering my mother so much felt there was no need to take care of their sidewalk because they lived in front of a garbage dump. But why don't they just clear their own sidewalk by throwing their stuff across the street? There is nothing to stop them.

On other streets, like the one just around the corner from where we live, there are a bunch of new and elegant apartment buildings. They replaced the houses that were there before. It's happening all over the city. For reasons of safety, *Bogotanos* are moving into apartment buildings with one or two armed guards outside. The sidewalk in front of each building has been rebuilt. There is no real way of coordinating efforts should anyone want to, for the buildings don't go up at the same time. And since many of them have garages underneath, some sections of the sidewalk are on something of an incline so cars can drive up and out onto the street without scraping the underside. It's easy to break a leg if you don't watch out.

It's not that people don't take care of their sidewalks. Many don't, of course, but that has probably always been the case. The real problem is that the sidewalks have been getting better, especially in the richer parts of town, those that I walk around in, and this has been happening too quickly.

The owner of a shoe store on the street below César's office window had his sidewalk rebuilt one Saturday morning. This man sells higher-quality shoes, and they're quite expensive. I can tell that he enjoys his store, and he is always there, with an assistant. He always open the shop on time, and I'm sure he stays late into the night to catch the last customer. His wife and children come to visit often. I hadn't noticed that his sidewalk was in bad shape, but the new one is clearly better and now much better than the ones on either side. It's easy to walk on. But the others seem a bit more treacherous than before, with their little irregularities and crevices here and there. The confidence I can get walking on his section of the sidewalk might not bode well for me in the next.

With the booming economy, sidewalks are being rebuilt everywhere. Entire sections of the city that were once residential have been commercialized. Tiny stores, many of them quaint little boutiques that sell one or two elegant items, bought perhaps on the black market or by a family member who travels abroad regularly or by a son or daughter who is a flight attendant, have sprung up in the most unexpected places. As each one opens up, the sidewalk is reconstructed, refashioned, to invite customers in.

Many new sidewalks are built of intricate patterns of brick and stone. Where once there was an apartment building with one sidewalk, there are now two or three stores on either side of a narrow passageway that leads to the apartments above. So now there are three or even four sidewalk patterns in one section of a block, each competing in beauty and quality with the next. And often there are huge, ugly iron rods jutting out from the cement to separate one sidewalk from the next. Rods, boulders, even chains, have been put in place by people who live there or by store managers who want to keep others from using their sidewalk, from parking on it.

The sidewalks have also been rebuilt to make room for parking. There has never been any real space for cars in Bogotá. They're stationed on the sidewalks in front of the new stores and in front of restaurants that were once private residences. A store owner can't make money if people can't park. Those who want to walk past, rather than in, are in trouble, for it's hard to make their way around the cars. Usually they're better off walking in the street while paying close attention to the cars that speed past.

There appear to be laws regulating the use of sidewalks in the city, but I don't bother to find out what they are. There is really very little that anyone can do. Even though the sidewalks probably belong to the nation, it hasn't built them. The owners of cafés have spent the money on renovation and feel they have a right to the sidewalks. They want their customers to be able to sit at their tables, just like it's done in Europe, even though nobody can walk past. The sidewalks are neither private property nor public lands. So the private domain prevails. Property-owning Colombians are competing against each other for what they consider to be their rights.

The way the sidewalks are run in Bogotá wasn't such a bad idea years ago, when there wasn't so much growth, even though my parents complained about them then. The system doesn't lend itself to change. It couldn't have been as bad as it is today when there was a measure of zoning and families tended to live in the same place generation after generation. Back then people knew each other and probably had a joint commitment to their block. They had some sense of their own small community. Or people felt embarrassed when others took better care of the sidewalk. But much of that has changed. Now anybody can build practically anything anywhere. Individuals have much to protect from the incursions of others. And they have to do so on their own.

I remember what a Mexican colleague, a very famous political scientist, told me when I asked her what she thought about Bogotá. She didn't hesitate for a moment. "It's as though the state, the government, doesn't exist." When I looked at her quizzically, she elaborated. "Everything looks disheveled, unkempt. The grass along the highways is not cut."

I smiled at her in a patronizing way, thinking that she should be able to come up with a better, more intellectual response. But she has a point. Now

I look back at Mexico City, and I recognize how much cleaner and better organized that city is and how easy the sidewalks are to walk on.

I don't go to the far-off neighborhoods of the south where poor people live. I used to know some of those areas a bit when I was in high school. Now the idea of going there scares me. I don't belong there, and right now I don't want anything to happen to me. I can't be thinking about myself. But most of those places don't have any sidewalks at all and probably never will. Maybe they're better off without them.

When I'm not in the office, or at home, I'm walking around the city, waiting, remembering, comparing, measuring the changes, seeing the life of the nation reflecting up at me from the sidewalks. I walk about three or four hours each day, maybe more.

I even get a few calls from old friends and acquaintances asking if it's me that they've seen as they drove past, as they were coming from work or going to the club. I walk the city carefully, on the balls of my feet.

NEWS

Every café and restaurant has its jetty, its strip of lit pavement. You pull in and an attendant comes to the edge. He motions you up to the curb. He finds you a mooring. You almost expect him to throw you a rope.

—Roger Garfitt

Yesterday, a little after seven in the morning, when Bogotá was enveloped in the fog that followed upon the rains of the night before, and the temperature fluctuated between 7 and 8 degrees (C), a man was riding his bicycle in a northerly direction along the Avenida Boyacá, where it intersects with the bridge over the Avenida Eldorado. Suddenly, unexpectedly, he raised both his arms in such a way that any innocent passer-by would have thought that the bicyclist was attempting to imitate the divers at the Olympics in Seoul.

His bicycle had just fallen into a hole located some three meters from the edge of the street.

—*El Espectador*

The citizen who is caught throwing garbage on the public street, or using it to satisfy his physical needs, will be subject to corrective measures that go from a fine to temporary imprisonment. In addition, the fronts of buildings and homes in Bogotá will have to be painted and fixed up, at least once every two years, for all owners are responsible for how their properties appear in front of public space. Moreover, the owners of empty lots will have to enclose them with brick walls, or other similar material, and make sure that they do not become garbage disposals or places of delinquency.

These dispositions are contained in a bill presented to the Council of Bogotá by Consuelo de Montejo. . . . If it is approved, property owners will be responsible for the state of their sidewalks and curbs. Thus, they will have to keep them clean, cutting the grass and trimming the trees. As far as the physical condition of sidewalks and curbs is concerned, owners will have to build them, out of brick, or cement, or otherwise complete them according to the norms established by their sector of the city.

—La Prensa

The Rebecca, the beautiful marble statue that adorns San Diego, one of the most centric and lovely parts of the capital city, finds itself totally forgotten by the district government. The fountain is practically dry, and these old shoes (seen in the picture) are a sign of how disheveled it has become. Bogotá does not have fountains and great sculptural designs like the other great cities of the world. The few that do beautify it, located in areas of much tourist attraction and modern urban conceptions, not to speak of their appreciable commercial value, are all, like Rebecca, in a lamentable and slovenly state of neglect.

—El Tiempo

Lack of discipline, indolence, and social disequilibrium are the principal factors behind the deterioration and the invasion of public space that can be seen everywhere in Bogotá, according to Otto Aristizábal, the district's attorney for public properties. The official offered to devote all of his energy to the campaign for the recovery of public space that has been promoted by *El Tiempo*. "The city," he stated, "has been converted into a ghetto of railings, gratings, chains, and locks. The common citizen has been denied his right to walk freely on the public streets."

—*El Tiempo*

TICO

FRIDAY, AUGUST 26

I'm giving up. I've waited two weeks minus one day. There is nothing to do. I'm leaving Bogotá today and going back to Charlottesville to prepare my courses at the university. I'm at a complete loss. Really depressed. I have no idea what has happened. Maybe all has been lost. I find no comfort in writing. Writing makes me think too much. It makes it more difficult to get through the days.

SATURDAY, AUGUST 27

Ulla calls early in the morning. I haven't even had time to unpack my tiny suitcase.

The call came in exactly two weeks after the last one, down to the hour. They want another meeting with César out in the hills. I'm light years away, feeling completely out of it, alone, surrounded by a community and a university going about their daily routines.

I think I can understand how Ulla and the children must have been feeling all this time in Houston. I'm about to jump on the next plane out.

César managed to put them off, hoping to get the real Eulises to call back so that they could negotiate on the phone. We've been talking to underlings. That has to stop.

MONDAY, AUGUST 29

They insist on a meeting, for that's the only way, the man claims, that they can deliver a message from the *patrón,* from the "boss." A message from Jake? What might it be?

We're anxious but don't feel hopeful that at this stage Jake could be sending us anything that will make things any easier. Yet maybe the instructions that we have been waiting for, the ones that we have expected from the very beginning, maybe they are finally coming.

No. It's too late. At this late stage I'm prepared to disregard them. We can't know what condition he's in. If he didn't negotiate before, he would only be doing so now because he was being forced to.

Even though I have a pretty good idea of what's transpired in those phone calls between César and the guerrillas, it's as though I know nothing. I don't have that feel for the conversation I get by being right there and then reading our meticulous transcript. I yearn for every word, every pause, each silence. That's the only way to figure out what's really going on.

TUESDAY, AUGUST 30

This time César and Norberto have a much farther road to travel. Ulla waits in Houston. I wait in Charlottesville. Vicente will call her first, and then she'll call me. The reversal of our roles is not to my liking, for I want my sister to get information framed in the systematic, piecemeal, coherent way that I am capable of.

The meeting was scheduled for 12:30. César made it back to Bucaramanga before the last flight back to Bogotá was scheduled to leave. But all flights were canceled because of the weather. So he rented a taxi for the ten-hour overland drive so he could be back in Bogotá early the next morning.

Now that I'm not around to watch César's every move, I can only marvel all the more at how he manages to do everything. His willingness to put his life on the line and his ability to think calmly and work continuously throughout it all never cease to amaze me.

While I spent a month or so pacing about the office and staring out the window, he sat at his desk for hours at a time taking one business phone call after another, never quite certain if the next ring would bring the voice of some guy asking about a hundred feet of pipe or Eulises. I watched in awe during the whole month of August. And César was doing all this for a man who was only his employer.

César was able to call from Bucaramanga before getting into the cab to let us know what had gone on. There is no message from Jake. They accepted the Polaroid camera and the cassette recorder César had taken along for their use when it comes time to deliver the final proofs. César explained exactly what kind of a picture we wanted, one with a dated newspaper clearly visible. Together they worked the recorder. We figured that they knew all about these things, but we have to make sure.

Apparently Eulises had kept insisting that our phones were being tapped. No more phone calls, he said. And they wouldn't budge from the three million. And we were to pay the first million in the next ten days, with the two additional million in two separate installments shortly thereafter. We'd had plenty of time, Eulises said, to collect the money. Also, they wanted addresses of the family in Bogotá and in Houston. Eulises said that the *estado mayor* of his movement had ordered him to inform us that from now on they would negotiate only with the family.

My time has come, but I'm not half as keen as I was at first. I don't think I can do a better job than César and Vicente have. But a member of the family might be able to convince them that our offer is for real, that we are not bluffing. I'll carry more authority. It's the only way of getting them off center. In any case, there is no choice. This is it.

WEDNESDAY, AUGUST 31

I've gone over to the History Department and requested a leave of absence without pay from the university, and I have canceled my classes. At least the guerrillas didn't call two or three days from now, when it would have been quite a bit more difficult for my students to find another course.

Cecilia and I will go out this evening to buy a pair of Reeboks. I need a new pair of shoes anyhow because my cheap running shoes have holes in them. And they're white. That's the only color I've ever used.

Now I'll buy a black pair. That way I can walk into the hotels to receive their calls and appear to be relatively well dressed. And I'll be able to better deal with the sidewalks.

And if I have to run, I'll be in good shape. I've always had this stupid feeling that the guerrillas have been watching my every move in Bogotá, following me, even though I never had any indication that there was anybody behind me. I did keep looking over my shoulder. At times I even got the idea that they were making sure I wasn't going to get into any trouble because they needed me to do the negotiating. Foolish thoughts. I also figured that they might kidnap me as well. That was a bit more rational. Anyhow, my Reeboks are going to come in handy.

THURSDAY, SEPTEMBER 1

César went out yet again. He informed them that a member of the family was prepared to fly to Bogotá to negotiate but would not travel out of the city and would not meet with them under any circumstances. If they wanted to talk to the negotiator, they'd have to do so on the phone.

We feel that they will be able accept these conditions. Nelson says that it is absolutely insane for me to go out there, and I now think he's right. I could be kidnapped as well, and however remote that possibility, there is no reason to incur the risk. In my heart I want to get together with them, to fight this thing out around a table, but that's not the responsible thing to do. Yet I figure I have a better chance of convincing them to see matters our way in person than I do on the phone. In any case, the option is always out there.

César left the meeting feeling that further negotiations could be carried out over the phone. But we can't be certain.

It took another two long calls to iron things out, at least from our end. Eulises himself made the second one. In both, Vicente gave them my name and told him that I was the wife's brother.

I am insisting that I be referred to as Don Heriberto. Tico doesn't quite do it, and I want them to think that the negotiations are moving to a higher level. It has already turned into a joke. César and Vicente are referring to me with exaggerated respect as Don Heriberto, and I in turn give them an assortment of honorary and professional titles. "*Ingeniero* Ramos." "*Doctor* Ortega, how are things in Bogotá this evening?"

Although the guerrillas keep insisting on another meeting, Vicente managed to convince Eulises that both he and César no longer had the family's authorization to negotiate anything at all. They were out of the picture.

To get things moving, we finally gave them the phone number in Houston and made preparations for answering it. It's been a huge debate, and I've really been the only one who has insisted that Ulla can handle a phone call from them without much trouble. But she'll keep the answering machine with the speaker phone on all the time. We have worked out a few responses she might use just in case.

Before the last call was over, Eulises let us know that things were no longer in his hands and that he now had to report to his superiors. We understand that we're moving up the chain of command. Eulises also said that they were having some difficulty or other and that it will take them a while to get back in touch.

JAKE

We moved on August 20. The next day at lunch Ricardo asks Mónica if she has the *pepas*. Apparently they were going to put the pills in my beans. I heard they were going to keep me shitting.

He told one of them, "Now, five minutes after he eats, when he goes to his hole, when he has to run, you all go with him so that nothing will happen to him." They were all watching. I was thinking of refusing the food. But I knew sooner or later I'm was going to have to eat.

I tried to feel if there was a different taste. I ate about half of it and waited for something to start happening to me. They kept looking at their watch. After about twenty minutes, Ricardo says, "He must have passed it; it didn't do anything to him." He said, "We'll try again tonight." He asked Mónica how many more *pepas* they had. She said, "I got two more."

Could I refuse the food and then admit that I'd been hearing everything? I wanted them to think I wasn't hearing nothing, that I didn't understand anything they were saying. That evening we go through the same thing. Then Ricardo said, "He must be immune to it. For some people it doesn't have any effect." That started giving me an idea that it was bullshit.

Then I lay in my bed, and they go off to the side and Ricardo tells them, "In the mail today I got all the information on *el tío*. About the house he lives in, the jewelry his wife has, and little by little I'll give you all this information, and then we'll do some studies together, and we'll ask him some questions." They started passing out information. The kind of business we did. Our house in Houston. Various kinds of things. This kept up for about three days. I figured this was information they could get anywhere; they could send somebody to look at the house.

Three or four days later, at night again, he said, "What we have to know is if he's got insurance, what his tie is with Texaco, and where his secret bank account is with all his millions." One of them said, "Well, let's take away his cigarettes and his coffee." The other one said, "No, let's make him sleep without a mosquito net or on the ground, let's take away his whole bed, look how comfortable he is, he's got the best bed in the camp. And let's send him to the river bottom; let him sleep down there."

They started on this thing that maybe Ursula would come out there. About two or three nights later, Ricardo said, "Huh, wait until you hear this. Three of our people went into his house in Friendswood. And you should see what a house. *La señora estaba durmiendo en la cama, y las dos hijas arriba, y Tony estaba también y Tomaso y el perrito. Y mira, estaba en el garaje un Mercedes que debe ser del señor, pero bonito, un BMW que debe estar de la señora. Y cuando le preguntaron a la señora donde estaban todas las joyas. Que eran todas en el banco. El día después uno de los guerrilleros fue con ella al banco y miró todo.*" And they left it open if they took the jewels from the deposit box. You know, they said that they had been to the house, and they described it pretty well, the Mercedes and the BMW and the dog. They had it down. That Tony had started to fight them, and they knocked him out with a pistol. It's very hard to stay still, not to say nothing, and take all that in. I had to keep reassuring myself that this was all talk.

He said that they'd gone to Galveston and talked to my mother. He gave an imitation of my mother speaking that was perfect. *E Santa Maria del Judice.* Italian and all. I mean, he had the accent just right. And they had gone to see my brothers. Charles did not cooperate at all. But when they went to Domenic's house, he went into another room and got a shotgun and kept them, and they got one of the guerrillas in jail. That they had gone also to visit your mother and she called them all kinds of names, *ladrones,* "thieves." That's just what your mother would have done. This came out in a period of three or four nights.

By this time I'm reeling. And then he said, "You know how much that guy over there makes? *El se gana 6.800 dólares al mes. Un millón ochocientos mil pesos al mes.*" That was exactly my monthly salary to the cent. They were hitting the figures just right.

One night they said, *"Ese Vicente Ortega, cuando fue el comandante en la oficina de ellos con sus dos sargentos,"* or whatever they call them, the three of them—the commander and two of his men—had gone over to the office in Bogotá. "*Cuando el comandante le sacó el archivo, Vicente le dijo no eso lo necesito, y el comandante con el revolver le pegó en la cara, y que Vicente luego se fue al baño y cuando se estaba lavando la sangre de la cara, sacó el lavamanos de la pared de la rabia.*" Now ain't that a perfect description of Vicente Ortega? Yes. Isn't that exactly what he would have done if they came into the office and went through the filing system and hit him in the face? Can't you just see him ripping the washbasin right out of the wall?

I didn't know what to do. Every morning I got up and knew what the whole day in front of me was going to be like. It was a very disagreeable thing, facing one more day of this type of existence. I started thinking of committing suicide. The days start running together. I have no clear idea of time. This had been going on for quite a bit. At lunchtime it was the same thing. They'd be called to attention, and they'd talk about what they were going to do. Then ten minutes later they'd get another idea: that they would walk me out and shoot me about two miles down the road.

Our Guerrillas, Our Sidewalks

They still come over to me and played checkers or play cards with me and give me cigarettes. Face to face they were still the same. Far away they were putting on all this pressure. The threat was always there that one night they'd get me in the center of all of them and start asking me questions about my business, my family, my money, my jewels, and everything else.

I never did get over it that they had all these facts. I'd halfway rationalized that they had not gotten this money and that they didn't come to the house, and that they didn't really have all this information, proof, as they said they did. Because then why would they need me to admit it? So they were never really sure how good their information was. It was hearsay. What they wanted me to do was confirm it. I never did. I never did respond. It was something in me. I'd made up my mind. Maybe it was part of my early army training. Give your rank, name, and serial number and nothing else. Don't give any information. But it was tough. It was some tough days. And you never were sure when the talk would stop and the action would start. That was their plan. Just keep me off balance. Maybe they figured I'd break, start talking, crying.

I said to myself, just don't admit to nothing. Don't ask them, where did you get this information? Play deaf and mute. And that's what I did. And, goddamn, that was the best thing in the world. I knew that once conversation started . . . and they felt it too, I guess. Once he starts asking about something, then we got him because it will all lead to other things. When they started talking, I would play solitaire more. I started working at getting the cards perfectly straight. It would take me an hour to do one game, to just concentrate on having the cards down to the millimeter, just perfectly lined up.

Ricardo was an expert at doing this stuff. I don't think the others were. Maybe Mónica. I don't know if they'd done it before. Maybe he had to a lesser extent. They were thinking that they would break me in a week. I heard Ricardo tell that to Mónica one time. "In a week we'll have him broke." Now was that for me to hear again? But when it went on for so many days, they knew they were going to get no response. I mean they tried everything, from indirectly threatening me with discomfort to death. It all fell on deaf ears. It probably frustrated them. I wondered whether they were afraid that their superiors would think that they'd failed.

There were points where they'd bring things up, and right away I would discard it. I'd say this is bullshit. All this thing is a fabrication of lies. But it's a funny thing. You know they're lies, and the next moment you believe them again. Because they were hitting so many things right. And I imagine

Jake

that when you're doing something like that, all you need is three or four good facts, and you speculate on the rest of them.

I was trying to prepare myself for any eventuality. If they were going to force me to write a letter, I made up a little scenario, saying all right, Ursula, give them the six million. Sell my part of the Hotel Lamar in Houston and other things like that. The Lamar was knocked down ten years ago. So that you all would know that it's bullshit. I had to put myself in different situations to think about how to respond. I had to keep doing it. It occupied my time also.

Maybe this goes on with other men that they take to a much lesser extent and much less subtle. Is this the way they get them to write letters? They knew that they had the man who had the power to do it all, and he wouldn't do nothing. They were getting no response from me.

TICO

FRIDAY, SEPTEMBER 2

César calls. I can tell it is an international call by that little click and a momentary silence over the lines. He's been receiving reports from Sabana that a small-time but well-known political boss has been coming around making offers.

"What kind of offers?" I ask.

"Well, this man is well connected. Everybody knows him. He works with the Mano Blanca. He says he can protect us, that he knows that the guerrillas are very influential in the area."

I've never heard of anything like the Mano Blanca. There are right-wing death squads in Guatemala with names like that, but not in Colombia.

I ask César who they are, and he tells me that they are groups that are trying to defend people against the guerrillas.

"You know," he says, "*son las derechas.*" "They are the right wing."

I want nothing to do with them. As far as I'm concerned, they are the real enemies.

I ask César if they are the *narcos.*

"Probably. There are connections there. They probably get money from them."

I scream something into the phone about having the supervisor tell them to go to hell.

César quietly informs me that we can't really do that.

"They are well connected," he repeats. "It's not convenient to have them as enemies."

"Okay, tell them that we are in a very difficult situation, that we can't really be seen to have a relationship with them while the guerrillas are holding Jake, that they have to understand that."

The guerrillas may even kill Jake if they think we are working with the death squads.

"Maybe the thing to do," I tell him, "is to thank them for coming around, for thinking of us, but to come back later when all this settles down."

César tells me that these are his thoughts as well.

JAKE

All at once it ended. Suddenly, just like that. I could feel it. It lasted more than a month, about five weeks. I think they stopped because they were getting nowhere and it was beginning to do them more harm than good.

During all this time that they were doing this to me, I was thinking more and more about the money. I halfway believed they already had six million dollars. Then I knew that it was impossible. You don't know what to think. And they wanted double that. If they really meant it, I was going to be there for a long, long time. Those sums were so ridiculous. I knew what they could do with six million dollars.

The more I thought about it, the less I liked it. I started figuring out how many men they could arm. A thousand dollars per man, or maybe two thousand dollars per man, that would be three thousand men that they could arm, or six thousand men at a thousand each. That was a disaster.

It got to the point where I didn't want them to get one cent. The feelings all ran together. I wanted to get out. I wanted to see my family again. But my freedom would give them more arms and ammunition, more power to be able to keep fighting. All I knew was that people were being killed, kidnapped, that many women and families were crying. I didn't want my freedom to give them more money so that they could expand their operations.

One day they were talking about this *emboscada*, this ambush of an army patrol. They were laughing about all the soldiers they'd killed. That got to me. But I didn't say anything. It was the only time that I heard them talking about their operations.

What in the world can I do? As more of these facts were brought out and more information was fed me, I kept playing the deaf mute. There were days where I wouldn't eat or drink and days I would think about suicide, trying to really make up my mind what I could do.

DYING

This photograph of Jake Gambini was taken by the guerrillas during his captivity.

JAKE

All I thought about in those whole days was death. I was trying to think of how to get out of this thing.

Close to my chair they had left a tree trunk about an inch and a half in diameter. The top was very pointed because of the way they cut it or stripped it off. It was sharp enough. I thought often about throwing myself on it, on my stomach, to let it go through me like a spear. I had all the steps figured out. Except I had one problem. There was this other little tree right next to it that wouldn't allow my body, the good part of my body, to fall where I'd know that I would be killed. I would shove myself into it, and I'd be hanging there like a stuffed pig and not hit any important organs. That would have been worse.

But there were many times in a period of about eight days that I wanted to do it. I mean, I'd make sure that the guard was away, and I'd say, okay, this time around I'll make the jump. I'd unbutton my shirt and open my pants a little bit where it wouldn't have anything to stop it. But then I'd always realize it was foolish. I couldn't do it that way.

I saw these pieces of tin can, an old sardine can. Took it, put it in water, and that night I ate it, swallowed it. And glass, little pieces of that, too. About three quarters of an inch long. I couldn't swallow it by itself so I wrapped it up in a little piece of toilet paper and swallowed it. Stupid.

Then I ate wild mushrooms. I remembered this father of a friend of mine who died choking on a piece of meat. They'd bring me these *arepas* [corn-meal cakes] and I'd make a big chunk in my mouth and swallow it without chewing on it to see if I would choke on it.

And there was this bush with long thorns. Nobody was watching me. I took some of those thorns and wiped them in my shit, and then I'd wrap them up in paper, and when it was dark I'd scratch myself with them. Trying to get typhoid or something. You do all kinds of crazy things.

After they stopped all their psychological things, a man came and asked me for a description of you. They wanted to know all about Ditha, too. I kind of decided that you were going to be doing the negotiating. We sat out there until about two in the morning. They asked all kinds of questions about you all and whether Ditha had small feet and, if she used cosmetics. Everything.

The next day they took some more pictures. After he left I didn't eat for about two or three days. Thought more about suicide. I started thinking more and more about not eating. I said, I've got to do something. And at that time I was angry at them, too, for the way they'd been talking about Ursula and the girls, Tony, Thomas, and bringing all these personal things into it,

143

you know, that they'd been in my house, kicked the dog. And I had to play the deaf mute. My only revenge was to keep them from getting any money. I had pretty well discarded the idea that they'd gotten any. The only thing that kept bugging me was the figure of my salary, but I figured they'd gotten somebody to tell them that. But at the same time I never could quite get over the thing of the six million. There was confusion. A hatred started coming up in me, a hatred that needed for me to find a way to get back at them.

I finally came to the conclusion to quit eating. That was the only way to do it. Starve yourself to death. This way, then, you might still have a chance of getting out if they get shook up. And if they don't, after a while you'll be in a coma, and you won't give a damn.

I figured that was the only way I was going to get them off center. I really felt that if they were going to see me die, they were going to do something. They were asking for way too much. And that was the reason there was no agreement. I had to say, hey, I've got to get them down. They had a chance of getting nothing.

If things got bad enough, they would give up on their ridiculous sum and make the best of a bad deal. If I couldn't even walk no more, they would have to advise you all, and then it would get out in public that I was starving to death. I was thinking that they could not let their image down. They told me so much about how much they cared about their image, how they treated the prisoners. They had to get the best of a bad deal. It's just like when I get into a stock deal, and I see after a while that the stock is only going to go down, why you get out and try to save what you can.

Do I do it fast and fail, or do I do it very slow and succeed? I thought that maybe forty or fifty or sixty days before I would go into a coma would be way too long. I didn't know if I could take it. And then I said to myself, yes, you can. The days will pass. They'll click off.

I wouldn't eat in two or three days and then eat a meal so they wouldn't think about it. I did that to see what I could and couldn't do and also to lose weight, so that when I picked out the date to not eat anymore, I wouldn't have any extra body fat to keep me going. I tried to make it as short as possible. My pants were getting bigger and bigger. I'd lay in bed at night, and I'd feel my stomach, feel everything go down. You waste to nothing; your bones all start coming out, your legs, your arms. A couple of times they cooked some chicken and offered it to me, and I'd eat a little bit, and just say I wasn't hungry.

NEWS

Tonight I am going to speak to you about a problem that has enormously preoccupied Colombians for many years. It's the violence. It is a violence that has sealed thousands of young lives, has filled with sadness many of the homes of humble people, and has made the progress of Colombia and the efforts of our respectable people very difficult. It is a violence that has left us nothing but blood, anguish, and pain.

. . . The Peace Initiative that I am going to propose to the nation is different from others. It has a clear beginning and end. Its execution requires concrete steps that have to be followed in a logical, previously determined order. It is a guide that contains precise deadlines so that step by step, within institutional channels and the necessary respect for the Constitution and the law, those who have taken up arms will renounce their violence and return to civil life. . . .

A democratic state cannot renounce the simultaneous use of generosity and firmness. These are not mutually exclusive actions. Thus, our policy of reconciliation is inspired by the principle of "an outstretched hand and firm pulse."

—President Virgilio Barco

I am in agreement with the proposal. Nevertheless, I see two difficult points in it: at the heart of the proposal lies the idea that the guerrillas want to stop being guerrillas, and this is not the case. Second, there is more emphasis in the proposal on the reincorporation of the guerrillas into civil life than in the political opening that they have been struggling for. There are few easy mechanisms through which to discuss issues, for example, like the nationalization of the oil industry. It seems to me that we ought not discard the possibility that the Peace Commission work with the government on this peace proposal. We have to let a little time pass, so we can all study it well.

—Monsignor Darío Castrillón, president of
the Commission for Democracy

The peace plan looks like it's been designed by a group of experts in international treaties, because it doesn't take into consideration that Colombia is living through a very serious internal conflict. It was done as though there already is a victor and a vanquished. It has been dribbled out to us, and has a lot of sentences that cannot be applied. It's very confusing, because you really don't know what it's after. The use of the Congress is not the most appropriate. The government recognizes that it has done nothing to dissolve the right-wing paramilitary groups in the country. We'll have to wait, but there's a great deal of confusion.

—Bernardo Jaramillo Ossa,
president of the Patriotic Union (UP)

1. Out of the necessity to come to an agreement on a social pact in favor of life, peace, and democracy, we salute the initiative for peace.

2. The proposal should be subjected to a clear formulation. It does not address broad national interests. It limits itself exclusively to seeking a solution to the armed conflict, which is understood as a confrontation between the National Army and the guerrilla movement.

3. We believe that the issues of peace cannot be limited to a military solution. Institutional, economic, political, and social forms of violence are present in many places throughout the country, largely because the State does not exist in those places, and due to its inability to find immediate and long-term solutions to these social conflicts. . . .

10. At the same time, Mr. President, we reiterate with patriotic sentiment our movement's desire for peace and social justice. Our movement does not simply seek a return to civil life. We are searching for peaceful means to bring institutional, social, political, and economic transformations to the nation.

Before you, we sign with firmness and goodwill.

Our Guerrillas, Our Sidewalks

Simón Bolívar Guerrilla Coordinator: Armed Revolutionary Forces of Colombia (FARC), 19th of April Movement (M-19), Quintín Lame Armed Revolutionary Movement, Revolutionary Party of the Workers (PRT), and Popular Army of Liberation (EPL)

—*La Prensa*

In the face of the political objective of the Barco government to make the guerrilla movement surrender, and to disregard its long history of struggle, the Camilista Union–Army of National Liberation, a member of the Simón Bolívar Guerrilla Coordinator, informs the Colombian people and world opinion of its unflinching decision to continue as a clandestine and belligerent political and military organization. . . .

From the mountains of the New Colombia. Camilista Union–Army of National Liberation (UC–ELN).

—*La Prensa*

The reform of the Constitution and the search for peace are inexhaustible themes for conferences, debates, presentations, and speeches. And they are successful because Audiovisuales, the television programming company, had planned to present a month-long miniseries with special weekly guests who were to talk on the subject of peace. Due to the high ratings, however, Audiovisuales plans to prolong the program into October. "Debates Over Peace" can be seen every Monday evening at 7:20 on Channel Two.

—*La Prensa*

Many of the cities of the country have agreed to celebrate the "Week of Peace" between September 25 and October 2. It's organized by the Company of Jesus, the Movement in Favor of Life, as well as other religious organizations. The objective of the "Week of Peace" is to take a series of elements and forms to communities that are removed from national decisions, which will encourage an interest in the search for peace through nonviolent means. . . . In each of these cities there will be a program of cultural and recreational events designed to identify peace and the ways in which it can be obtained. The celebrations include conferences, bonfires, floral wreaths, concerts, paintings, festivals, movies, and plays, all of which will bring together the entire population, and especially children, to create in them a consciousness of peace in Colombia.

—*El Espectador*

The controversial "red telephone" between the presidency and the general headquarters of the FARC and the M-19 out in the mountains has just been modernized. The old radio-telephone, through which countless messages from Jacobo Arenas and Carlos Pizarro have passed, has been exchanged for a modern and sophisticated system, which has, among other advantages, sound amplification, digitalized frequencies, computerized memory, and a directional antenna. It is expected that after the favorable responses that these two guerrilla groups have had to Senator Alvaro Leyva's peace initiative, the telephone will be very much in use as the year draws to a close.

—*Semana*

TICO

SATURDAY, SEPTEMBER 17

In Charlottesville it feels like we're never going to hear from them again. They're at it. Silence. Or are they?

Does the president's peace plan have something to do with it? Do they not want to be negotiating with a family while they're claiming to consider Barco's plan? They don't really care about these sorts of things, do they? I can't believe they even think about them. But how long are they going to keep us waiting this time?

Maybe they're trying to figure out who I am. But wouldn't they have done that a long time ago, even before taking him? They will know I am a historian. Will they read my book? I've published a few articles in *El Tiempo* that are critical of the political elite. Maybe they will make the connection and decide I'm not their enemy. I keep thinking that this might help the negotiations, but every time the thought crosses my mind, I realize that I'm kidding myself. It's just like Jake thinking that they wouldn't kidnap him because he treated his workers well.

I try to stay home so I won't have to answer awkward questions, but I still run into people at the supermarket or the gasoline station. And I go to the university soccer games. My friends and acquaintances are kind, thoughtful. They treat me gingerly, with kid gloves, as if I am about to break. They don't quite know what to say or ask.

Women feel less uncomfortable around me than men do. They quickly ask about my sister and especially about her children. The anthropologists seem less ill at ease, perhaps because they have been in enough bizarre situations themselves to know what it might feel like. They ask me direct and perceptive questions about what's going on. But usually it's a "I thought you were in Colombia. How . . . ?" I answer lamely that we are waiting. I try to stay home and play with the children. "Will you play with me, Daddy?" "Yes, Emilia. I'll play with you." We wait.

MONDAY, SEPTEMBER 19

It's been almost three weeks. I haven't really been thinking anymore. I guess I'm kind of like a zombie, just going through the motions during all these days.

TUESDAY, SEPTEMBER 20

The phone rang in the office in Bogotá today. They accept me as the negotiator. They will call back, either on the twenty-third or twenty-fourth, Friday or Saturday.

Maybe we are back on track. They lead the way; we follow. We never know where we are going, what we will be doing. I'm really in a daze. Will I be able to make a difference? Is this for real?

FRIDAY, SEPTEMBER 23

I'm off. I can wait no longer. It's a horrible flight. I have a bad headache and keep wondering if I'm going to throw up. I don't eat anything, just a Coke at the airport in Miami.

Tico

There is a message for me on the stairwell. I call Vicente. The guerrillas want me in a hotel room that night. They'll call then or the next morning.

I kiss my mother; stuff my mouth with the tiny, delicious, open-faced sandwiches with which she always receives me; and run out as soon as I hear the car outside. I tell my mother that nothing is happening. Her hands are grasped in front of her, almost in prayer. As I leave her there standing by the window, she must be thinking that we are about to get him back.

I walk into the hotel room at 9:30.

Vicente and César have always worked from printed scripts. But I feel that words on paper will get in my way. It's like in class in a lecture. My notes often get in the way of what I'm trying to get across.

I know that I need to think about what the voice is telling me and construct responses accordingly. I'm confident that I will say what has to be said.

But Nelson quietly talks to me, making sure I know the ground rules, don't go off half-cocked. He's never quite trusted me, and I can't say I blame him.

The call comes in at 9:45. Since the beginning I have been a calm voice of reason. Now I'm blustery. I want to establish a tone that differs from the familiar one that we have grown into with them. It's not that I plan it. It just happens as soon as I hear the voice.

I don't refer to him as Eulises. There's to be no personal relationship with this man. This is strictly business. I speak as little as possible. I listen, letting him talk; I provide little or no information. The situation they've put me into, I let him know, is not at all to my liking. I offer up a few nonaggressive, light vulgarities here and there to establish I don't know what. I guess I just want him to know that I speak Spanish like a native. That I am Colombian. They had asked about my Spanish, obviously wondering whether they'd be able to communicate with me. I guess they don't know very much about me at all.

He speaks correctly, properly, respectfully. The connection is good, loud and clear. The man is calling from Bogotá. We've moved up the chain of command, up to an urban commando, to headquarters, to the leaders perhaps.

The man on the phone wants some personal information about me. I figure it's irrelevant and tell him so. Maybe I'm also a little bit scared to tell him. I don't even give him my last name. I feel stupid. He knows my name. He's got to know at least that about me. And they must also have checked with Jake, with others. This is stupid. Deep down inside I want him to know who I am.

The caller is just making sure he's talking to the right guy and even tells me as much. But I refuse to answer his questions. He must think that he's dealing with some kind of an obnoxious upper-class intellectual, if not an actual idiot, that he's going to have a difficult time with me. He's been given a bum assignment.

They are not moving an inch from what we have referred to during the long weeks as "the three." After carefully preparing the way, saying most everything that has to be said, I raise our offer by a higher increment than before. It's the figure that we had decided on back early in September.

It's a good faith effort so they understand that now the family is talking and that we are doing everything we can to deal forthrightly with them. I go up 15, not 10, million pesos. We're up to 105 million. That, I tell him, is as far as we can go. And I want a quick response, for I need to leave the country again. I'm not here to waste my time. I have my job to return to. Responsibilities. I'm trying to change the pace of the negotiations.

He listens. But he wants to send us something. Do I have an address? You know where to reach me, I tell him. I'm frustrated. What kind of a game is this guy playing? What's he up to? He says he'll call back, perhaps in two days. Same place.

César, Nelson, and I get out of the room in a hurry. It was stuffy in there. The contact went well. I have been open to negotiations but authoritative as well. We got our new offer to them. The negotiations are on again.

We're off to call Ulla. "Hi, Sis." At Vicente's apartment I drink more than two rum and Cokes, the first real booze I've had since June 24. I feel good because I've done what I had to do.

But haven't I lost an opportunity? Maybe I could've have reached out to this guy instead of putting him off so much. I mean, I know all about them, about their struggle. . . .

No. I've done the right thing. I've got to stick to the rules. Personal questions don't matter here. I can't let any of my own ideas enter into this. This is strictly business. And they don't care anything about me or my ideas.

Jake was wrong to think that they would not kidnap him because he treated his workers well. I am doubly wrong to even imagine that my sympathies for them, my views as a historian, would make them negotiate more softly with us.

How stupid of me. It's amazing how dumb we can become, how we can fantasize all kinds of ridiculous things simply because we want them to become real.

The weekend lies ahead.

Tico

MONDAY, SEPTEMBER 26

Getting into the hotel is the worst of it. I really don't want Nelson around because I know that they're watching our every move. And there's only one entrance to this place, and they must know what Nelson looks like by now. If they know someone else is in the room with me, they won't trust us. But Nelson insists, and Ulla has taken his side. He wants to listen to every word and then transcribe the conversation. He spends hours at it. I'm the historian, but I couldn't care less for the transcriptions. They don't tell me a thing.

The call comes in just as he promised. There's nothing new. He only wants to know if I am indeed going to travel. I want to, I tell him. He doesn't have an answer for me yet. They are doing some research to decide what to do next. I tell him I will do everything I can, whatever is in my power, to bring this thing to a quick solution. I can stay a few more days.

He has me. He knows it.

Should I have told him I was leaving? Might the negotiations have broken down again until I could get back?

No. I think I've done the only thing possible. Nelson agrees.

WEDNESDAY, SEPTEMBER 28

Silence. Oppressive.
I can't remember what I did today.

THURSDAY, SEPTEMBER 29

A note arrives that's addressed to me, last name and all almost correctly spelled, and a Polaroid photograph of him.

Mephistopheles himself, thin and with a long beard and a cigarette in hand, stares out at us from the wilderness, from the other world.

Their note insists on "the three" and reiterates that they are convinced that the security forces are helping us.

Why do they keep insisting on this? Just to keep us off balance? To make sure we don't try now to get in touch with the police? Why bother sending us a picture? We know they have him. Are they trying to soften us up? Or is it merely a goodwill gesture?

Nelson is reassuring once again. He lets us know that we should be glad it's a picture. We are being treated well. He knows of a case where the family received a finger in a box through the mail. We spend hours with the picture, looking for I don't know what. It appears to be about a month old. It was probably not taken with our Polaroid.

The note also gives us instructions for the next phone call, day and place but no time. Next week. We have a five- to six-day wait ahead of us. There's nothing to do. We're back in the grind. They're calling all the shots.

TUESDAY, OCTOBER 4

We try everything in today's call, all kinds of arguments and gambits.

> THEM: Well, look, we are going to go down to 2.8 million.

> ME: No. No. No. No, *hombre.* I mean, that is . . . I mean for us there's no difference. It's all the same. Do you understand me?

> THEM: Aha. Aha.

> ME: That is, that is to say there's no difference. Those figures are so unreachable for us that the difference between one and the other is nonexistent. Do you understand?

At the end of our four-minute conversation we agree to go back to our people, to see if something can be done. I have let him know that we might be able to go up to 115 million pesos if they agree to that sum as the final one. He orders me to yet another hotel room to await another call in three days. I ask, almost pleadingly, whether he can call earlier. Tomorrow? No, he says. The day after. Morning or afternoon, I want to know. Morning, he says, off-handedly.

I'll do almost anything to cut down on those hotel hours waiting for the phone to ring.

THURSDAY, OCTOBER 6

It is a long morning, maybe the longest so far. The phone doesn't ring. I just sit. The silence is hardly bearable. He's playing with me, letting me know he's calling the shots. The bastard. At twenty minutes after noon the clanging sound of the phone makes me jump. I sit back down, wait a few seconds, calm down.

> ME: I'm very happy. I've accomplished much on this end.

Tico

ME: Remember what I told you last time? Well, I've been more
    successful than I thought. I think we'll be able to get all of it, all
    115, and bring this business to a close.

Nothing doing. It's the most confusing conversation of all. He keeps talking about some kind of a problem, and I simply can't figure out what he's
referring to. And he keeps talking about trust. We'll get something in writing, he says. Wait for it.

I can't figure out what the hell is happening. What's all this stuff about
trust? I mean, we've been talking for months. They have to trust us by now.

It's got to be Nelson. That's it. They know we're getting professional help
in this. Damnit! Here I am talking to the guerrillas, and they don't trust me
because I've got this gringo helping me. This is ridiculous.

But that doesn't make much sense either, for they have to know that plenty
of people get professionals to help them. They should want that. It sure beats
having to deal with some hysterical family or a wife who really loses it.

But nothing is working. I've had it. I feel lower than ever before. Nothing we
do seems to help. I can see no way of making any kind of progress. We are at an
impasse. I don't know what's happening. The tensions are showing. Damn
them. Who the hell do they think they are? I'm really starting to hate them.

GUERRILLAS

After me, like a malignant shadow, was *la Violencia*. I arrived at a
town, and another one, and there it was, waiting for me, as
though trying to get me to move on. And if it hadn't yet arrived
because the road had been long, there it would be a week later.

—Tirofijo

Shortly after Gaitán's death, they assassinated my father. . . . I was
only three or four years old when the Conservatives killed him. I
remember that mother had bought some cans of sardines to eat
on our trip. That day we were definitively leaving Ulloa, Valle,
where I was born. We were leaving there, banished by *la Violencia*.

Just minutes before we were scheduled to begin our trip to
Cartago, somebody knocked on the door of my house. A guy
asked if my father was there. He said he needed a letter of
recommendation from him in his capacity as a Liberal leader of

Valle. Dad went out to the door. When he lowered his head to get his pen out of his pocket and sign the letter, the guy shot him. He fell. The guy fled. All the Conservative notables came by afterward. A priest, who is still alive today, was among them. They shouted, asked if Fayad was good and dead. "Otherwise, we'll really shoot him up," they screamed.

He smelled of death. It was deafeningly hot. Mother served us those sardines for lunch. Since then I haven't eaten sardines. They disgust me. They don't bring back any memories. They simply make me nauseous.

The whole town knew that they were going to assassinate Dad. His future death was talked about in the cafés; it was spoken about on the streets. But just like in García Márquez's *Chronicle of a Death Foretold*, nobody told him they were going to kill him because they all thought that he knew.

—Alvaro Fayad

Our entire family was Liberal, and those who were born, well, they were Liberals, too. All of us, my father, my mother, my uncles, an endless chain from which no one could escape. It was like a knot of pure tradition. This is not something that can be explained, or at least we didn't come close to an explanation. It was all already written down. Let's say it was the destiny of each one of us, like the sign of the cross that we all inevitably carry on our foreheads. Our whole family was *Gaitanista*.

—Tirofijo

On March 13 [1986], at noon, Fayad asked his bodyguards to leave him close to his apartment in Bogotá, in the Quinta Paredes neighborhood. His wife was there, and a child, Raúl Rosero's son. Raúl is a well-known composer. That afternoon Fayad made a few phone calls. The intelligence services detected his voice through some kind of an intercepting mechanism that identifies voices with the help of a computer. If it identifies the voice according to a pattern, it immediately finds the telephone from which the phone call is being made.

They detected Alvaro, and immediately surrounded the whole area. After five in the afternoon they came into his apartment. Fayad had a machine gun. But it seems that in an effort to save his wife's life, he told them not to do anything to her, that she was pregnant, that she had nothing to do with the struggle, that it was only his thing. Everything indicates that the guys consulted with higher-ups, with those who could make these kinds of decisions. Then they received the order to kill them. They apparently told the boy, who was seven, "Take a last look at your mother; this is the last time you are going to see her, because we're going to kill her." Then they killed her, and then they killed Alvaro. Two bursts of machine-gun fire went through his chest. From some neighbors it is known that there was no exchange of bullets.

—Antonio Navarro Wolff, leader
of the M-19

The Conservatives killed my three uncles: Daniel, Juan, and Antonio Marín. They killed Daniel with a gun and a machete in Anserma. They killed him in front of his eleven children. They cut up Juan's belly. He's the uncle who talked to me about Gaitán, and who would give me twenty cents if I would shout *Viva el Partido Liberal.* He was so fat, all that yellow grease, horrible, it just came out. . . . They took me to see all that. Antonio was in Obando with one of his sons, who was seven or eight at the time, when the Conservatives shot him. Before he died he told my cousin: "Tell your mother that they killed me, and that she shouldn't let them steal the mules from her." That's what my cousin told me, crying. They did, after all, take the mules. Antonio was one of the uncles that I loved the most. He was brave, and he stimulated my rebellious ideas.

—Iván Marino Ospina, leader of the M-19

Even Iván's [Marino Ospina] enemies, those who in Cali and Bogotá raised their glasses at their parties when Iván died, have to recognize, and they do, that he died according to his principles, valiantly, with dignity, without allowing himself to be handled, without letting them humiliate him.

Even Belisario [Betancur, president of Colombia, 1982–86] appeared to be happy when they killed Iván. He made it obvious in a letter he sent to some people in Valle who had asked him for a harder line [against the guerrillas]. He said, "Soft in form, hard in content." As if to say, look, we're the ones that killed Iván.

—Antonio Navarro Wolff

Two weeks after the *nueve de abril* [the day of Gaitán's assassination] I turned eight. I knew already at that time who Gaitán was. In my house we talked a lot about Gaitán. My mother has been a Liberal activist all her life. I was interested in Gaitán since I was a kid. I heard his speeches. . . . His death affected me very much.

Gaitán was killed by the oligarchy. And they killed him because he wanted to start a democracy. Gaitán had managed to revive the popular movement, and it was beginning to have unpredictable dimensions. And that threatened the interests of the Conservative oligarchy that was in power at the time. Gaitán awakened in the *pueblo* the belief that they could win. He taught them that one day the power of the poor would triumph over the power of the rich. That was going to happen. That's why they killed him. That's why the government of Ospina Pérez drowned the mass movement. That's why he armed the politicized police. That's why he repressed. That's why he started *la Violencia*. That's why they threw the *campesinos* off the land. That's why people took up arms. That's why three hundred thousand Colombians lost their lives. That's why they continue to die. That's why, maybe, we, too, will die. Because in this country there is no democracy. Here we will have to achieve democracy through the use of arms.

—Jaime Bateman Cayón

They would come around asking for someone, but nobody had seen him leave. They asked for such and such a family, where their bones had gone off to, but nobody would say; nobody wanted to testify whether those bones were still walking. Our neighbor, he ran away, fled; we don't know in which direction.

We don't know where he might have taken refuge; he didn't say good-bye. There are times when you don't say good-bye.

—Tirofijo

TICO

FRIDAY, OCTOBER 7

Don Guillermo drives me to the airport, just as he has most of the other times that I've left. I can count on him to pick me up early, before 6:30. The flight to Miami leaves after 10:00, but I always get to the airport at least by 7:00, about forty-five minutes before most of the other passengers arrive. That way I get through quickly, with little tension, and can sit down, read the newspapers, and watch as the other passengers stand in long lines before the Eastern Airlines counter.

And I want to give Don Guillermo the business. His niece works as the maid in my mother's house. She was with Ulla for years before that. He used to drive Jake around quite a bit, especially to the airport. I'm sure my brother-in-law always gave him substantial tips.

"I wonder how he is."

Those are the first words out of his mouth once we greet each other, talk a bit about the weather, the traffic we are encountering.

"Have you heard anything?" He asks quietly, without wanting to be pushy and not really expecting much of an answer.

"No. Nothing substantial," I answer. "But apparently he is doing okay."

"I drove him to the airport that last time. Did you know that? Who would have thought that something like this would happen to him? He is such a good man."

"It can happen to anybody. All they want is money."

"How must they be treating him?"

There's a long silence. There's little I can say.

"He used to fall asleep back there in the seat. He was always late. They would call from the office for me to be there at a certain time, but he would not be ready. And then we had to rush to the airport. I'm talking about domestic flights. You are like him with this flight to the United States. He arrived for this one just as early as you. But afternoon flights or domestic flights, that was something else. But he knew I would get him there on time. He would rest back there, fall asleep."

"Yes. He could fall asleep almost anywhere."

"I made little noises, you know, to wake him up as we were getting to the airport. I would watch him through the mirror, this one here."

He moves his head in the direction of the rear-view mirror, never taking his hands off the steering wheel. I figure Jake snored on those trips to the airport. But Don Guillermo doesn't mention that.

"One day he woke up as I had to swerve to stop from going down a street. Right up here at this corner. The *universitarios,* the students of the university, were on strike, and they had closed the street. They were throwing stones and burning buses—you know, what they do every time they go on strike. He woke up. He asked what the problem was. I told him, and he went back to sleep. And we arrived at the airport on time.

"When the girls came last summer, for vacation, *el señor* told me that I was to take care of them, to take them everywhere. He gave me his car. The Mazda. He gave me the instructions. And I did. Yes, I took them everywhere. To the houses of friends and shopping and at night, too. Every day."

We are getting close to the airport.

"He wakes up real early in the morning. Isn't that so?"

"Yes, I think so. Around four, maybe earlier."

"To work?"

"Aha."

"And he would go jogging, too, right?"

"Yes, that is what they say."

"*Cómo estará?* I wonder how he is."

JAKE

I thought quite a bit about the two brothers with the Irish Republican Army who committed suicide that day in an Irish jail, starving themselves to death. I calculated that it would probably take me about eighty days to really go under. I'd probably get into a coma in sixty days. The first of November would be about thirty days, the first of December sixty days, the twenty-fifth of December was going to be eighty-five days. I had made up my mind that at Christmas I was either going to be out or dead or at least in a coma.

I felt that I'd had a good life, a full life, and I was very happy with it. And if this situation was going to continue much longer, I'd rather be dead and gone. Finished. Not cling on to a life that is useless or meaningless or dependent on other people's whims or their likes and dislikes. Is

life so important that you have to live that way? How long was I going to
be there? Another six months? Another year perhaps? Maybe I'd have
come mentally deranged.

On October 2 or 3 I cut it all out completely. I prayed to the good Lord
to give me the strength to be able to go through with it. Not to be tempted
or that hunger pains or thirst would get to me. I decided not to tell them
what I was doing. I was thinking they would try to feed me through the
veins. I didn't want them to be preoccupied at all. That would give me a few
extra days. I was spinning my wheels there. They knew exactly what I was
doing. After the first two or three days Ricardo walks through my place, and
he tells them all, "Well, today I'm not very hungry. In fact, I think I'm going
to go on a hunger strike." He said that to them. He didn't say that to me.
And they would all eat and come over and say, "Boy, that was good." They
started keeping notes after seven or eight days about everything I did, if I
played solitaire or looked to the sky or talked to myself and when I went to
piss. They offered me water, and *panela* [clumps of brown, unrefined
sugar], and fruit. I did as if I tried to eat, and didn't.

One day Sonia takes two or three oranges and makes an orange juice,
puts it in a cup, and brings it to me. It was very inviting. I should've been
smart and took my little sip and put it aside like I always did. But for some
reason it rubbed me wrong. And I said, "No, no thank you." She said, "No,
take it." "I told you I didn't want it." She went off in a huff. In about an hour
or two, I said to her, "I'm sorry I got mad about that orange juice." She said,
"Ha, if you want it, fine. If you don't want it, that's fine, too." That was the
only time I ever talked harshly at any of them.

It got to be a challenge to see how fast I could lose weight. It gave me
some pleasure to see how skinny I was getting. It's a terrible thing. But I was
working very hard to get skinny, to lose weight. I was getting good results.
They used to give me two thermoses of coffee a day. Now one thermos was
more than enough, and I had quite a bit left over, and most of that I spit out
anyway. I wanted to dehydrate to make it go faster. I gave up all pretense of
just smoking one pack a day and just chain-smoked all the time. At night I
would wake up and put my head and arms out of the mosquito netting and
smoke. Ricardo used to mention it to me. He said, *"Tío está durmiendo muy
poco ahora. Está fumando toda la noche."* "Uncle is sleeping very little now and
smoking all night." And he'd tell me how many times I'd smoke. They were
getting worried.

They gave me a pocket book that they got there, a book on love, taking
place in Boston, from the year 1870 to 1900, 1905. It was a thick book, and

I read it in a day and a half. They couldn't quite understand how I could read it so fast.

I was finally doing something. I was finally accomplishing something. I wasn't dependent anymore on people on the outside or on them or on anybody. I was back in control of my own destiny. Nobody could do anything about it. I was back. It was out of their hands and out of everybody's hands.

It was me again. That give me some pride, inner pride. I was able to say to myself, "Fuck you, motherfuckers. Take the food and shove it up your ass. I don't need nothing from nobody. You want to take away my mosquito netting at night, go ahead and take it. You want me to sleep on the ground, I'll sleep on the ground. You all will never break me now. No way."

They knew it. And I told them. I said, "I'm going to solve the problem for everybody. When I die just make a little hole there and bury me. A hundred pounds of dead meat is worth nothing. You all will not have to worry about me anymore. My family won't have to worry about me anymore. Nobody. And I'll be at peace."

I said, "Look, Ricardo, do you think I have a will to live? What I wish for every morning is that you would receive an order saying that we can't make a deal for this guy, so put him against the tree and shoot his ass. That will get me out of this misery a lot faster."

I said, "Do you think I'm scared of death? Death to me is nothing. Right now, the mood I'm in, death to me is the beginning of a new life because I'm completely tired of this life I have right now. I have no desires. No nothing. The only thing I want is to get out of this. I'm finished."

We all die. My family would have been hurt. They would have suffered for a while, but a short period of grief and mourning is much better than two or three years of uncertainty. You'd find out. I really didn't think that they would just bury me out there and not say nothing.

I don't know. That's one of the risks I took. And I considered that risk very much. I wasn't too afraid of my body showing up dead. That would have been all right. Then everyone picks up the trail of their life. That's normal.

I came to the conclusion that if I didn't eat, I wouldn't have to shit. That gave me great pleasure. At first I wondered how many days I would last before I couldn't get up no more, and I asked myself how I would go take a shit if I couldn't get out of my bed. That was dumb because if you're not eating anything for days, you're not going to have to go. When I came to that realization, I felt much better because I knew that I could just lay there in bed and nobody would have to do anything for me. That was quite a relief for me.

You know, they watch you every minute, twenty-four hours a day. But I found the way to bug them, annoy them, make them worry. All at once it

Jake

wasn't hey, we got this man, and that's it. All at once I had control. It took me a while to get there, but I found the way. Not completely. But I had control over certain phases of my life.

TICO

WEDNESDAY, OCTOBER 12

Not only is something wrong; nothing's right. The rules simply don't apply. Only Nelson keeps believing that they do. The conversations with him are becoming strained. He keeps saying that they'll come down suddenly, out of the blue, and when we least expect it. The moment will come when they will realize that they have no other choice.

Yes. They will call. They have to. They need us. We have the money. Hey, it's only a business. We'll come to terms.

But, no. I know that this isn't working right. Either something has happened to him, or these guys are bent on getting millions. Christmas is beginning to loom in front of us. Six months? That's some kind of an average, isn't it? Six months isn't all that long for a Colombian kidnapping. Right? Maybe ours will last longer.

Damn!

TUESDAY, OCTOBER 18

It looks like we can't go on. I think Ulla has had it. She's pretty desperate. She tells us that it hasn't worked, that she's convinced that the guerrillas will not negotiate with us unless we move up. We've been wrong all along about the kind of money that it would take.

Has she always felt that we were not doing this right? The whole thing is unraveling, and I don't know what to do.

We were on the phone all day yesterday. I talked to Nelson. Ulla did, too. And conference calls. And Vicente. César, too. Nelson and his people don't budge. He says they will come down. He has helped us so much and is so knowledgeable. Ulla has always listened to him more or at least as much as she has listened to me. He's been through it. And he knows all kinds of cases. But I'm starting to think that we have misjudged this whole thing from the beginning.

Jake doesn't fit any of the categories. He's not an *hacendado* or a politician. He's a foreigner but doesn't work for a big company. He's an owner. Nelson's people have never had a case like this before. This is unique. Maybe our original ideas and their advice, which together seemed so logical at first, are all wrong.

But Nelson's point is clear. If we change, if we offer more now, the guerrillas will know, or they will think, that there is more there to be had. Instead of us getting Jake back earlier, he will be out there even longer. The guerrillas will just string us out indefinitely.

What can I say? Where do I get the strength to argue against Ulla? What right do I have? I don't know if we are doing the right thing. Do they really want two million dollars?

I think that Ulla is thinking about offering them almost twice as much as she had originally thought of. We would be close to a million. How's she going to come up with that kind of money?

I really don't want to know. That was clear to me from the beginning, and it makes so much more sense now. I've got nothing to do with the money. I only talk money with the guerrillas. I follow instructions. I'm just a regular old history professor.

But Ulla wants to know what I think. I'm really at loose ends. Do we continue as we have been, or do we change? I don't know, but we're breaking. There's no question about that. Ulla's had it. The guerrillas have us. I feel helpless, for we are going to give them so much more power over us. We will show our weakness, and then they can really string us along for months. How do we put a stop to it?

But maybe Ulla is right. Maybe they figured on a sum from the beginning, a million, perhaps more, and they are determined to get it. If we don't start moving up quickly, we may have no movement in months. They're in the driver's seat either way.

Who am I trying to kid? They've been in control of all of this, of us, right from the start. They've known all along exactly what they were going to do and when and how and for how long, and we have just been reacting, thinking that we knew what we were doing, that they were reacting to us.

What are we going to do?

We can't do anything unless they call. Maybe they won't call for a month. What good are our decisions then?

Tico

JAKE

We made the big move to the fifth camp. It was October 15 or 16. It took about four or five days. It was an easy move. Ricardo told me they wanted to get me closer to where I could be freed. Maybe he was right. We passed through quite a few villages and small places where there might be ten or twenty houses. I could hear people talking, and they were greeting people. But they had my head and my hands covered so the *campesinos* couldn't see that I was white.

I got bad saddle sores. I ate some *panela*. A few clumps of *panela* a couple of times a day would give me the energy to make the horseback ride, keep me from falling off. It wouldn't put any weight on me. Substantially it was not food. It might have been calories, and the calories were being burned off anyway. Every hour or so they asked me if I wanted more. They found the one thing that I would eat.

I didn't know why they were moving me. Every time they told me anything about being released, I figured it was a ploy to get me to eat. It wasn't critical yet. This was about fifteen days into the hunger strike. Ricardo said, "You know, you haven't eaten in quite a few days." I said, "Yeah, I'm just not hungry." He said, "Yes, but it's not natural." He said, "You know how long it's been since you've eaten?" I said, "Yeah, it must be about eight or nine days." "Oh, no," he said, "it's much more than that." They were counting. They had it all down. But he didn't tell me how many days. I wanted to get that out of him but couldn't. But I knew. I counted by the weeks. From this Sunday to that Sunday. I started on a Sunday.

When we got to the other location, they finally let me listen to some shortwave radio. He let me use his little Sony. I was able to listen to whatever I wanted. I always had hopes of finding Armed Forces Radio. I knew exactly where it was because I'd been listening to it for years. Never could get it. I was very disturbed about that and thought, doggone it, you must be in a location that you can't get it; it must be because of the mountains or something. I'd listen to BBC and Voice of America. The World Series was over by then, so I'd get the football scores. And some stock market reports. Discussions on Dukakis and Bush, the merits of both. Or I'd just listen to music. That would make the day pass a little bit more reasonable. I'd use it for about an hour in the afternoon and then give it back. They were trying to get my spirits up.

The first day we were at the new camp, a man I didn't know came to see me. He brought me this handwritten letter from the leadership of the movement. He read it to me. It was two pages front and back. It said that they were sorry to hear that I'd lost my spirits and that I wasn't eating very much, but that I had to get my strength back, that I would feel some elation by surmounting such odds and getting out alive. Negotiations were going on, and it wasn't their fault that I hadn't gotten out. They were doing everything they could, but that they were having problems with Colombian intelligence and the DEA. They said they couldn't figure out why they were involved, and that the family wasn't being very cooperative. I said, "Fine, it doesn't make no difference to me. If you all are maybe asking for too much, that is you all's problem. You all will have to come down some, think of something that will be paid. There's a problem somewhere."

I have nothing to say.

The guy handed me the letter. I said, "No, what do I want that for?" He said, "You might want it when you get out." I should have taken it. You would have liked to read it. But I couldn't. I said, "Oh, I doubt that I will ever get out of here. I'll probably get buried on the side of that little hill over there, about ten yards from here." He left that same evening. I said to myself, well, looks like somebody's taken notice.

About two days later another man comes. If he wasn't a doctor, he could have been a psychologist. He was real suave. We talked. He asked me how I was feeling. Why was I so depressed? We talked a little bit about hunger. He said, "We'll probably have to give you some *suero*, serum, intravenous feeding." They'd ordered about fifty or sixty bottles, brought them in a big sack. And I said, "Well, I really don't need any *suero*. I feel good." And he said, "Yes, but you're getting very weak, you're losing a lot of weight, and we're all worried about you." And I said, "Well, giving me *suero* isn't going to make me eat if I am not hungry. I can't resist you all. But I protest that you are giving them to me." I said, "The *suero* won't keep me alive very much longer. You can't keep a man alive in a clinic if he's not eating. You might give him a few days extra by not letting him dehydrate." So he said to Ricardo, "Okay, don't give them to him. He doesn't want it."

He told me they had ways of getting a small portable TV with a generator. I told him, "I don't watch television." So he told Ricardo, "Does he have any reading material?" And Ricardo said, yes, I have this book that I was given quite a long time ago that I was supposed to give to him when he gets out. It was the book on the Italian cities. I saw that Vicente had written in it and told me that when I got out, we'd meet in any town that I'd pick. But then I saw that it came from a bookstore in Charlottesville, so I knew who had gotten it, how it had gotten down to Bogotá. That gave me more strength in my feeling that you were doing the negotiations and were directly involved.

Jake

I had no pains. None. I wasn't thirsty. No stomach cramps. The Good Lord was with me. When they'd bring me a meal, I'd sit up. I'd look at it and I'd know that they were all looking at me. I'd light up another cigarette. And finally I'd try to eat. If it was beans, I'd put a bean or two in my mouth. If it was peas, the same way. Or rice. Whatever it was. If it was just soup, I'd take a spoonful and spit it out. Put the plate at the end of the bed, and say, damn, I can't swallow it. That gave me quite a bit of elation. With every meal I knew that I was getting closer to my goal. I could feel their sense of disappointment as I missed another meal.

I knew I was getting weak because to go urinate, I'd have to hold on. And my piss would be quite dark, sort of reddish. To get there I had to cross this big tree trunk. It got so bad that Ricardo had to cut it in half to give me a passageway. I knew I was dehydrating because I would be urinating a lot more liquid than I'd be taking in every day.

I'd sit on a log in the stream or a rock and get undressed slowly, pour cold water on top of my head. It was so cold, but it felt so good and refreshing. It shocked you into feeling good. I'd put some of the water in my mouth, spit it out. I guess a few drops would go down my throat. You might call that cheating, but it was all right. I'd wash off, soap myself. I couldn't stand. I'd notice how skinny I was getting. God damn, I'd say to myself, how in the world can this be happening? I'd wash my feet, my underwear, and I'd dry myself. One of the guards would come over and hold me when I tried to put on my pants. I'd tie them up with a little piece of rope that I'd found to keep them from falling down. I'd put on my socks, my boots. They had to hold me going up.

In the whole time I was out there I never looked into a mirror, so I had no idea what I looked like with my beard and my face and my hair. They trimmed my beard once or twice, and they trimmed my fingernails a couple of times.

I thought about my life. This was a hell of a way to go. Here's a man who has been fairly successful in life, with a family and a wife that loves him, who enjoys food and wine and drinks. Here I was in some forsaken hillside of Colombia, and I didn't even know where I was. Twelve or eight people guarding me. And the height of irony was that I was starving myself to death to gain freedom. Maybe I would die on this forsaken hillside and even be buried here, and nobody would even know.

Other thoughts entered my mind. Of all ridiculous things, food. Here I was, I hadn't eaten anything and really drank anything in about twenty-five days, and I'd think about all the different restaurants we'd been to in different parts of the world. Like some little place in Italy that gave you a tremendous meal. It didn't bring any hunger pains to me thinking of this. This is the funny thing. It didn't make me desire food. I'd also think that if I ever got out, what I would cook and eat. I thought about cooking rice and milk, putting raisins and *panela* into it to make a cold rice pudding. Mixing milk and bananas and ice cream in a blender and drinking it down.

They told me they were making real progress. They did not want me to be in that condition. I really think they wanted me to feel that they wouldn't mistreat me. They told me, "We can't let you go home like that. We can't let your family see you in this condition." But they also knew that I had done this on my own. They could always say, "Well, didn't we always give you food?"

This is what helped me. If they wouldn't have given me these meals that I could refuse, maybe I would have gotten hungry. Three times a day. I looked forward to it. The time started passing almost faster. Waiting for breakfast in the morning, waiting for lunch, dinner.

The days would just click off.

The morale of the camp started going down. Things were quieter. There were not so many jokes. They went around with a longer face. They were not sure if in my weakened condition I would catch some kind of a disease or a fever or malaria or anything else. I imagine they might have been worried about what their commanders would say to them, blame them for what was happening. All those who came to visit me asked me if I wasn't eating because of the way they were treating me.

Two or three days later another man came in. He was a joker. He told me a few jokes, and I sort of smiled. And he says, "You don't like jokes very much." I said, "No. I never really enjoyed jokes too much and in this situation much less." And he says, "Maybe what we can do is send more people that can stay here and talk with you, and let you pass the time talking. Maybe this is your problem." I said, "No, I like my solitude."

The next day they killed a pig. They cut it up, the guts and all, and it smelled good, and everybody was really eating it up. They brought me a plate of it along with rice. The joker put down his plate, and said, "Let's make a bet. Let's see who can eat the most." I said, "No. Let's make another bet. Why don't you stay here two or three days and see who can eat the least?" He went on his way about a half hour after that, wished me good luck, hoped that I would get my morale back.

They were taking notice. Something was going to be done one way or the other. You could see it in their attitudes. The comment of this one guy, *"Vamos a fracasar. El negocio va a fracasar."* "We're going to fail. This deal is going to fall through." They were getting worried.

Jake

When the joker left I told Ricardo that I was completely tired of this situation. I want to get out of it. I told him I lost all desire for living. For women. For art. For business. I couldn't care anymore about anything. The only desire I had was to join my maker in heaven. And he would tell me, "Well, what about your family?" And I'd say, "My family will be all right. I think the worst has already been passed for them, with the shock of the kidnapping. It's been so long now that it doesn't make much difference." He just walked away. They really didn't know how to respond.

My mind would wonder. I don't think it was hallucinations, but I was wondering about how I would handle the whole situation if I got out. What would I do with my life after that? During those days I made certain decisions. I would never go back to Colombia. The only time I would go back was if your mother died there, going to the funeral. That's it. Maybe in later times, if things changed, to visit them in the cemetery. That's about it. For the respect that I have for your father and your mother. I made other decisions about the company. But I didn't know what the situation was on the outside, if the company still existed, if we had a house.

TICO

WEDNESDAY, OCTOBER 19

We were on the phone until late last night.

We're putting off a decision. There is a temporary consensus among us. We are going to wait a few more days, and if we don't hear then, we'll do something.

It's not clear how many days we have agreed to wait. Nobody wanted to state anything real definite, to fix a time period. We really haven't decided anything. Ulla has given us a few more days, that's all.

Damn! It's their money! Why am I arguing that we shouldn't change course? What right do I have? This man's life is in my hands.

But is it? Do our decisions carry any weight with them at all? Besides, we haven't done anything. They don't know what we're thinking. For all they know, we might not be too keen on getting him back. I mean, they don't know anything about us. Right?

Or do they? What do they know? How much research have they done? You keep hearing these rumors that they figure everything out beforehand, who is who, what the family is like, what the personalities are. Everything.

Did they do that with us? Why wouldn't they have? Of course, they did. This is a big kidnapping, one of the biggest. They did ask for five million dollars.

I've got to think. But there is not much to think about. There's nothing to do. What happens if we change our minds? What do we do then? How in the world do we let them know that we want to negotiate?

Maybe we could spread the rumor in Sabana. I don't know how that would work. Vicente seems to feel that it's possible, even easy. The guerrillas are everywhere. Maybe it's as easy as walking into a crowded bar in Sabana and telling the first person you see that the Gambini family wants to talk to them. They'd get the message, maybe even quickly.

THURSDAY, OCTOBER 20

Cecilia practically screams at me to get on the phone. "It's Ulla!" There is a wide look of expectation on her face as she thrusts the receiver at me. It's early in the morning, not yet 10:00. The guerrillas never call that early.

"*Llamaron*," Cecilia blurts out. "They called."

Something has happened. I don't have time to think whether it's good or bad.

"Tico, we have just received a wonderful call. I just can't believe it. It's over. He said, '*Hemos aterrizado*.' 'We have landed.' Tico, they have come all the way down! They have agreed to our offer! I just can't believe it. It's over! It's over!"

So close. We were on the verge of breaking down. It was a matter of days, maybe hours. I don't think we could have gone on like this much longer. But it worked. We've won. How close can it get?

I breathe deeply and close my eyes, listening to Ulla's excitement.

They haven't exactly agreed to our offer, but they have come down, way down, all the way to less than the half-million we have been angling for. It's as though they knew from the way we were negotiating what we would finally settle for.

Has Nelson been right all this time?

I listen to the conversation. It's on Ulla's answering machine.

CÉSAR: What can I tell him? Tell me something so I can tell him.

THEM: Tell him that yes, that we are going to settle this *pronto*, but not for what he has said.

CÉSAR: Aha.

THEM: Tell him to see if he . . .

Tico

There was a slight pause, a dead moment as a coin was being inserted. He was calling from a pay phone somewhere in Bogotá. There were certainly some people standing behind him. Could they hear what he was saying?

THEM: . . . if he can come up with something more.

CÉSAR: Well, I'm not involved in this anymore, but I would say that you should bring something, too, something more realistic, no?

THEM: Yes. That is why. Yes. We have landed a little bit, no?

CÉSAR: Correct. I think that is good.

THEM: It's just to see if you can be a bit more just in this situation, no?

CÉSAR: Aha.

THEM: Now. That is to say, we have landed. We are no longer going to ask for what we have been asking.

CÉSAR: Aha.

THEM: We want this to be settled at 150.

CÉSAR: How much?

THEM: 150.

CÉSAR: 150?

THEM: Yes.

César couldn't understand what was going on, what they were asking for. The figure didn't coincide with anything they had been saying before. And they had switched from dollars to pesos.

CÉSAR: 150. We're talking in Colombian, right?

THEM: Yes. Yes. Yes. But of those 150 we want 300, ah, 300,000 dollars. In dollars.

CÉSAR: Aha.

THEM: And the rest in Colombian.

CÉSAR: No. But you are telling me 150 what, professor?

César refers to everyone as professor. The *guerrillero* was no exception.

THEM: What?

CÉSAR: You are talking to me of 150 million pesos?

Our Guerrillas, Our Sidewalks

THEM: Yes.

CÉSAR: Ah. Okay. That is 300 in dollars and 200 in . . . ah . . .

THEM: No. No. Three hundred in dollars and the rest in pesos.

The rest was somewhere between forty-six and fifty-three million pesos, depending on the exchange rate they were using, either that of June 24 or today's. They would get more with each passing day.

They talked a few more brief moments. They had referred to real figures over the phone. Months of negotiating were resolved in a few minutes over a telephone wire. And all those months where they didn't want to talk on the phone. What's going on? Why the sudden change? Nelson can't quite believe it either. It's unorthodox, to say the least.

And he kept insisting on doing things quickly. Get the money, he said. Call him today; call Heriberto today so he has more time to get the money.

There is no question about it. They want to close a deal quickly. Why? Why? What has made them change their mind? What's happened?

CÉSAR: Okay. Perfect.

THEM: All right.

CÉSAR: All right. Then . . .

THEM: I'll call you back this afternoon.

CÉSAR: All right. Until then.

THEM: Okay. Good-bye then.

TUESDAY, OCTOBER 25

We are on the phone with them all the time, like teenagers who have suddenly discovered each other. Constantly. It's as though we feel we can't let go of each other. At least that's how I feel. I want constant communication.

It takes eight calls to work out all the details. We continue to negotiate, not because we aren't prepared to pay the price they are demanding, but because we have to be consistent. We can't just suddenly agree to what they want. But the differences are not substantial. They know they will get close to their 150 million pesos—460,000 dollars or so.

And we have to deal with the final proofs. I have to demand them.

I didn't yesterday. When the time was right, I blew it. I didn't get a chance to broach the subject. I kicked myself for prolonging it. Not today.

ME: Listen, *hombre*, we have to figure out a few details.

He doesn't want to listen. He talks about the upcoming general strike and other problems they are having and the condition of the roads. It's raining too much out there, he says. But he's angling for details on how to make the transaction right then and there, talking to me. He wants to finalize the whole thing. We are close to the end. He wants to talk to César to give him the instructions.

ME: All right, but you guys are ready to do this?

THEM: Of course.

ME: Then you have the proofs for me?

THEM: Yes. *Listo.* Ready.

They aren't what we want. After pushing him, he admits that the pictures have no date on them. I tell him what we want, and I let him know that he should know these things. After all, they're a serious organization, right? And we have even given them a Polaroid and a cassette recorder and told them what we wanted.

THEM: No. No. But we are already talking about this. To do some
      things. We have trust here.

ME: Yes. Yes. I trust you completely.

THEM: Well, then, what is the problem?

He's nervous. I have never heard him speak so quickly before. He's breathing hard. Something is wrong. The more nervous he gets, the less I trust him.

They don't want to give us any proofs. Jake's dead. That has to be it. Why else would they not want to follow the rules? They can't produce a picture with a good date on it. It's over.

I insist. Rules, I tell him, are rules. It will take two weeks, he says. I tell him that's fine. I have no problem with two weeks. Two weeks are nothing. Then he says ten days. When he knows I'm serious, that we won't budge without the proofs, he lets me know that we'll hear from them in eight days.

THEM: Tell me. And you, where did you learn all these things?

ME: Look. This man is of my family, and I have to do everything I can
      to make sure everything goes well.

THEM: Yeah, sure. But you all were told to ask for those things.

ME: Let me tell you something. I wasn't born yesterday, you know?

He hangs up. We have both lost our composure. It's the first time. I regret my last statement. I think about it and think about it. It feels as though I've transgressed, as though I have insulted a close friend. And I keep wondering whether they're going to get angry.

Nelson tells me to stop worrying. I didn't say anything insulting. "We're close to the end. Don't worry. They're not going to forget about all this merely because of something you said." I know he's right. But my words keep coming back to me.

I'm not thinking about his voice. I'm trying not to think about why it is that they don't want to give us the proofs. Eight days!

Another flight back to Charlottesville.

JAKE

At about one o'clock in the afternoon of October 31, Monday, Halloween, they received word that somebody was coming in. I believe he was the man of highest rank who had come to see me. He's the one who had come to see me on about September 15, and told me to be careful when I was going to the airport and not to give any of my jewelry. With that he set up my fake release three or four days later and all the psychological stuff.

When he saw me he was very surprised and agitated. He told me, *"Tío,* you're looking terrible. The last time I saw you, you were in full health, your weight was good, your morale was good. Now you're completely down." And I said, "Yes, but don't forget that was quite a long time ago, and nothing has happened. I'm still here."

He said, "Well, we have been talking to Heriberto. We had lost contact with him, but now it's all back, and everything looks like it's going very well. We have much respect for him. He's very smart." And he said, "Tell me, he's a history professor, isn't he?" I said, "Yes, and I think he might have written a book and a lot of papers."

And he said, "Well, the negotiations are going well, and I think your release is pretty close." I said, "Close? What do you mean by close?" And he said, "Well, fairly soon." I said, "Well, how long?" I tried to pin him down. Then he finally said, "Eight days." This is the first time I asked how long. To try to get a commitment. It wouldn't have meant anything, but anyway for my feeling. And, you know, I don't think I demonstrated any joy or anything like that.

He said, "Yes, but now they want proof. We have to take some pictures, and you will have to talk in the tape recorder." They brought out a magazine, *Cromos*. And he said, "They want a picture of you with this recent magazine to give absolute proof that you're well and mentally alert." I said, "Fine." He told me to read everything on the cover and two or three different pages with the page number and everything. I thought they were carrying it to excess. I started reading in this poor Spanish of mine.

I talked into the tape recorder. I wanted to get across to you all, or to the outside, that I was not eating and that I was ready to go ahead and die. I wanted my family to understand that dying wasn't anything. I was at ease with my situation and not to worry about me. I said that my family knew me well enough to know what I was doing. And I said, "Thank you very much, Tico, for everything you are doing, and give my love to the family." And then I turned it off.

He looked at me, and said, "*Tío*, or *señor* Gambini, we can't send that tape like that. They'll think that we are trying to pressure them into a settlement with your words. We don't like to be like that." I said, "Give me the tape back." I said, "Tico, I'm being given all the food I want. In fact I'm being asked what I want to eat. I'm just not hungry. I am being treated very well, and I have everything I would need if I wanted." I gave it back to him. And I said, "Now, that should satisfy everybody."

He took some pictures with that Polaroid. They had taken pictures of me before. But this time I was holding a recent magazine in front of me that would date the picture. Deep in my mind I started saying, well, there might be something to this that he's telling me. This might really be something.

But I couldn't let myself get elated. Even though it might have been true that they were getting ready to make a settlement, if I would start eating, maybe they might change their mind and keep me longer again. I kept up the way I was. This is the same man that had tricked me before. He's the one that set up that fake release.

He told me he had to leave. And he did. Boy, he took off. He left at 4:00 or 5:00 that afternoon. They never did that; come and go in one day. He was in a hurry. He mentioned that they had to get the proof to you, that you all were waiting.

Inside I was in a state of turmoil and agitation. I was thinking, well, they got nervous, and they want to get rid of me. They don't want to have a corpse on their hands. That's what got them off center, to make the move, to make an offer, or to get down to a more realistic figure.

I said to myself, Jake, you can't stop now. I was really afraid that I would still be there in eight or nine days. I prepared myself mentally that I was not going to be released. But deep down I hoped that I wouldn't still be there, that I would be free.

TICO

THURSDAY, NOVEMBER 3

They call right on the eighth day, early in the morning again, just after 9:00. Have we received the package? No. He says it will come.

Three minutes later there it is on the secretary's desk: a picture and a long tape.

He's dying. He's stopped eating. He's given up on life. He doesn't mind death. I can't believe it.

I listen to the tape recording on my phone. His horrible Spanish.

Jake says something about me knowing him well. What's he trying to tell us? That he wouldn't really kill himself? That he would and we shouldn't worry? Is that why he is thanking us? Is he saying good-bye?

I don't understand. I can't understand him. Not enough. Not now. How can I understand anybody in a situation like that? And I don't want to think. I just want to go through the motions. Do what I have to do. Take it step by step, one after the other. Got to get it done.

But there it is. He's done it. Everything we always feared, it's right there in front of us. We always knew that he was going to do something. But stop eating? Is that what he's done? Something like that. I never thought of that. What's he doing? Killing himself? Starving himself? Has Ulla always worried that he would do something like this?

What in the world am I doing in Charlottesville waiting? And out of town, at a field hockey game, enjoying myself until late afternoon?

Those damn proofs! Why did we insist on them? Eight days. He's starving himself, and we are waiting around for a picture. We're killing him. I know I should have trusted the guerrillas. They want to return him to us before he dies on them.

I'm slowing things down. Is he in pain? Conscious? What is he thinking about us?

Got to stop. Got to stop thinking. Do what I have to do. Think of the guerrillas.

We are so close to them. Their immediate interests and ours are identical. We both have to make sure that there is life in his body. We've known this from the beginning, of course, but this is different. This is real. Together, they and us, we have to work against a common foe, against time, against him, against this man who has refused to eat, who is about to die on us.

They didn't want to go through the final proofs because of what he had been doing. They're afraid of how we will react. Would we conclude that our trust had been broken? Would we think they had tortured him? Deprived him of food? We might go public, even publish the photograph in the newspapers. They were no longer in control. And they must have worried about what might happen to him during those additional days in which he was still their responsibility.

But they could've reacted differently, used his condition to their advantage to pressure us. Look, they might have said, the man is starving himself. There is nothing we can do. Come up with the three million by next weekend or he's dead. Just look at his picture. You have his voice. He's told you that it was his decision, not ours, that we have been treating him well. You know what he is doing. We're sorry. We certainly did not want things to end this way. If you don't pay, you'll be killing him, not us. They could have told us that they had a lunatic on their hands. But they didn't.

They didn't. We're not dealing with simple kidnappers, with *criminales comunes*. They are *guerrilleros*. It's as though the entire guerrilla ideology is encapsulated in his physical condition. They take people away, after all, fully convinced that it's their moral right to do so. They don't torture their captives because doing so is not part of an objective economic and social transaction and because they are morally convinced in the rightness of their actions.

The man I've been talking to on the phone is not a common criminal. He's a man of convictions. He's convinced that what he's doing is right, that it's good, and that he has history on his side. He has Marx on his side. He's the good guy, and I'm the bad one. He's taking from the rich to fight for the poor. I'm not evil because of who I am as a person, but because of the position he believes my family holds in society. When he talks to me, he isn't talking to me but to a certain category of person. Categories. He knows all about me without ever having met me, without knowing anything about me.

The *guerrillero* has to deal with me, with us, for the greater good of his movement and his nation. He needs the money to keep his struggle going. He's the one who is lowering himself. He feels that the rich live off the poor, that the exploitation of labor is the basis of the class distinctions of Colombia. They are fighting to bring them to an end. He represents justice and I, greed.

I'm acting in a way that goes against everything he thinks is right. I'm trying to get my brother-in-law back while giving them as little money as possible. Not only are we rich, but we're unwilling to give up some money to save one of our loved ones. All my actions must confirm his beliefs. Mine is a self-ishly materialistic conception of the world in which I put a price on the head of a family member. That's the way we act. When his revolutionary movement comes to power, they will get rid of people like me.

Suddenly I can see his world again, just as when I mourned Camilo's death as a teenager. I can feel his anger and his passion to create change, make the revolution, turn everything around. His Colombia and mine really aren't that different.

I can hear the few critics who are left in Colombia who are calling life here a savage form of capitalism. There aren't many laws and institutions by which those who are down and out can claim any rights. The poor, especially the rural poor, are out in the cold. I've known about this Colombia all along, of course, but now I can feel my own anger about it coming back. If it weren't like this, then the guerrillas wouldn't be out there. Jake wouldn't be out there. I'd be leading my life.

Savage capitalism. That's it. Those two words encapsulate it all and tell me everything I need to know about Colombia. It's almost like a revelation. I can really sense that the market has been a disaster in Colombia because it is back with such force, existing all around me on the streets.

But it's in the mountains that it really has a meaning, for that's where it's had such a long history. Those three Andes mountain chains filled with people fighting for land, for a way of surviving in endless frontierlike places in the face of overwhelming odds, without much law or government or police forces to depend on. It's been a constant fight for private property.

I can see the tiny little plots here and there of coffee smallholders, small owners trying to keep their places in the international market, families, men, women, and children, young and old alike, picking the beans on those steep inclines, fighting off others who want to grab hold of their little tract of land, their treasured *minifundio*. Rugged individualists all of them, those who have a little, or a lot and those who don't have much of anything but are trying to get their hands on something. Hardworking individualists. What else could they have become?

They've been out there since early in the nineteenth century. Before coffee they competed for gold in the many riverbeds of the valleys. And they worked in tobacco and rubber, following the booms and busts of the international market. And after coffee it's been cows and ranching that have made their lives so precarious, forcing many of them off the lands once again. In the struggle for land, human life in Colombia has been devalued. It's almost as though those who have a chance of getting more, new local

elites perhaps, think nothing of throwing others off and maybe even ending
their lives.

But it was coffee that really transformed the countryside, setting people
to scramble for whatever pieces of land they could get their hands on, stak-
ing out a claim, and thrusting Colombia into the modern world. For many
of those coffee workers, their pieces of land have been getting smaller over
time, not only because they have lost some of it to others, but because
they've had to inherit pieces to children, who have an increasingly difficult
time making it. So families have been forced to fight not only against others
but often among themselves as well for what has been theirs.

There's been little government, but the political parties have been there
all this time. They are the only thing that rural Colombians in the highlands
have been able to grab onto for a measure of protection and defense or as
a means of getting hold of someone else's land. Liberals and Conservatives.
So the politicians have been able to make deep inroads into the countryside, where rural people have cloaked themselves in the mantle of the two
parties, becoming one or the other, seeking their best chances, finding perhaps that a local boss with influence in the town and hopefully beyond it is
a Liberal and that with him their life chances and those of their offspring
might improve a bit.

And others out there might find that in their town the people who seem
to count are Conservatives, so it's that party they turn to. Or others might
want to seek the protection of God and the church, finding there that their
local parish priest is a Conservative bent on banishing from the area all
those who are Liberals, those who can be construed to be without a belief in
God. And it turns out that the more of those alleged heathens are thrown
out of the area, the more land there will be for those who remain, those
who now adhere more fervently to the Conservative Party than ever, for they
know how they have managed to get ahead in life. Small landholders are
pitted against small landholders, little people against little people.

That's the main reason the rule of law has not prevailed—because the two
parties have taken over the role of government in the countryside. Instead of
one set of rules that at least is intended to cover everyone, it's all been turned
into a partisan struggle. Rather than setting the basis for uniting people
around a common set of expectations, national, regional, and local leaders of
the two parties have divided Colombians into warring factions.

Because more often than not out there, it does pay to adhere to one
party or the other. And the more people do so, the stronger they make
those politicians, those priests, those intermediaries between local areas
and wider politics, those men who make the system work by tying it

together. Thus the violence begins to grow from the bottom up, becoming an integral part of the daily life of people out in the countryside.

And there's more, so much more. It's not only party labels and identities that tie small people to Liberals and Conservatives in their town, in district capitals, and in far-off Bogotá. Together many rural people, especially those who own some property, share a view of the world with regional and national political elites. They are in it together, knowing full well what they are doing. They've been fighting over access to land, for a place to survive.

They're all using their wits, their minds, figuring out what to do, with whom to make alliances. So it's not a question of some people craftily hoodwinking ignorant and superstitious peasants into a whole series of strange beliefs about how evil all those other people are so that the peasants will go out and kill those others. That's what a lot of elites like to believe, and many academics, too, because that way they can simply say that it's the ignorance, the backwardness of rural Colombians that makes all the violence possible, that makes people fight against each other. What these elite politicians and thinkers are really doing is blaming the victims for the violence that destroys their lives rather than blaming the entire system itself, the rural capitalism that engulfs everyone.

It's the easy answer, and it leaves the elites off the hook. The violence is not their fault. They can say that they have nothing to do with it, for it resides in others, in poor and thoughtless peasants. I grew up learning about that belief. Everywhere I went, whatever I read, everything told me time and again that the Colombian people are perverse, violent. That's just the way they are, we were told. My guts always informed me that it wasn't so. It couldn't be. Maybe that's why I spent so many of my young years in high school reading about Adolf Hitler and the Nazis and the concentration camps—to prove to myself and others that violence was worse elsewhere, especially among Germans, who fancied themselves so civilized. My father, a German, agreed with me. He always told me that he supported the German people but not the Nazi state. And I answered likewise. I support the Colombian people but not the government. Now I know it's more than a question of the government.

Much more. Together rich and poor and all those many out there who are struggling to be in between believe in making it in the market through the individual ownership of land. It's the belief in capitalism and the savage practice of it that hold the nation together and render it asunder.

The man on the phone knows most of this, even though he probably focuses on those many who lose their land and have to move farther away. I also keep thinking of those who have fought for what little they have had and managed to stay where they are, breathing life into the two traditional parties. I'm pretty sure that for him it's more nearly a struggle between the haves and the have-nots. But there is so much that we can agree on.

Once again, now, it feels almost as though we're on the same side. But I can't be with them, not anymore, maybe not even then. It was probably all a romantic illusion, the fantasies of a bourgeois boy. I felt those stirrings, and they pulled at me strongly, but not strongly enough.

And now? Now I know I can't be with them. It's not just the kidnapping, this one and others. I can sense that I've left the guerrillas behind, that there is just too much that they don't understand anymore. Yes, there it is again, that knowledge that they have been out there too long. Too much has changed that they can't know about. The voice on the phone doesn't have a sense of it, even though he lives in Bogotá. I'm sure he doesn't see it.

I shake myself into listening to the tape again, but it's no use. My mind drifts back to the mountains and to Bogotá, to far-off Bogotá. I can see the plots of land, a complex mosaic of colors and fences from valley to valley, some sections getting larger, but most turning smaller, becoming more distinct. They're like the sidewalks, tiny pieces of individual territory. Yes.

I am beginning to sense something that I've sort of known before but haven't seen. Now the knowledge is overwhelming me. It's all connected, rural and urban. The violence in Colombian history that has been made possible by the struggle for tiny plots of land is now being reproduced by city people confidently walking the sidewalks, pursuing their own private futures. For they are the ones who allow the government to sit back and do little for those who have less than they do and for those out in the countryside. The politicians know that urban people will remain quiet. So whatever happens to poor people happens to poor people. And the upper class of Colombia survives happily, comfortably, knowing that there won't be a revolution in Colombia.

But it's not quite that easy. They have bodyguards, and they live in secluded parts of the city. No, they're not comfortable. They're living in fear of being robbed or killed or kidnapped.

But the people walking the sidewalks aren't against them, the rich. They are trying to survive in a world molded by the rich, trying to grab a piece of the pie. They know what they're doing, and they are doing it with their eyes open. I've seen them walking the sidewalks with that glimmer in their eyes. They're just like the rural people. Neither of them have gone into their lives with their eyes closed, ignorant, not knowing what they were doing or why. It's what I keep trying to teach my students. Regular people are not dumb, nowhere, never.

Our Guerrillas, Our Sidewalks

This is something that the voice on the phone does not know, cannot know. He probably thinks that city people are dumb, don't understand what the real world is like. He still thinks that most Colombians are against the elites, and he must feel that city people are being lied to, that they have their eyes closed, and that it's simply a matter of telling them the truth, of letting them know how thoroughly they are being exploited by the elites. He hasn't seen the city. He's too far away. Yes. He's been out there too long.

Capitalism has engulfed us all, and it's just so much stronger than the guerrilla who is talking to me can possibly imagine. It gives too many people the chance to dream, to act on those dreams, and to become a part of a society that is also amazingly unequal and violent, where one person has to distrust another.

And that's not all. If the people walking the sidewalks ensure the growing inequities, aren't they also the ones who make it possible for the guerrillas to keep operating? They are separating themselves, moving away from the countryside, trying to forget it, believing even that it's full of a bunch of ignorant peasants who don't know anything other than killing. City people aren't telling the government or the political parties to do something for rural people. With poor and helpless *campesinos*, with more and more land-less peasants around, the guerrillas will be there, too, fighting for them, seeking to defend them, and in the process making a life for themselves. And kidnapping people.

City people support the government, whether actively or passively. They know where they are going. The sidewalks keep the guerrillas from coming to power. And the sidewalks keep the guerrillas alive.

It's not that I expect all those people to do something. What can they do? They can't stop walking.

It's all beginning to make sense. All this time, during these many days since he's been gone, people who had places to go to kept telling me not to worry. We would get Jake back. This is normal, they said, and went back to their lives. It happens to everybody, they said. I remember saying it, too. It's Colombia. We live with it. Life goes on. Now I can really understand why so many Colombians kept telling me to ask them about other things. Work. A direction. It's the belief in work, in the idea that people can make some-thing for themselves in society, that allows them to focus on their own pri-vate lives. They can live without thinking about what happens to others.

The thoughts flood over me. But we've got things to do. I'm not going to listen to Jake's voice anymore. I can't concentrate on anything he says. No emotions. There's a task ahead of us. We have to do this quickly. We're rac-ing against time. We've got to get him back. Now!

Tico

NEWS

It's a case that deserves one of the first places in the books of world records, and it ought to make an appearance in the annals of peculiar forms of crime. Yesterday it was revealed how a sports and recreational club managed to rob 316,000 cubic meters of water in ten years from the city of Bogotá.

Miguel Ricaurte Lombana, manager of the city's aqueduct, and a team of researchers dedicated themselves to figuring out how it is that 42 percent of the city's water disappears without a trace, while thousands of people in the marginal sectors of the city, and in outlying municipalities, have no water. The successful results can be traced to the fact that the team of investigators wanted to find out how, in one case, the Royal Racquet Center, an exclusive club that offers five racquet games (tennis, squash, racquetball, paddle, and badminton), has a number of sports fields, a gymnasium, turkish baths, a swimming pool, a sauna, a dining room, and huge water heaters, and its members shower as many times a day as they wish, could sustain all those services without its own well.

—El Espectador

The tragedy is that there is capitalism but without its corresponding ethic of individual responsibility. It's thus a savage capitalism . . . free enterprise without the equality of citizens.

—Salomón Kalmanóvitz, economist and
historian

We might do well to remember that Alejandro López stated sixty years ago, when the nation's "take-off" toward industrialization and modernization was in full swing, that our biggest problem resided in the lack of a "secular ethic," an ethic of citizenship. With the acceleration of industrial development and modernization toward a mass society, this deficiency makes itself ever more perceptible as traditional customs and vices . . . conspire against an effective social solidarity. The *pueblo* is not respected, the common folk are not respected; even though our legal institutions of public rights affirm that sovereignty resides in the nation and that the people are the "principal decision-makers."

—Rubén Jaramillo, philosopher

"Violence and corruption are typical of developing capitalism," the author Mario Arango told me. "*Narcotráfico* is no more immoral than the slavery that contributed to North America's growth."

—Alan Weisman

Yet throughout my visit to Colombia, a number of prominent Colombian economists, lawyers, politicians, and journalists tried to convince me that the gangsterism in their country was an intractable fact of life. . . . It was an argument that was endorsed by no less a figure than Jaime Child, Colombia's eminent Marxist economist, who told me, "In great capitalistic enterprises there always is a certain amount of illegality and violence, and that is the situation with the *narcotraficantes.*"

—Howard Kohn

We've lived a century and a half of independent, republican life within formal institutions that were never filled with the actual content of rights and duties. . . . Moreover, they weren't able to generate a tradition of behavior that might correspond to the liberal ideology of the Constitution. The substance of the "res publica," the certainty of a common good, deteriorated. Today we live the exaltation of egoism, an abandonment in which our citizens take justice into their own hands in order to defend the last bastion of their identity: their own personal financial well-being.

—Carlos Gutiérrez, philosopher

Fiction becomes real when people distrust each other so much that they prefer not to think, or not to say what it is that they're thinking. Then it just becomes a habit to repeat what others say, especially what those who offer some kind of tranquility are say-ing. And fear makes people seek help among those who have influence, money, or arms, and they repeat what those people would have them say. If someone repeats what the military is say-ing, he has the protection of the military, even if he is stating a bunch of absurdities. If someone repeats what the National Guer-rilla Coordinator is proclaiming, even though it's nonsense, he has the protection of the guerrillas. In the end, the search for truth matters little. What counts are the slogans of those who can liberate us from fear.

—Francisco de Roux, SJ, director of CINEP,
a Jesuit research organization

Our individual liberties are drowning in a sea of impunity. From it great evils have developed, such as the degeneration of the public good and the egotistical tendency to evade the law. According to William Jaramillo López, the former mayor of Medellín, the insti-tutional crisis is born of the individualistic tendency to search for "fractions of power" in a selfish manner, and without regard for the law. This can only lead to a state of anarchy.

—*El Espectador*

It seems that we criticize one another just to get the feeling that we are destroying something with our own hands, rather than to present an idea, to think things out, to determine what is good. It is a most peculiar form of critical expression: to attack, and hopefully in as cutting a way as possible, whether it be in the plastic arts or in literature. This is a temptation that all of us Colombians have, and that we don't always wish to overcome, because we are, perhaps, a "culture" that feels permanently harassed, threatened (by Colombians, of course).

—Santiago Mutis, intellectual and poet

ULLA

Did he give up on us? What did he think? That we weren't trying? It was out of our hands. He was doing something and not giving us enough time to help him. He had given up on us. I knew underneath that he would always think that we had tried our best. But we weren't communicating. We weren't working together. He wouldn't know.

Tony told me he was doing this on purpose, to get out, to get the guerrillas to let him go. But would he go to the extreme of starving himself? If that was what he was doing, he had to go all the way. He couldn't just stop. It was either all or nothing. I knew he couldn't last forever. A day or two was a long time. Could he die just a few days before getting him back? He wouldn't have known that we were able to do something for him, too.

But Tony was just saying that to make me feel better. He was always trying to make it easier on me. I wanted to agree with him. But I knew. I knew he was doing it on purpose, to die, to get out of that situation. He was depressed. I know what it's like for him not to have his liberty. Not do what he wants to do. To be cooped up is a terrible thing for anyone, but he has always been a free soul. And he is so family oriented. I know that was killing him. He always told me, I'm not afraid of dying. I've led a good, full life.

We didn't know when he stopped eating. We didn't know how many days he had left. We had to get him out fast.

TICO

FRIDAY, NOVEMBER 4

The guerrillas needn't have worried about how we would react to the picture and the tape. I knew nothing was going to happen to him. I know they wouldn't starve him. A dead hostage is worse than no hostage at all. They need him alive and well.

I'm feeling better.

This is it, our last round of negotiations. It's no longer a matter of producing arguments, playing roles, being hard or soft, making a mental script of what I'm going to say, or choosing the precise words, the appropriate tone of voice, asking Nelson for advice, guessing what the man on the other side of the telephone wire is going to say, or guessing at the hidden meanings of the things he doesn't say. All we have to do is fine-tune the final sum and the final logistics.

Once again I am the first one out of customs after a Friday flight, but this time there isn't anybody even close behind me. I run all the way. The customs official waves me through. Vicente and Jimmy are waiting, the car ready to go.

Vicente thrusts a square piece of yellow paper into my hand. "The picture," he says. "Look at it."

I don't want to. What's to be gained? I don't allow myself a good look, or to think much, and I say something about it not being a very good picture.

"You can't see anything too clearly," I mutter. But it's scary. The date is sure clear enough. I thrust all feelings aside. He's coming back. It's just a matter of details, of hours.

They take me straight to the hotel. My mother knows that I will be coming in late, and Vicente hands me a key to the house.

"What hotel?" I ask.

When Jimmy tells me, I smile. Once I let the man on the phone know that I didn't particularly like being put in downtown hotels. It was too hard to get in and out, with the traffic and all. This time they've picked the one that's farthest out, way to the north. They're being more than accommodating.

But I also know that there will be less to see on the street below. And I do prefer, for myself, to be downtown. I hate all those new elegant hotels to the north, with rich people all over the place and tourists.

He must have smiled to himself when I told him so many days ago that I wanted to be in the north. Sure, he thought to himself, that's the part of town where these people belong, where they feel comfortable.

I walk into the room, and César and I shake hands. He looks tired and pale. He is shaking his head back and forth slowly.

They haven't called yet. We wait, silently. There is nothing to say. We are to expect a call either tonight or tomorrow morning.

César, Nelson, and I wait for the phone to ring. It doesn't.

I decide to stay in the hotel overnight. Maybe they'll call at 6:00 in the morning. He told us he wanted to be able to get a hold of us at any time. Every minute counts.

The room is small, and it has a low ceiling. There isn't a lot of air in there. It gets stuffy quickly. The double bed pretty much takes up what space there is, leaving little room to walk around, to pace back and forth. It's the most expensive hotel in the city, but a sickeningly pungent odor of a cheap bathroom detergent fills the room.

I've got stomach cramps. The odor doesn't help.

Our Guerrillas, Our Sidewalks

JAKE

Days of smoking. Reading from the book on Italian cities. I would read about two towns in the morning and one in the afternoon. Solitaire. The days passed. I would think, well, is it going to happen? I tried to observe everybody, to see if there were any changes in the routine that might indicate that we were getting ready to leave. Eight days would have been Tuesday, November 8. I wasn't sure if we would leave on that day or if I would actually be given over on November 8.

In the meantime I would also listen to the radio. Voice of America and the BBC. Bush was beginning to draw ahead of Dukakis. I didn't make any comments. I mean, we talked about the election a little bit. They wanted Dukakis to win. One reason is because Bush supported the contras in Nicaragua.

I was getting weaker. As I was bathing I could see the two guards observing me, seeing how skinny I was, wondering how much more weight I could lose. The days passed. Friday, Saturday, Sunday, Monday. I started thinking to myself, well, it looks like it might have been a trick again. Not yet. I said, don't think that way until about Tuesday. In fact keep up until even further. He said eight days, but it can be longer. In fact, Ricardo told me it could be ten, fifteen days. I kept on, played my cards, read the book, smoked, kept going.

TICO

SATURDAY, NOVEMBER 5

The window is large, one huge pane offering an unimpeded view. I'm up at 5:00, standing here in front of it, waiting for the dawn. I know Jake is up by now, too. But I just look out the window. I want to see the city.

The sun reaches Bogotá quickly, pretty much at the same time each morning, somewhere between 5:45 in the summer and 6:05 during the rainy months. Unkempt, dressed in yesterday's sweaty T-shirt and crumpled pants, I stand at the window for an hour or longer before breakfast arrives, making out the shapes of the city and its surrounding mountains, rejoicing in the knowledge that in a few moments I will see what I know is there. The whole city comes quickly into view. I watch, waiting to see when I can begin to make out the Hilton, a thin, elongated structure just to the north of downtown, some fifteen miles away. We've been in there, too. That's where

Jake

we found out they wanted five million. I watch as the outlines of the mountains emerge. The fog is lifting.

It's but a matter of time, and the view will improve. And the day will come to an end. Each day that passes will bring us closer to getting him back. Each day has to be gotten through. How many more do we have? Two? Three? A week? I can't even begin to guess. There are no rules now.

I look for the strength of the winds, the clarity of the air, the size, form, height, and color of the clouds.

At 10:00 Nelson arrives. He watches television. He'll look at anything, all the while working on his papers. The tube is always on. For me it's background noise.

César comes in and promptly falls asleep on the bed. I don't know how he manages it. He will almost certainly be the one to get on the plane, to carry the suitcase full of money out into the hills. I try to read but can't even get through the newspapers that are strewn all over the room. There's no news that counts. I have the window.

The phone wakes César. Nelson turns off the television. I look down at it from my place at the window and let it ring three times, time to breathe deeply. It is 11:20 in the morning.

ME: Hello.

THEM: Yes?

ME: Yes.

THEM: How are you?

ME: Very well. And how are you?

THEM: Well, *más o menos.* So, so.

ME: Good.

THEM: Tell me something. . . . Did you receive? . . . Did you get something?

ME: Yes. I received the package. Everything is fine.

There's a longish pause. He doesn't say anything.

THEM: Yes?

ME: Yes.

Another pause. He's nervous. He's expecting some kind of an angry explosion from me. He probably figures that he's in for a severe scolding.

Our Guerrillas, Our Sidewalks

THEM: Well, yes. We are very sorry for this last thing that's happened.

ME: Yes, it worries me a great deal, too.

THEM: But they tell me he's okay, you know, as a result of the news.

ME: Good.

THEM: But we need to do this quickly, to hand him over.

ME: Yes, I thank you very much.

The call lasts seven and a half minutes. The voice keeps talking about Jake's health, that he is getting better, that I know him perfectly well, that he is in a good mood now.

I'm not listening. We still have to work out the final sum and talk about how the transaction might best be accomplished. I work at getting him to commit to returning Jake to us in as short a time frame as possible after they've gotten the money. Six hours? He seems to agree to twenty-four. That's good. But twenty-four hours? What in hell will we do with ourselves during those twenty-four hours, having lost total control over everything? Where will they leave him? How will he get in touch with us? I insist on the precariousness of the situation.

ME: Can you leave him close to a clinic?

ME: Can you hand him over to a priest?

ME: How about leaving him in a town?

ME: I mean, you can't just leave him on the road somewhere. He'll never make it.

THEM: Don't worry. Don't worry. He's feeling better. He's getting stronger. Don't worry. We will do what we can. But we have to be careful, you know. Safety. Safety.

ME: When can we do this? We're ready.

THEM: How long will it take you to get going?

ME: Four hours. Four hours. *Estamos listos.* We're ready.

We are giving ourselves an extra hour. Everything is prepared. Every last detail has been seen to by Vicente and César and Jimmy and Nelson.

ME: When? Tomorrow?

THEM: No. Not tomorrow. Well, maybe. We'll see.

Tico

ME: When?

THEM: I'll call you.

ME: This afternoon? Tomorrow?

THEM: Maybe tomorrow.

ME: At what time?

   I watch for the rain, predicting where it will come down first and guessing when it will start pelting at my window. By the strength of the rain I estimate the level that the water will reach in the little creek that runs alongside the street in front of the hotel. It rains in the early afternoons in Bogotá. This year has brought as much water from the sky as Colombians can remember, and we've begun to wonder whether God is punishing us. I worry about the weather. We will be using a small twin-engine plane. We can't afford any storms.

   We're going to stay here until a little after 3:00, just in case something comes up, some change in plans. It's dark by 6:00, so nothing can be accomplished after 3:00. We aren't about to do this in darkness, especially not with a small twin-engine plane.

SUNDAY, NOVEMBER 6

   He calls at exactly the same time, just as he told me he would: 11:20. The call turns out to be only ten seconds shorter.

   He seems relaxed. He is calling only because he agreed to. There's nothing going on. It quickly becomes obvious that he has nothing to say. I insisted he call, and he has complied. It's been a pattern. Every time I asked him to call earlier than he had told me he would, we gained nothing.

   He quietly put us off. There is some kind of a problem. They will solve it, he says. Not to worry. I hear children playing in the background. Guerrillas have children, too. Is he calling from his home? Where does this man live?

   THEM: Make sure the plane has plenty of gasoline. We're going to
      need it for another trip.

   THEM: You have everything prepared, right?

   ME: Yes. We're confident that we will be able to accomplish
      everything.

   THEM: Okay. We trust you, you hear?

ME: Yes. Of course. We also . . .

THEM: Okay. Then.

ME: . . . trust you.

THEM: *Listos.*

ME: I'll await your call.

We wait until 3:00, knowing it's no use. But we can't leave. We just sit there.

MONDAY, NOVEMBER 7

The morning is bright and clear, a great day for a plane ride. We wait. Today is the day.

I eat my usual breakfast at 6:30. Then we munch away at heaps of junk food: peanuts, potato chips, pork rinds, warm Cokes, and mineral water. The room doesn't even have a small refrigerator. Room service seems like a grotesque kind of luxury, and we don't want anyone coming into the room in any case. We've moved the table around so as to have better access to the phone. Wires are all over the place.

I wonder what the hotel people think is going on in our room, even without them knowing that we're waiting for a phone call. I guess that if anybody even thinks about us, they will conclude that we're trafficking in cocaine. But then maybe the hotel is used to our type of dealings. Maybe the operators even listen in, comparing one case to the next.

No call. Monday comes and goes. We have no explanation for it. We leave the room at 5:00, staying on just in case.

I go to the airport with Gisela, my cousin, to pick Ulla up. I wanted her to come tomorrow so she wouldn't have to wait in Bogotá with nothing to do. But she insisted, fully convinced that today was our day.

"Hi, Sis. How was your flight? No. No call today."

JAKE

Monday afternoon about four or five o'clock, I'd already refused my meal. They had noticed that somebody was coming in. It was the two guides that had come with the *comandante*. One of them, the smaller one, came over to me, and said, "*Tío, ya,* we're going. We'll have something to eat, and we're going." I said "Fine." Ricardo gave orders to get all my stuff together. They were preparing something to eat. Sonia came to me, and she said, *"Tío, va a comer algo?"* And I said, "Yeah, give me a little bit of rice, and boil me an egg, and give me some coffee with *panela.*" I had to. I had nothing in me.

In the meantime Ricardo had sent one of the men across the river to get a horse. Everything was made ready. They bundled up my stuff. I tell everybody good-bye, you know, wish them good luck and they wish me luck, and shook hands, and I told them all thank you for the treatment they had given me. I said good-bye to Ricardo. We embraced. There were three or four of them around. The rest were on guard duty. I told them all, I said, "I hope one day you all will find a peace here, that all of you will be able to get on with your lives and get out of these woods, go on with your education, or do what you all want to do." Ricardo was happy. He had a smile on his face. Was he happy because the deal had finally been made, or was he happy for me because I was going to get out? These people are not completely without feeling.

We started going up the hill. One of them held my arm. Ricardo, Juan, and Tiberio were going to come with us. Apparently the plan was to cross the river and walk to the site they wanted me to get to. They were talking about walking all night long. They wanted me there by about twelve o'clock the next day.

We waited up on top for about a half an hour for the horse. Ricardo was getting nervous, and so were the other two guides. They wanted to be on the way. Ricardo told me, he said, "Can you walk? We are going in the direction the horse is coming." He walked close by me so in case I fell, he'd catch me. We went about five kilometers. Maybe four. It's hard to say. Some of it was rough terrain, up and down. Finally, going through a small trail, they heard the horse coming, and it was Tiberio. He told them, "There is no way we can cross that river." He said, "I just barely got across, but it is rising more, and the water is way high. It would be very hard to swim across, and anything could happen if the *tío* got knocked off the horse, as weak as he is. We can't do it." There was a lot of agitation, and of course, I was agitated, too. We were going to turn back.

I was on a down. I said to myself, oh, shit, I got fucked again. Was the river up? By all the evidence, it looked like they had swum through high water. Or were they just tricking me again? Ricardo said, "We will have to leave tomorrow after the river is down. By noon it should be down. We'll leave." And so the other two men left, and Ricardo, myself, Juan, Tiberio, we went on back. Everyone down below in the camp was very surprised to see me. There was one man already sleeping in my mattress. So he got up, and they put down the sheets again, and we set everything down. And I said to Ricardo, "Maybe we should have tried." He said, "No. There is no way I could risk anything happening to you, not at this stage. We have been waiting so long. Let's wait for the river to go down."

I went back to bed. If I would have been a man that cried, I guess I would have cried. I laid in the bed, and I prayed, and I said, Lord, your will be done. And I went to sleep.

RETURNING

TICO

I took a long, hot shower. As I was getting out just before 6:00 to go and stand before the window, I thought I could hear the phone ringing. Dripping wet, I ran out of the bathroom and leaped over the bed, leaving the towel somewhere behind me.

The tape recorder was not on. This is pretty much the way I remember the conversation, and the rest of that long day. I did no writing, not until days later. I couldn't.

THEM: Good morning. I have had trouble reaching you.

It was him. I thought it was him. But my heart was pounding so fast that I couldn't really hear well.

THEM: I told you to be there at all times.

ME: I've been in the shower.

THEM: Yes, but I also called last night. We could have done this yesterday.

He was lying. We could have done nothing after 5:00. Unless their plans had changed. Had their plans changed? Had they always known they would do things differently?

THEM: *Listos*? Ready?

ME: Uh. Uh. Uh. Yes.

THEM: What is the matter?

ME: Uh. Nothing. We're ready. But César is not here.

THEM: It doesn't matter. The instructions are simple. I will tell you; you tell César.

He quickly told us what to do, down to the kind of clothes that César should wear. I was getting only the first part of the plans. César was to fly to Sabana. I didn't know what would happen next. All I knew was that our plane should be there waiting for additional instructions, presumably for another flight. They were making sure we couldn't bring the police in.

THEM: Remember, this is the most complicated part of everything.

ME: Yes.

THEM: You have to do everything just as we have told you.

ME: Yes.

THEM: Good.

ME: How long will this take?

THEM: From our end, four hours.

That was the first piece of hard information I had ever gotten from him. I calculated. Four hours and four hours, our side and theirs. I had instructions that took us up to 10:00 in the morning. César would be back to us by 2:00 or a little later. Maybe we could get a phone call from him by 2:00. We were looking at eight hours. Once César was back, the long wait for Jake would begin.

THEM: This will probably be our last conversation.

ME: Yes, I understand.

I felt cold. An uncertainty I hadn't felt before came over me. I had gotten to know him over the weeks. My days had been spent in anticipation of his voice. We could always count on him to call. And this was it. Without hearing from him again, I no longer had any influence on what could happen. It was out of my hands.

ME: Okay. I will stay here at this number, just in case.

THEM: Fine.

ME: I will stay here until I hear from César, or from you, in case something happens, and you need to get in touch with me.

THEM: If that is what you want.

ME: Good.

THEM: *Adiós.* Good-bye.

ME: Good luck.

He was gone.

I called César. An hour later four of us were in the room making sure all the details were in place. Nelson was the first to arrive. Vicente picked César up. They left for the airport together. Vicente would return to the office so nobody would think that anything was going on. And that way the guerrillas would have two places to call if they needed to. Nelson and I stayed in the room.

The phone rang at exactly 10:00. I expected it to be Vicente telling us that the first part of the mission had been accomplished. But it was him.

THEM: What is the matter? What are you guys doing? He hasn't arrived.

ME: That is not true. The plane left Bogotá at precisely the right time. He should be arriving exactly now. If something has happened, I would know about it.

THEM: He has not arrived.

ME: When were you informed of this?

THEM: At 9:50.

ME: Check with your people again. He is there. He is scheduled to arrive at 10:00.

THEM: The plane? Is it the right one?

ME: Yes. Exactly the one you asked for.

THEM: Does it seat four passengers?

ME: Huh?

THEM: The plane. Does it seat four passengers?

ME: Ah. Ah. I don't know. Three or four.

At 10:20 Vicente called. César had indeed arrived on time and had received further instructions, but the second plane that was to take him on was not there. It had not arrived as scheduled. And Vicente couldn't reach the pilot. He was either on his way or hiding from us.

The pilot chickened out at the last moment. He sent someone else to fly the plane. But he was the best in the business and knew the area like nobody else. He knew Jake and could be trusted. We had had a long meeting with him in Bogotá, ironing out all the details. I wanted to explode. "If I ever see the bastard, I'll wring his neck."

The plane arrived, but it was a half hour late. We were at least thirty-five minutes behind schedule. Would the guerrillas think we were up to some funny business? Would this ruin everything? I expected another call from him. We geared up to wait until 2:30, or 3:00 at the most. The plane had landed somewhere else and taken off again. We knew as much. The pilot was in communication with his boss. We demanded they stop talking. We didn't want the guerrillas to think we were trying to figure out where they were and what they were up to. That was the end of our communication with them.

I was totally at a loss. We were no longer in touch. There was nothing to do. Again. But this was worse. I sat down to write. I couldn't. There was no way of concentrating. I could hardly remember what had happened since the phone had rung. I kept walking, pacing. The room was so small. Looking out the window.

CÉSAR

We flew to this small airport about twenty minutes away. The directions they gave us on the phone in Sabana were fine. We had no problem finding it. It wasn't an airport exactly, but a pretty good runway with a hut next to it. This was their place, and you could tell that they used it a lot. There were a whole bunch of them there, and some weren't armed. They just looked at me, and most of them said, hello, but nothing more than that.

One of them came up to me and asks me if I'm César. I think he was the youngest of them all. Just a kid, not more than twenty years old. He told me to follow him, and I thought he was going to take me to their *jefe*, to their leader.

I carried the suitcase. A little ways down into the trees, when we were alone and the others couldn't see us, he told me to stop and to put the suitcase on the ground. He told me to walk away and sit on a stump some thirty feet off in the distance.

The boy was looking down at the suitcase. He took a good long look at it. It was as though he didn't seem to think it was large enough. Then he lifted it as though weighing it.

He put it down and knelt over it as he opened the zipper. I was standing off to the side watching. The kid smelled the bills. He rifled through them like he was the most experienced bank teller in the world. He had done this many times before. He knew exactly what he was doing. He went through batches he'd taken out at random. He was not interested in the pesos, only the dollars. He took out a few bills here and there, touching them carefully, holding them up to the sun.

"No. No. I don't like it."

I didn't say anything. I didn't know what was happening.

"No," he said again, slowly. "I don't like it. *Esto no me gusta.*"

I thought my heart skipped a beat. Was this whole thing going to fall through? He was going to take the money and say we cheated, we didn't bring enough, and we would never see *el señor* Gambini again?

"It's all there. Count it." That's what I told him. I'm pretty sure that's what I said.

"No. Some of these are fakes. *Chuecos* [counterfeit]."

"No problem," I heard myself saying. "Just separate the bad ones out. I'll take them back to Bogotá and replace them for you. No problem."

The kid looked up at me. He put the bills back in the suitcase and closed it. He smiled.

He was just checking. I had done the right thing.

TICO

It started to rain at about noon. At first it was a heavy downpour, and then the waters came down lightly but methodically. The clouds hung heavily over the city. Would César be able to fly back?

People walked briskly through the rain up and down the street in front of me. I counted their steps. It took a little girl three times as many steps as a young man to cover the same distance. Did she get three times as wet? I watched as pedestrians circled away from a huge puddle in the street as they saw that cars were approaching. The sidewalk was being periodically showered with mud and water.

Our room was on the sixth floor. I could see faces, expressions. On the sidewalk just in front of me stood a man and a woman partially hidden at times by a small tree that kept getting in my way. They stood looking at each other, talking, confronting each other, hardly aware that it was raining. But I knew that they could feel the rain, for they periodically cleared their eyes of the water to better see each other. That at least is what I thought at first. Her hand moved toward her eyes more often, until I realized she was crying. They were arguing, fighting about something. I hadn't seen them arrive, so I didn't know if they ran into each other on my sidewalk or had been walking together until they could no longer and had stopped to talk.

They were there for an hour, maybe a little longer. They arrived a little bit before 2:00. At least that was when I first saw them. They moved ever so slowly from right to left, away and toward each other, in the direction of the tree. By the time they went their separate ways, he had backed up perhaps as much as five or six steps. But it wasn't that she was gaining ground. He was the more aggressive of the two. She wanted to touch him. He talked.

She received his words and struggled to answer. He seemed to be accusing her of something. He got really angry, even shoved her a bit a few times, then gently put his arms on her waist, as though half-embracing her. Then he moved away again, getting angry all over again.

I watched transfixed, first on one foot, then on the other, as my legs got tired. But I knew why I watched. I didn't want them to leave. I wanted them to argue right there in front of me. It's not that I wished them any harm, but I had no control over their emotions or their private lives, and if it wasn't right there, they would certainly be arguing somewhere else, somewhere where I couldn't see them.

Two women came by, each with an umbrella. The four figures recognized one another. There were polite greetings all around. The umbrellas were in the way, so I couldn't see much of what was going on. But I could see my couple. Their backs were toward me. Their arms circled each other. They embraced lightly. It was over. The spell had been broken. The anger my couple felt was gone. The ladies would leave, and so would my couple, realizing that it was raining, that they were getting wet, that their conflict wasn't so great after all, that it could wait. They would leave, thrusting me back into the room, back at the clock. It was after the time. It was after 2:30.

But no. As soon as the ladies left, the man and the women took up where they had left off. I watched thankfully. Then the inevitable happened. He gave her a lousy little peck on the cheek, turned on his heels, and walked away. It really was a lousy kiss. She stood there for a few moments watching him walking away, and then she, too, turned around and left. Neither of them looked back, at least not where I could see. I turned around and looked at Nelson. He pretended to be at work on something. Our eyes didn't meet. The next time I looked, three o'clock had come and gone.

The minutes dragged. I was hooked into the time. I could see each minute pass. There was nothing to keep my mind on anything else. I looked down at my notebook and couldn't understand how I had ever been able to write anything. I just wanted to shove off every thought that came to my mind.

Something had gone wrong. I didn't have the strength to keep the thoughts from coming. The money was gone. So was César, and Jake was not coming back. We had lost him. It was too late. There was no good reason for us not to have heard from César. Were they going to use our plane in some kind of an offensive? Or, maybe he was coming back today in the plane with César. Maybe that's why the *guerrillero* had asked about the number of passengers. Maybe they had this whole thing worked out. No, they never did that. It went against all the rules. Why should they take the risk? Was Jake that weak? Was he gone? Was he going to make it?

The phone rang once. I had the receiver in my hand before the first ring ended. It was the hotel. Did we want the room cleaned?

The phone rang again. Ulla. "Tico? Have you heard anything?"

I barked back at her. "No. No. Got to keep the line open. I'll call you as soon as we hear."

I couldn't believe I had screamed at her. She was just sitting there at home with Mother, not knowing anything, farther removed from that phone than I was. What did my mother know? What was she thinking? How was her heart?

It was going to get dark soon. We had to think about the next day. Did the new pilot have a family? How would we notify his wife? What could we tell her? We needed a cover. Nelson went downstairs to call Vicente and started the preparations for another day. We set a limit of 5:15. Vicente was to call the room, and we would call it a day. There was nothing we could do. Nothing.

I looked out the window. It had stopped raining. It was clearing up a bit. The sun even peered through the clouds here and there over the city. I couldn't understand how the sun could be coming out.

CÉSAR

The *guerrillero* told me we were going to fly back, to get back on the plane. I didn't quite believe him. Why would we be flying back to Sabana? It didn't make any sense. I thought it was all over.

We got back in, and he got in the back seats again. He directed the pilot toward some coordinates on a huge map he had spread out in front of him. That was the best map of the area that I'd ever seen. There was a small clearing in the jungle. The boy pointed it out to us.

"There. Down there. That's where we're going."

We began to descend. The pilot circled the area. "No," he said. "I can't land there. We'll never make it. It's too small. It's not a runway at all. We are going back."

I could hear the boy behind us putting the map away. That's when I saw the gun. He put it against the back of the pilot's neck.

"*Aterrice,*" he said, softly, "Land."

I was sitting there next to the pilot, looking down at this tiny spot in the jungle. It didn't get any bigger the closer we got to it.

The pilot was sweating. I tried not to look at him. But the kid was just as calm as could be.

As we got closer to the landing place, I saw a bunch of men all around, and I realized that it was really rough. I mean, this wasn't a landing field at all. And it was rough. I thought the plane was going to tip over because of all the big bumps. The plane was shaking uncontrollably as soon as it hit the ground.

I knew that the strip was short, that we might be in the trees any second. So I closed my eyes. When we came to a stop a few seconds later and I opened them, all I could see were these huge dark green trees right in front of us.

JAKE

I hear a noise at about 3:00 or 4:00 in the morning. Somebody shakes me awake. It's Ricardo, and he says, "Get ready; you are going again." I saw the same two men. They said, "They want you there today. You have got to be there today. We have a boat waiting for us."

They were doing some cooking. They had let me sleep more while they were preparing things. They had all my stuff ready. It was going to be those two men and myself. Ricardo and that whole bunch were going to stay behind. I said good-bye to Ricardo again and told him he had treated me decently. I certainly didn't hate him or wish him dead or nothing. And I wished them good luck, and I meant that. I got on the horse. We rode off to the river, and there was a boat. The river was high, very high. I could see that we would have never been able to cross.

I knew that there was going to be a move. Something was happening, but I wasn't sure what. There were three possibilities, really, and I had to look at all three of them. Number one, I was going to be released. Number two, we were going to a site to meet somebody from the company who would tell me to eat, either Vicente or César or even you. Or three, they were just handing me to another group.

We got on the boat. Two men came out from across the river. I could see that one of the men, a younger fellow, was in charge. We went down the river about a quarter mile. At a house they let me off. One of the guides that had been coming in and out of the camp said they were going to go back to pick up some people and get some coffee. "We will get you some coffee," he said. They came back with a boat full of about six or seven people. Everybody looked me up and down, and we all went down the river together. It was an aluminum-type skiff with a motor on it. Pretty fast. And the guy who was driving it knew the rivers, the sandbars, and the curves real well. They offered me some food and I said, "No, I'm not really hungry." Finally I had a little bit of fruit.

We went on down the river and finally got to a place with a high riverbank where I could see that somebody had been stacking up wood, to load on boats, I guess. We all got off there. They helped me get off the boat and sat me down on a pile of lumber. They said, just wait. I think it must have been about a six- to eight-hour trip. We got there around two o'clock. I tried to see what directions we were going in. But it was a little bit overcast, and I couldn't really see the sun that well. And then I was trying to see which way we were going according to the current. At one point we were going downriver, and at another point, though, we were going upriver.

As I was waiting there, finally I felt a hand on my shoulder and turned around. It was César. I said, "How are you doing?" And he said, "Fine. How are you doing?" And I said, "Fine." And then, I don't know, I guess he said, "We are going to go." Because even when I saw him, I didn't know if it was to get me out or just talk to me. I was getting out. Yes.

CÉSAR

We waited. I didn't know why. They were just lounging around. *El señor* Gambini didn't say anything. There was no expression on his face. I mean, none, nothing at all. He just sat there and looked out in front of him, straight out into the distance.

At first I thought they wanted to make sure we left when it was so dark that we wouldn't be able to call the military and tell them where to find these guys. Then the *guerrillero* told me that they were working on the airstrip, that he wasn't sure that it was level enough for the plane to get enough speed to get up in the air.

I couldn't figure out what their plans were.

TICO

The phone rang at 4:55. We both jumped and stared at each other.

"It's good news," Nelson screamed at me. "It's too early for Vicente's call. They have heard."

"We don't know nothing," I responded.

I knew I couldn't expect good news and get nothing. One more time and I would break. My entire body ached. I slowly picked up the phone. Vicente was breathing so hard that there was hardly any way of making out his words.

I didn't know if that was good or bad. Nelson was listening on the earphones. He was giving me the thumbs up. Vicente seemed to be saying something about a message having come through to the office from the control tower in Bucaramanga. It was from César. They were coming in. They were flying in to Bogotá.

They. Plural. Two people. It wasn't only César. We were to go to the airport to pick them up.

Them. Not him. Two people. And César would never ask to be picked up if only he was arriving. He was too modest to ask for favors. I couldn't see out the window. The tears kept flowing. It was over. The flight was scheduled to arrive at around 6:15.

I don't remember hanging up, but I was on the phone to Ulla. She already knew. Jimmy had called. He was crying.

"Is he really coming in?" Ulla asked me.

"It looks that way, Sis. But we can't be absolutely sure." I was trying to speak as slowly and calmly as I could.

Suddenly I felt completely in control again. The wait was over. Something had happened. But I didn't want Ulla to be too certain that it was over, that Jake was coming back. Could she go on if all this was false news? Could I?

"Could they be sending him in with César?" she asked again.

I thought about the four-seater. But why four? I told her I'd call from the airport the minute there was more news.

"Why are they doing this?" she asked.

Maybe he was dying. I couldn't tell her that. But it had to be on her mind, too.

Nelson and I ran out of the room, leaving it just as it was, and grabbed a taxi as we hit the street. I couldn't tell if it was raining. The driver knew the fastest way to the airport. I didn't have any idea where we were. The city has really grown.

I couldn't believe it. It had happened. He'd done it. He had gotten himself out. He'd changed all the rules. My brother-in-law. We always knew he would do it.

He figured it out. He did the one thing that would force the guerrillas to give him up—take himself away from them. He was depriving them of a body, eliminating the merchandise.

And he got the guerrillas to deliver him to us at the same time that we gave them the money. I don't think it's ever been done before.

This whole operation today had been orchestrated by the guerrillas. All of it from beginning to end. They had planned it all. They had made sure that he made it back alive.

What an operation! He was coming back. Those guerrillas! Boy, luck had been with us.

No. It wasn't luck. The rules had worked. We did everything the way we were supposed to. We had gotten him back. Everything was fine.

NEWS

Last year 29 kidnap victims were assassinated. This year the number has already risen to 64.

—*El Tiempo*

Last night in Medellín the police liberated Helena Olarte de Echavarría, 83, and María Helena Echavarría de Robles, the wife and daughter of the entrepreneur Carlos J. Echavarría. Doña María Helena is the wife of Francisco Robles, the president of Par-Publicidad.

Five of the kidnappers were killed by the police as they attacked a house on the carrera 65D with calle 28, to the south of Medellín.

The ladies recounted that they were kept in a "hut, they treated us all right, gave us to eat, and gave us medicines. We knew we were kidnapped in a place close to the airport because we could hear the noise of the planes. We were locked up in a hermetically closed room, without windows or a bathroom."

—*La Prensa*

Every thirteen hours in Colombia, a person falls into the hands of kidnappers.

—*El Tiempo*

Thirteen *hacendados* were kidnapped last week by a column of the FARC that violently took over two farms in Vichada. . . . The multiple kidnapping of members of two families took place at 11:00 in the morning of September 28th, when almost thirty insurgents arrived at the farms.

—El Tiempo

Only 12 percent of all those kidnapped in 1987 were rescued by the security forces. And this year the situation is even more dramatic: only 6.5 percent have returned to their homes as a result of the actions of the authorities.

General Maza Márquez, the director the DAS [Administrative Department of Security, the Colombian equivalent of the FBI], attributes this impotence of the authorities "to the lack of cooperation from families. Since a kidnapping involves the life of a loved one, all of its civil character and value disappear."

—El Tiempo

JAKE

The man in charge, who apparently had come with César, told me to get back into my red overalls and into my tennis shoes. I separated out the things I was supposed to take, and he went through them again and took out some things. I didn't know how we were going to go. I was assuming that César had gotten there by river also. Then he told me that there was a plane.

At about 3:30 or 4:00 the man in charge told us that they had forgotten to bring my papers and my belongings. He said, "I'm going to send someone to get them. We will have to stay here tonight, and you all can leave in the morning." César said, "No, it's not important. You can send them to me." And I told him, too, "Just send them when you can." Then he asked César, "When is he leaving?" César said, "Tomorrow." They wanted me out of the country. They said that to César and to me, too, I think, halfway. They had my *cédula* [identity card]. And that was the question that came up. How was I going to get out of the country without my residency papers? César told him that we would be able to take care of that, not to worry. So many things were going through my head that I imagine I was oblivious to a lot of things that were said.

Our Guerrillas, Our Sidewalks

The guy was very intelligent, savvy, a young fellow, apparently well educated and in complete control. He said, "You, the people that work for you, the company, nobody will ever bother you again." He told César, "Now if you all get any notes or letters or threats, you let us know because we will never bother you all again."

It was quite a long walk over to the plane. It was a rough strip, almost like a field that had just been plowed. That is all it was, with trees at one end and the sides all cleared away. It was in the middle of the jungle. It looked like they had been working on it no longer than a couple of weeks. And I saw the little plane over there. As we started getting closer, I recognized the pilot. He had taken me to Sabana de Torres quite a few times before. I had quite a bit of confidence in him.

We got there. I shook hands with them, thanked them, and wished them luck. César and I got in the back seat so that we could give weight to the plane and get it lifted up. The pilot got way back to the edge of the strip and gunned his motors.

We started down the strip. It was rough. He was pushing for all it was worth. Kept pushing it. Then we hit a bad part and slowed down and then got going again. We were fast approaching the end of the strip. We could see the pilot was getting worried. He was sweating. Could he get that son of a bitch up? I guess we all kept a tight asshole. He got it off the ground, and we took off.

There was my exhilaration. I knew we were gone. That was it. I'll never forget that moment.

I said, "Okay, I'm free."

I said a little prayer and got old César's hand and just tightened it or tightened it on his leg. And I said, "Well, thank you." And I thanked the pilot. Let's not kid ourselves. I was ready to die, but I was very glad to be alive. I felt a sense of triumph. I was very happy knowing I would see my family again.

Goddamnit, I felt like I could conquer the world. I felt a sense of triumph. I felt very happy knowing that I would spend Thanksgiving and Christmas at home. It's a feeling that very few people ever get in their life. Maybe this is one of the reasons a man like me works hard, to do things, to get the sense of elation when you get it done. We overcame.

Jake

TICO

The cab raced to the airport. I looked out the window. There was nothing left to do but wait for him to arrive. But I was feeling differently. Strange.

We were getting close to the airport, and I was about to see him, but I felt like I wasn't quite there. Insignificant.

All that time, the trips, the arguments about how much to offer them, the telephone conversations. All those tape recordings, trying to figure out what the voice was saying, the nuances. The contingency planning. The newspaper clippings.

For nothing. It hadn't made a bit of difference. It had all been for nothing.

What rules? He had broken them all. There had been no rules here. He'd done it all. I couldn't believe it. He'd gotten himself out.

It was as though I'd been cheated. Not quite. But still.

Did the guerrillas feel like this, too? Not the way I did?

It didn't matter. Of course not. He was coming back. He was free. Ulla and the kids would have him again. But he was the one who did it.

He'd never had any doubts about who he was. He always knew what was right. Everything I'd been working for all these months was about to happen. I was about to see him. But it felt as though we were at a greater distance than when he was out there. It was as though I wasn't really there. I'd been wiped away. All those rules for nothing. He did it.

JAKE

I looked down to figure out where we were. César told me we were going into Bucaramanga. I told César, "Tell the pilot to order me some cigarettes and something to eat, fruit juices, some milk, some sandwiches. I might be a little bit hungry," I said. I told him to order me some Marlboros.

I asked César if my mother was still alive and your mother. Had anybody broke into my house in Houston? Into my apartment? Had any of the guerrilla groups been up in the office and hit Vicente? Then I said to myself, it was all bullshit. It was all bullshit.

Then I asked, "How much?" I wasn't quite sure what he told me. He motioned with his fingers. I didn't want the pilot to hear. Felt great really, physically, mentally. I might have felt a little weak, but not that much. I might have almost been able to go jogging. Put on a few pounds and I'd been ready to go.

The cigarettes they brought me in Bucaramanga at the airport were not Marlboros, but that was all right. I smoked and ate a part of a sandwich and had some fruit juice. It was terrible, just all sugar. But they did bring me a couple of fresh oranges, and I ate those. César and I talked about various things, trying to catch up, you know.

TICO

We got to the airport early, at least twenty minutes too early. I paid the driver a hefty sum for his efforts. He stayed to watch. He knew what was about to happen.

We waited. A plane taxied in our direction before 6:15. The man at the hangar told us it was the plane we were waiting for. It stopped. I didn't know what side the door was on until it opened up and César got out.

"*Cómo está? Cómo está?*" "How is he? How is he?" César moved his hand slightly from side to side. So, so.

I could just make him out inside the plane saying something to the pilot. He got out slowly. We didn't help him. He had on his red J. C. Penney coveralls, the same ones he had had the morning he was taken. There was a cigarette in his right hand.

Standing in front of us was a man I had known for almost twenty-five years. He was smaller than I remembered him. He looked old, cavernous. I embraced him, softly. My arms went all the way around him. I looked into his huge eyes. They were bigger, a lot bigger. They were clear, full of life.

"Thank you. Thank you. Thank you." he said.

Then I asked him, "Have you eaten?"

I detected a slight smile on his lips. His left cheek seemed to move a bit. But I couldn't be sure. The beard was huge. He looked at me. There was a diabolical glimmer in his eyes. I ran off to the phone.

"Ulla, he's back."

JAKE

Got into Bogotá and landed at that little hangar we always used. You were there, and you introduced me to Nelson, who was off to the side. Talked to you, said, thank you.

You all told me that Ursula was in town.

At first I was a little disturbed, but then I was glad. All my children were fine. Everybody was fine. What a day. Jesus, what an adventure. What a way to end thirty years of working in Colombia.

TICO

He was down to 115 pounds. It was almost as though he took pleasure at how much weight he had lost. He wanted us all to know how little he weighed. He'd probably been up to about 180 when they took him. I think it's the coffee that saved him. He hadn't eaten anything in I don't know how many days, about a month, maybe more, but he had taken sips of coffee all the time. He didn't dehydrate. But coffee? I can't imagine.

He had to see a doctor. Vicente had some phone numbers written down on a white piece of paper. Instead, I asked him. It was a mistake.

"Do you want a doctor to come?"

"No. I'm fine."

I asked again.

"No. Shit, I feel great. Never felt better. We can wait until Houston."

For the past months I had been making decisions. Not all of them, but some. Now I was asking and letting someone else decide. Ulla insisted, too.

But everything seemed so different from the way it had been just hours before. He was back. He was making the decisions, just as it used to be. He could indeed see a doctor tomorrow or the day after if he didn't want to now.

And Nelson wasn't with us to keep us focused, to maintain the discipline that had been our daily lives during all these months. He'd really done a great job for us. The man never wavered, and now that I think of it, it really was comforting to have someone around who had been through these things many times, who had a broader sense of them. Nelson should be with us. He's been part of it.

But we're too relaxed. And we didn't really want a doctor to come. There had been so many intermediaries, so many unknown people between him and us. We needed to close off the outside world, round out the circle.

That's what he wanted, too. Everyone was to gather around. He wanted to thank us. To talk. To tell us what had happened. He wanted a party.

Jake called friends and family, his children, his sister, his brothers, who were all far away in the States. They were to call his mother, to tell her he was well. And he had made all kinds of plans while he was out there, for himself, his family, and for everyone else. He wanted to tell us all about them. There was work to be done. Time had been lost.

We asked my cousin Gisela to bring some fried chicken. There was wine. I had a Scotch or two. He ate and drank red wine. We took pictures. One with him and each one of us. And group photos, too. Polaroids. Bad pictures. Nobody had given any thought to recording the event.

Slowly we began to leave, not wanting to let this moment pass, yet knowing that Jake and Ulla had to get to sleep. The others went off to party some more. I went home. We had to be up by 5:00 to get everything ready for the trip. I had to get some sleep.

JAKE

I took that disastrous shit. I felt like I had to go. I sat on the toilet, and I felt that it wasn't coming. It was hurting. I put my fingers down there and pulled that goddamned piece of shit out with my goddamned fingers. I tore my asshole.

So stupid. I mean, when I felt like it wouldn't come, I should have told Ursula, and we could have gotten an enema or some oil to put up in there, or hot water. Then I would have come out through the whole thing never having felt any kind of a pain.

I had a halfway idea that it was the glass or the tin coming through. But it was just a plug there. I hadn't had a bowel movement in three weeks. Whatever possessed me to go down there with my fingers, to actually force it out? Ursula suffered with me. She knew how much I was hurting. And when she saw me stripped down, she cried. I was skinny.

It was pretty stupid of me not to see a doctor. But I felt good. Jesus Christ, I felt great. You come through an ordeal like that, you have all your people around you. I mean, who needed a doctor? I hadn't been sick.

There wasn't anything in the apartment for me to take. I never have taken any kind of painkillers. I tried some suppositories and tried to go to sleep. I couldn't. There was just no way I could go to sleep. I was just so hyped up. Ursula finally dozed off.

I got up. I started going through all my files, picking the ones I wanted to take with me, and going through the kitchen, setting aside a bunch of things I wanted to have sent to the States. I had to get back to work, to do something.

Here I am. I've been sleeping and resting for four and a half months.

TICO

"Piles." "Piles." Those were the first words out of his mouth as he opened the door of the apartment for me shortly after 6:00. "Tico, would you believe it?" He also said something about pain.

I had never known him to feel any kind of pain. It has something to do with a high threshold. Some people just don't feel pain. When I was a teenager, I remember that Jake could keep his finger over the flame of a candle longer than anybody else. It was a physiological sort of thing.

"What a dumb shit I am," he muttered to himself as he puttered around the apartment packing things. Ulla told me he hadn't slept. She didn't look so great either. He talked all night all about his experiences. Talked and talked and talked. But he was in pain. There were drops of sweat on his forehead.

He wanted to go back to his office, to pick up a few personal things.

"What about those steps?" I asked him.

"Shit, no problem."

I didn't think he would make it up to the fourth floor, up all fifty-one steps. We walked behind him, prepared, I think, to catch him and all the rest of us. I remembered then that he didn't weigh much anymore. We could hold him. I was more out of breath than he was when we made it to the top. I sat down. He went straight to his office, to look for his things. There was no time to waste.

He and Ulla drove to the house to say hello and good-bye to my mother on the doorstep. Then it was straight to the airport.

JAKE

I must have looked bad. I was dressed in a gray sweatsuit. I had that wild beard. I didn't think a beard would grow so fast. I guess fingernails and hair in a situation like that grow much faster. Because I had a tremendously long beard, considering it had only been four and a half months.

Some of the people in first class on that Eastern flight were nervous all the way up to Miami.

I ate a tremendous amount of food on that plane. I just ate everything they put in front of me. I think Jimmy had a few cognacs. We all felt great, except my back end kept hurting me.

I had to go to the bathroom a few times. Liquid was getting out, it was seeping through, so I put some towels there. I sat down on a pillow, and that helped a little bit. I was taking some painkillers that you all had gotten for me at the airport. I could hardly sit in that airplane. Hours. It was a long flight.

We get on to Miami. Somebody said something about a wheelchair. They wouldn't let me do nothing for myself. I wanted to carry a bag or something. Nobody would let me do anything, treated me as if I was fragile and was getting ready to break.

I thought I'd have a little problem when they compared the passport picture to my actual looks. The guy looks at the picture and he just says, "Fine, okay." That was so funny when my own son and Lillian, my own sister, don't recognize me, and this guy with the passport just says, "Fine." Maybe he was so shook up at seeing me. It looked like everybody cleared away from me as I passed by, opened up a path. And this guy, he just said, "Welcome back to the States," like they tell everyone else. And I felt like telling him, "Buddy, you don't know how welcome I feel."

At home I tried to shave my beard. And I couldn't get those new type razors to work, because I wasn't pulling them down. Finally I found an old razor. But my cheeks were so hollow that I couldn't get inside the holes to get all the hair out. But once I had shaven and combed my hair, Ursula said I looked a lot better.

TICO

I guess that Don Guillermo, the taxi driver, had seen him standing on the sidewalk in front of the apartment building. It must have been just after 6:00 in the morning. I hadn't seen the dark, wine-red 1968 cab drive past, and neither had any of the rest of us. But early the next morning, while he was taking me to the airport, Don Guillermo told me that he'd seen him.

"I saw him. I'm almost sure it was him. He looks different. He lost weight. Right?"

"You did?" I asked impatiently, not believing him. "You saw him?"

I was sure we had managed to get him out of the country without hardly anyone seeing him. We had even gotten special permission from the authorities so that he could fly out without his documents.

"I was just passing by," Don Guillermo answered hurriedly. "Pure coincidence. I was looking for my first ride."

I knew that he didn't usually start out that early, and in any case he was miles from his home, and the residential street wouldn't get him his first client of the day. But he had seen him. There was no question about it. Don Guillermo has all his facts straight. How Jake was dressed. Who was with him. The long black beard. The time.

A cold sweat came over me. Lots of people must already know of his release. For months we worked to keep everything quiet, to negotiate in secrecy. It was the only way to survive. For months I worried that someone was following me or that our phones were being tapped. And now suddenly people were finding out before they should.

"How is he?" Don Guillermo asked me.

"Fine," I said. "Fine. Just fine."

He wanted to know everything that had happened. I couldn't tell him. But long silences didn't fit either his mood or mine. Nor could we just talk about something else.

"I wonder how he is," Don Guillermo said slowly.

"He's fine."

"How will he be?"

"Fine. He's a strong man."

"They must have treated him very badly. He looked so thin."

"No. No. They treated him well. They gave him everything he wanted." There was another silence.

"You know that he would have wanted to see you," I said to him. "Right?" He nodded his head slightly, as though in agreement.

"But it was a very complicated situation," I added quickly. "We didn't have a lot of time."

He nodded again. My words weren't enough. He didn't quite believe me.

"You are going to see him?" he asked.

"Yes."

"When?"

"Soon. First I'm going home. Then I will see him."

"Will he come back?"

"I don't know." I knew otherwise.

"You tell him, please, that we are all thinking about him. Yes? And that we wish him the best."

Our Guerrillas, Our Sidewalks

"Yes. Yes. I will tell him."

My nervousness was gone. A sense of relief invaded me. It was a calmness so deep that I could tell I hadn't been breathing well for a long time.

I started to inhale slowly and deeply, many times, until the pit of my stomach hurt. I felt drowsy. There was no reason to worry. All was well. The news hadn't hit the papers the day before, and there was nothing that morning. Not too many people could know. I thought about the words that Nelson had kept saying again and again once we knew it was all over.

"It's history! It's over! It's history!"

Indeed.

Whatever could happen no longer mattered. Nothing more could happen. Normality was returning to our lives. Our brush with the violence was over. It was history. I was getting closer to the airport. Colombia was receding. The edge was gone.

I said good-bye to him and gave him all the money I had in my pockets and walked into the airport. I could sense that my country was no longer in my gut. I didn't give a damn. Yes, people were still getting kidnapped. Right at that moment somebody somewhere was probably being taken away. But I couldn't feel a thing.

It must be that attitude that so many others had, all those who haven't been kidnapped or whose loved ones have returned safely. I was trying to force myself not to think about Colombia.

Campesinos were being killed. Yes, I knew. I felt a twitch in the bottom of my stomach. But I was leaving. I guess it was a slight twitch. There was nothing I could do about it. *Campesinos* were being killed. They were always being killed.

There it was. I could sense it. That feeling that I thought others had, months ago when I first came back to Colombia and saw all those people walking around, all those smiling people, making a life for themselves, walking the sidewalks.

But I wasn't smiling. But I felt so good, so relieved. Maybe I was smiling. No. But I sure didn't take a little step to the side as I walked into the airport to see the reflection of my face in one of those huge windows next to the doors. I thought about looking. And didn't.

There was nothing all those people walking the sidewalks could do. What had I been expecting from them? Why had I been so surprised when I saw them?

They were living. Walking. Going places.

Damnit. Jake was back! To hell with it all. We had paid our dues.

Our brush with the violence was over.

Tico

LIVING

JAKE

I got up early, as usual, about 3:30, 4:00. Made my coffee, went outside, got the *New York Times,* sat outside, smoked a cigarette, drank my coffee.

I looked out, sitting on the wall on the entrance to the driveway. It was a beautiful morning. I gave my thanks to the Lord for letting me be there and that everybody was all right. How lucky I was to be able to sit there, drink this coffee, have a cigarette, and read the paper.

As I opened it up, there it was. All the information about Bush winning the election. I was happy. I felt like nobody else could feel any better than we did. He had just won the election, and I had got my freedom.

You know, ever since I had gotten out, I had always been with somebody. One, two, three, or four people. But at this time in the morning, I was out there. I was just by myself. Really had time to think about it, to know the real meaning of being out. Quite a feeling. Yes, indeed. A man every once in a while needs his privacy.

NEWS

The generalized climate of violence in this country has gone beyond the bounds of individualized drama. The common citizen also feels affected. The violence produces a state of confusion, of uncertainty, anguish, and fear. People protect themselves by avoiding the subject.

—Martha Lucía Uribe, psychologist

Much more than of the mountains, the violences that are killing us are of the street. . . . Colombians are killing each other more as a result of the quality of their lives and their social relations than in an attempt to gain access to the control of the State. . . . The proportion of dead and injured from subversive actions, compared to those of other forms of violence, has not surpassed the 7.51 percent reached in 1985. . . . In particular, crimes against human life and personal integrity showed a net gain between 1980 and 1981 in urban areas, at the same time that they diminished in rural areas. Between 1982 and 1985, these same crimes rose significantly in the cities, while they continued to decline in the countryside.

. . . These violences threaten the anonymous citizen, the millions of Colombians, more than do the guerrillas or the *narcotraficantes*. If the State were more concerned with maintaining high degrees of legitimacy, and to constantly seek the adherence of the citizenry, these forms of violence would be the focal point of official policies. For these are the forms of violence that question the very efficacy of the State and the validity of the institutions of the country.

—Report of the Commission for the
Study of the Violence

It's not a question of war. In 1995 the most frequently asked question in Colombia will have to do with the manner in which this or that relative, a father, a mother, a grandfather, died. And the most frequent answer will leave behind it a trail of stupor. He died assassinated because his automobile cut in front of another one. He died because he looked at someone the wrong way on the bus. He died because the next door neighbor didn't like his dog. We live, like in Faulkner's novels, in the era of rage. Our style, at least in the city, is aggressive. Our arrogance expresses itself in our scowls. And our aggressivity in the way in which we press the trigger.

—*La Prensa*

Colombian *campesinos* know they will be the ones to die. Some of them are killed because they don't cooperate, others because they do. They're killed for speaking up, or for keeping quiet. They're killed on a commercial bus while traveling from one town to another, or at the town's party. That's the way it happens, just as it did during *la Violencia:* of those famous three hundred thousand dead that are always being talked about, how many were soldiers, or policemen, or guerrillas, those Liberal guerrillas? This is the way it has always happened in all our civil wars, beginning with independence, and all the way through the 19th century.

—Antonio Caballero, columnist

The desolation of the victims of *la Violencia* knows no limits. In this country people feel that they do not have an institution that they can resort to. There is a generalized atmosphere of abandonment.

—Guillermo Sánchez Medina, psychiatrist

That day it hit me that I had witnessed a murder being planned and had done nothing about it. A week earlier I would not have thought this possible; now the idea of doing something had not even occurred to me. What could I do? Asking for details struck me as imprudent, and the police would pay little attention to a story about a murder not yet committed. More than that, the *sicarios'* [hired killers] story hadn't seemed to me like murder. I had severed the connection between the four men in my hotel restaurant and the imminent death. . . . After only ten days in Medellín I was thinking about violence in the passive voice, as something that just happens to people.

—Tina Rosenberg, journalist

CÉSAR

I walked out of the office, down the stairs and into the street. I had taken only a few steps before a man came up to me and said hello.

I didn't recognize him. I had never seen him before. He seemed to know me because I heard him call me by name, first and last. Respectfully. I mumbled something and tried to step out of the way.

Then the man said something. "How is *el señor* Gambini?"

I was noncommittal.

"No," the man said, "we just wanted to know how *el señor* Gambini was in Houston."

Suddenly I knew. "Fine. He's well. *Está bien.*"

"Aha. Good. We're glad to hear that. And how's his health? Has he recovered?"

"Yes. Yes."

"Good. We just wanted to make sure."

The man turned around quickly and was gone.

TICO

SATURDAY, JUNE 17, 1989

I'm sitting in Alderman Library with *El Tiempo*. A long article on the kidnappings glares up at me. The writer seems to have done quite a bit of research. My eyes focus quickly on a familiar name somewhere in the middle of the story. This time Jake's last name is spelled correctly. I have the feeling that the journalist knows what he is talking about, even though the dates are way off, the year is wrong, and so, too, is the name of the company.

> In July 1987, the ELN kidnapped Jacobo Gambini, the president of General American Pipe, a petroleum company. The company refused to pay the *rescate,* and his body was found in a grave in Sabana de Torres.

For a split second I come to doubt what I know. We got him out. I mean, he got himself out. Right? Right. He *is* alive.

Still, I almost believe the story and have to catch myself, even though I know all about the way news gets into the newspapers.

That day back in July flashes in front of me, when I was sitting at the Miami airport and I learned that he had been killed and his body mutilated and burned. Reading the news again makes it seem simply too real. Too possible. The printed name. The information. For a tiny moment before I can gather my thoughts, he is dead. It ended as we had feared all along.

I get up and take a walk through the library, then up to the fourth floor and out. I need to inhale the fresh spring air.

After the relief comes anger. How the hell is anybody going to write the history of Colombia for this period with those kind of newspapers? I thrust my arms into the air, oblivious of all those walking around me.

There is no objective truth to be had. We can't rely on anything. What good is it all?

Then slowly I start to smile. I don't know quite why at first. I begin to understand, and it seems all too fitting. We worked so hard to keep all this secret.

Silence is the way to survive Colombia. His release didn't get into the papers, and only our friends know what happened. There are only rumors about.

The guerrillas know, of course. They were the only ones we were ever really able to count on in Colombia during those months. Nobody else could come to our aid. They even came to César afterward to ask about Jake and see how he was doing. The guerrillas know, and they haven't told anybody either. A few important higher-ups in the police know. They aren't talking either. To them Jake is just another statistic. For all anybody knows Jake is dead.

Yes! I like that. Nobody can harm him that way.

This is it! To be publicly dead and privately alive. This is indeed the way to survive Colombia. To live life in total silence. No harm can come that way.

The news in *El Tiempo* is just great, just what we need and want. Jake is dead. That way he can keep on living.

I am chuckling to myself as I walk briskly over to the cafeteria for a cup of coffee. Then as I sit down I begin to realize just how horrible I am feeling. Was I really laughing to myself just moments before? Now I am even finding it hard to breathe deeply.

I have come to the most terrible conclusion. It is everything that I am opposed to. To live in silence and walk our own path through life, only taking care of our own, that's exactly what I have always been most opposed to.

A public voice is what Gaitán fought for. He wanted everybody to be able to speak and be heard, to have a place and be accounted for. And Camilo, too. That's what Camilo was all about. And the guerrillas. Long ago, that's what they were fighting for.

Looking down into my cup of coffee, I realize that I am thinking about the guerrillas in much the same way as I have long thought about Gaitán and Camilo. They are dead. The guerrillas are also gone. They have lost themselves out there in the mountains during all these lonely years. Their voice has been drowned out in the violence of Colombia, in their violence. The guerrillas are dead, finished.

Something more begins to dawn on me. It feels like a tiny kernel of new knowledge. Is it making me look at Colombia in a completely different way, or does it just seem that way?

My thoughts run ahead of me. Suddenly I know that in Colombia we can live with the guerrillas, that we are at one with them. We understand them so well and so deeply precisely because they are kidnappers, because they take prominent members of society, because they come for us. And there is more. We can't blame them for what they do to us. Their actions are nothing more than a logical step, one that is so obvious and so easy.

Those who have become rich and powerful in Colombia, from coffee growers to cattle ranchers to cocaine barons, know that they have exerted their will on the countryside. They have taken the land of others, and when necessary, when those others fought back or did not move, they deprived them of life as well. And they have done it for so many decades out there, so often, and with such impunity that not even the government has done much to stop them. They have acted freely.

So the guerrillas and the kidnappings aren't a surprise to anyone. They are simply a form of payback. The guerrillas are dispensing a measure of raw justice by taking back some of the resources of those who are rich and powerful. And rarely do they kill those they take away. The guerrillas are now little more than an obvious and even inevitable reaction to all the violence in the countryside.

Retribution. That's what it is. After all, that's how the guerrillas see their actions, how they always refer to the kidnappings. And this is how we can easily understand them, whether we agree with what the guerrillas are doing or not. Savage capitalism and kidnappings are different sides of the same coin.

Retribution. That we can understand. That's why we accept the kidnappings so easily. We can tell one another to relax, for we can't react with moral outrage. On what grounds? We participate. It's not just that we don't have any choice but to negotiate with the guerrillas to get one of our own back. It's business, not politics and not morality.

Jake understands what the guerrillas are all about, no matter how much he disagrees with what they did to him. He even said that at one point, when he remarked on the poverty that rural people live in. He knows what leads people out there to become guerrillas. He has a good sense for why they took him.

And it doesn't much matter that he and many others like him are moral and honest people who have never taken anyone else's land. Were those thousands of people who lost their lands over the years, who lost their lives, not also moral and honest? And what have all the good people of Colombia done over the years to put a stop to the violence?

So we tell each other to accept reality when one of us is taken away. It's the world we have made, and we live in it, for we can survive it.

The old words ring in my ears. My words.

"Hey! Don't worry. This will end well. It always does. The guerrillas are responsible people. They have to maintain their image. You'll get him back. They will take care of him. Don't worry. Nothing is going to happen to him. Negotiate. Go ahead. It's only a business transaction."

The old words seem to have a whole new meaning to them.

Have I not thought about the kidnappings in these terms before? Is this really new knowledge that I have inside of me, or is it simply a deeper kind of understanding of what I have always known? I can't really tell.

Our Guerrillas, Our Sidewalks

Is this how Jake has always understood the kidnappings? Why he never bothered to get kidnapping insurance, figuring the insurance would come out being a larger expense than any ransom that might have to be paid?

No. Not him. Jake's different. If he ever thought about it like this, he certainly doesn't anymore. And he sure didn't act like his kidnapping was simply a business transaction when they had him. No. He's as different as can be. Jake sees it all in moral terms. I remember those words of his on my tape recorder, coming back to me again and again as I transcribed the interview.

"It's wrong," he said.

That is his view of it, plain and simple. Kidnapping is wrong. It is about the worst thing that can be done to a human being, such a terrible human action that it's hardly worth surviving. And Jake can't understand how the Colombian people go along with it, how they can still believe in the guerrillas.

What Jake understands is that nothing good can come from kidnapping. If the guerrillas think that they can kidnap people, that they have the right to treat a human being like that, then there's no telling what they will think they have the right to do once they have more influence, once they win and come to power. Evil can only beget evil.

Is this why I'm thinking of the guerrillas in the past tense? Because Jake has shown me how wrong they are? Is there now no difference between his ideas and mine? Does it make any difference that I see the kidnappings and all the violence of Colombia in terms of history, the past, and the growth of the market, of capitalism? Does it make any difference that I see the sidewalks and he simply walks on them? Am I saying anything more than he is? I can't tell.

Isn't his clear moral vision the really meaningful one?

I can't keep my mind from churning this idea around.

Doesn't he have the absolute truth?

Are all my ideas and all my historical knowledge just ways of messing up that truth? Am I simply trying to make something understandable that shouldn't be understandable? Maybe I am even making it acceptable, making it seem inevitable. Maybe this is why it always seemed so strangely easy for me, and for so many others in Colombia, to tell friends to relax when one of their own was kidnapped.

Am I trying to make the kidnappings seem less horrific than they are, less grotesque, by seeking to explain them?

Jake knew from the start that what was happening to him was wrong. Jake looked his kidnappers in the eye and said, "No, I'm not going to go along with this. It's wrong." His truth allowed him to act according to his principles. He was able to look at himself and decide that he wasn't going to be treated like a piece of meat, like a commodity, like something to be exchanged. His beliefs made it possible for him to look death in the face.

He's different. Jake does not live in silence. He has a public voice.

I don't know where to turn. At the very moment when I feel that I have learned so much more than ever before about Colombia, about the guerrillas and the kidnappings, even about history, my thoughts are crashing down all around me. I am beginning to doubt everything I know, the very ways in which I think, in which I was trained to think as a historian.

Am I just making the truth relative?

I don't have answers to my questions, or at least I don't want to reach any answers right now. I turn my mind quickly back to the past, to history, to all those years of guerrilla struggle. These thoughts seem more comfortable. It appears that I can do more with them.

What *would* have happened had Camilo not been killed out there? What would the history of Colombia look like had the guerrillas remained revolutionaries? Could we have lived with their politics? I don't think Jake could have, even had they not become kidnappers. Their politics violate his sense of freedom. Could I have lived with a revolution?

One thing is certain. Successful revolutionary guerrillas would have been something that the upper class of Colombia could not have lived with. The elite would have fought the guerrillas had they remained revolutionaries, instead of surviving next to them, as the rich have done for all these years. The elite understands that a successful revolution will eliminate them.

Which side would have won?

I sit here in the cafeteria in Charlottesville as in a daze, with my eyes tightly closed and my head in my hands, seeing circles, round forms with figures hovering around them, men talking and laughing, joking around those tiny round tables in the cafés. And that wonderful, rhythmic music from the corner record store is dancing around in my head.

I want to focus my mind, to think about politics. I want to listen to public voices.

But there aren't any left.

POSTSCRIPT

It's been six years since he was taken away. Much stays the same in Colombia. Much changes. It's quieter now.

Like many times before in our history, a public exhaustion sets in. The hemorrhaging takes its toll. During this year's presidential campaign, the Liberal and Conservative candidates do not talk much about either the guerrillas or the cocaine capitalists. Mainstream politicians are quiet. The election brings the lowest voter turnout in history. The people are not paying much attention to what little it is that the politicians might be saying. The people are quiet, trying to survive. As before, Colombians want to be left alone to work and to make something of their individual lives. The election is won by a calm and pragmatic Liberal economist with bullets still lodged in his body as constant reminders of the public violence that is being left behind. Colombia's long-standing democratic institutions survive and continue to exist next to the regional influences of the guerrillas and the economic power of the cocaine capitalists, neither of which seeks the overthrow of those institutions.

There is much loss of life. The homicide rate remains constant, although some claim that it is rising a bit in the cities. Many say that it continues to be the highest in the world. As before, most of those who kill know those they kill. The loud public violence among armed groups turns more quiet. The quiet private violence of daily life goes on. Those who kill are convinced that they will not be prosecuted even if they are caught. The judicial system remains paralyzed. Impunity is widespread.

One of the nation's beloved soccer stars on the national team is shot to death early in the morning as he leaves a restaurant with his fiancée. The gunmen inform him that they are displeased with his performance in a World Cup game against the United States as they pump twelve bullets into his body. Most people hope that the cocaine capitalists who lost many

229

millions betting on the national team are responsible for the shooting. Crime caused by money seems more palatable than crime caused by crazed national fanaticism. But anybody can be responsible. The culture of violence knows no limits.

The economy grows at a rapid clip. Wealth is everywhere. Conspicuous consumption remains the order of the day. Our sidewalks are worse, although some are much improved through individual effort and private financial expense. The streets are packed with people going here and there, and the cafés are filled with men talking. Music is everywhere. The deep foundation for a high rise building that is under construction a block from our home caves in. People and cars on the surrounding highways fall into the gigantic hole. Newspaper pictures taken from surrounding buildings show a bombed-out area, as though the city were at war. The surrounding sidewalks are gone, too.

The cocaine capitalists of Medellín help bring about the emerging calm by orchestrating a horrendous bombing and assassination campaign against civilians, the police, the media, and high government officials. The government fights back, freezing assets, impounding homes, and organizing elite hit squads to get the leaders. The years 1989 and 1990 bring the most deaths.

Four of the six presidential candidates in the 1990 election are shot to death. They are all men of the Left, including Luis Carlos Galán, the standard-bearer of the Liberal Party. One of these reformers, Carlos Pizarro, who is the last commander of the M-19 guerrillas, finds his bullet while he is high up in the air, sitting comfortably on a commercial airliner, as he tours the nation campaigning for the presidency. The killer knows that he, too, is to die before the plane lands.

The bullets come from the Right, from the violent cocaine capitalists, the paramilitary defense squads, their friends in the military and in government, or some combination of some or all of them. Two violent cocaine barons lose their lives. José Gonzalo Rodríguez Gacha is shot in 1989 along with his son. Pablo Escobar is shot in 1993 when he has only one bodyguard left to protect him. The threat from a violent Right is much diminished.

At Luis Carlos Galán's funeral, his young son hands the Liberal Party over to César Gaviria, a soft-spoken and pragmatic politician with nothing like the social vision of the deceased leader. Gaviria continues the pro-market policies of his predecessors while devoting little thought to social expenditures. And he oversees the writing of a new constitution. Although not many citizens seem to know what the renewed law means, or how their lives will be affected, few feel that the new charter is any worse than the previous one, which lasted for more than one hundred years. It might be better.

For the drug barons the document is a huge step forward, for it declares extradition to be illegal. An understanding exists that allows the government and the cocaine capitalists to survive together. The new entrepreneurs can stay in Colombia and work, but they are not to be politicians. Politics is to remain the domain of the traditional politicians. Led by astute investors from Cali, the cocaine capitalists quietly make money exporting commodities throughout the world. They sell heroin now, too. Their profits quietly underwrite the campaigns of the politicians.

The drug barons no longer need to spark the imagination. They still their own voices. With the violence from their Medellín counterparts out of the way, the New Right survives with silent ease. As before, Colombia has surrendered to the forces of the market, to the export of valuable goods.

After many of the M-19 guerrillas lose their lives in battle and it becomes obvious that a military victory will not be coming, the leaders decide to turn in their guns and turn into politicians. Many of the old guerrilla leaders lose their lives on the streets of the cities. After initial electoral gains in 1990, the Left is of little consequence, gaining only a few thousand votes here and there. It is quiet, barely managing to survive.

The guerrillas are still out there in the mountains, even though some have given up. Only those of us who are in some way directly affected by them pay much attention to what they are doing. The encounters between them and the military are few and far between. They avoid each other and survive. Their revolutionary voice has not returned. Our guerrillas rule over diverse regions of the nation.

In one round after another of peace negotiations with the government, the guerrillas assert that they do not engage in kidnappings. In 1991 at least 1,717 people were taken, far more than the 1,000 or so in 1988. "With many families reluctant to notify the police," reports the *New York Times* on August 16, 1992, "the real number could be much higher." A new organization lobbies for kidnap victims. Gabriel García Márquez and the nation's major intellectuals sign a written declaration opposing the kidnappings. The government sets up a new anti-kidnapping police unit. There is a law in the books that says that the government will freeze the assets of families that negotiate ransom settlements. The kidnappings continue. Statistics are hardly kept anymore. Nobody needs them. Nobody wants them.

The guerrillas keep their word, once again. They leave us alone. No one comes again. An eerie calm settles over the company in Sabana. Jake does not return to Colombia. He rises each morning by 4:00, as before. He spends hours on his rose garden. He cooks. He eats and diets. He's healthy. He seems unchanged.

Only his diary has stopped. A detailed journal of each day's events over almost thirty years comes to an end on that morning in June six years ago.

Mine begins.

SOURCES

Page ix: Tirofijo to Arturo Alape in *Las vidas de Pedro Antonio Marín Manuel Marulanda Velez Tirofijo*, Bogotá, 1989, p. 19.

Pages 10–13: Jaime Arenas, to Germán Castro Caycedo, *Del ELN al M-19: Once años de lucha guerrillera*, Bogotá, 1980, p. 31; "Antonio," to Olga Behar, *Las guerras de paz*, Bogotá, 1985, p. 269; Arenas, to Castro Caycedo, p. 21; Jaime Bateman Cayón, to Patricia Lara, *Siembra vientos y recogerás tempestades*, Bogotá, 1987, pp. 107–108; "Pacho," to Behar, p. 281; Alvaro Fayad, to Lara, p. 95; Bateman Cayón, to Ramón Jimeno, *Oiga hermano*, Bogotá, 1984, p. 31.

Pages 19–21: Manuel Reyes Cárdenas, in *La Prensa*, August 22, 1988; Rafael Ortíz, to Martha Harnecker, *Unidad que multiplica: Entrevista a dirigentes máximos de la Unión Camilista–Ejército de Liberación Nacional*, Quito, 1988, p. 152; Iván Marino Ospina, to Lara, p. 165; Bateman Cayón, to Lara, p. 183; Felipe Martínez, to Harnecker, p. 77; "Pacho," to Behar, p. 284.

Pages 42–45: *El Siglo*, June 28, 1988; *El Tiempo*, June 28, 1988; *El Espectador*, June 30, 1988; *El Tiempo*, June 30, 1988; *Daily Progress*, July 3, 1988; *Houston Chronicle*, July 3, 1988; *Houston Chronicle*, July 3, 1988; *Houston Chronicle*, July 5, 1988; *Houston Post*, July 17, 1988.

Pages 54–56: Bernardo Herrera, in *El Tiempo*, October 16, 1988; Enrique Santos Calderón, in *El Tiempo*, September 18, 1988; *La Prensa*, September 2, 1988; *El Tiempo*, August 27, 1988; *El Tiempo*, September 27, 1988; *El Tiempo*, October 16, 1988; *La Prensa*, August 26, 1988; *La Prensa*, October 4, 1988; Roberto Mutis, to Behar, pp. 263–264.

Pages 59–60: *La Prensa*, October 20, 1988; Report of the Commission for the Study of the Violence, *Colombia: Violencia y Democracia*, Comisión de Estudios Sobre la Violencia, Informe presentado al Ministerio de Gobierno, Bogotá,

234

1988, pp. 196, 197; Ortíz to Harnecker, p. 37; César Gaviria, in *Semana,* May 17, 1988, p. 33.

Pages 68–70: *La Prensa,* September 1, 1988; *La Prensa,* September 7, 1988; Howard Kohn, "Company Town," in *Rolling Stone,* April 6, 1986, p. 72; Santos Calderón, in *El Tiempo,* September 18, 1988; Alan Weisman, "Dangerous Days in the Macarena," in *New York Times Magazine,* April 23, 1989, p. 44; Anonymous landowner, in *Semana,* May 17, 1988, p. 33.

Pages 90–91: Street graffiti, on the walls of the author's high school; Santos Calderón, in *El Tiempo,* September 22, 1988; *La Prensa,* October 2, 1988; Roger Garfitt, "Notes from Abroad: Bogotá, Colombia," in *Granta,* 29, Winter 1989, p. 251; Street graffiti, seen in many places and a well-known saying as well.

Pages 102–103: Santos Calderón, in *El Tiempo,* March 17, 1988; José Francisco Jattín, in *La Prensa,* October 5, 1988; *La Prensa,* October 5, 1988; María Teresa Herrán, *¿La sociedad de la mentira?,* Bogotá, 1986, pp. 183–84.

Pages 129–131: Roger Garfitt, p. 247; *El Espectador,* September 28, 1988; *La Prensa,* September 27, 1988; *El Tiempo,* September 23, 1988; *El Tiempo,* October 5, 1988.

Pages 145–148: Virgilio Barco, in *El Tiempo,* September 2, 1988; Darío Castrillón, in *El Tiempo,* September 3, 1988; Bernado Jaramillo Ossa, in *El Tiempo,* September 3, 1988; Simón Bolívar Guerrilla Coordinator, in *La Prensa,* September 13, 1988 (the document was signed on September 6, 1988); *La Prensa,* October 6, 1988; *La Prensa,* October 5, 1988; *El Espectador,* September 22, 1988; *Semana,* December 13, 1988, p. 27.

Pages 154–158: Tirofijo, to Alape, p. 55; Fayad, to Lara, pp. 57–58; Tirofijo, to Alape, p. 50; Antonio Navarro Wolff, to Lara, p. 247; Ospina, to Lara, p. 240; Bateman Cayón, to Lara, pp. 79–80; Tirofijo, to Alape, p. 91.

Pages 182–184: *El Espectador,* October 4, 1988; Salomón Kalmanówitz, in *El Espectador,* October 2, 1988; Rubén Jaramillo, in *El Tiempo,* August 14, 1988; Weisman, p. 46; Kohn, p. 68; Carlos Gutiérrez, in *El Tiempo,* August 14, 1988; Francisco de Roux, in *El Espectador,* October 2, 1988; *El Espectador,* September 9, 1988; Santiago Mutis, in *La Prensa,* October 5, 1988.

Pages 207–288: *El Tiempo,* October 16, 1988; *La Prensa,* September 8, 1988; *El Tiempo,* October 16, 1988; *El Tiempo,* October 4, 1988; *El Tiempo,* October 16, 1988.

Pages 221–223: Martha Lucía Uribe, in *Semana,* December 13, p. 80; Report of the Commission, pp. 18, 27, 18, 170; *La Prensa,* October 5, 1988; Antonio Caballero, in *Semana,* November 1, 1988, p. 32; Guillermo Sánchez Medina, in *Semana,* December 13, 1988, p. 80; Tina Rosenberg, "Murder City," in *The Atlantic,* November, 1988, p. 22.

Page 224: *El Tiempo,* May 29, 1989.

ACKNOWLEDGMENTS

This book did not start out in its present form. At first I attempted to construct chapters from the sources available to me, including my own daily notes and many hundreds of newspaper clippings. I had four chapters in mind. The first would offer a historical background of Colombia. The second was to be a history of the guerrilla movement. The third would recount the contemporary scene in Colombia at the time of the kidnapping, and the last chapter would tell the story of the kidnapping of Jake Gambini. And I intended to write a brief introduction and a conclusion.

This was the only way that I could think of telling the story, for as a historian I have been trained to write in chapters. After a long while I discovered them to be bulky contraptions inhibiting the active emergence of diverse voices. Once I was inside the chapters, I found it difficult to get others to speak for themselves. My hand in the construction of the text was turning out to be too heavy. While Jake was speaking for himself in Chapter 4, I was speaking for the guerrillas and for everyone else in the rest of the book and in "his" chapter as well. The disparity between our personal drama and my inevitably academic treatment of the guerrillas and others in Colombia kept growing larger. This was turning out to be our story, with Colombia and the guerrillas as a distant and often even convenient background. Neither Jake Gambini nor I wanted it so.

I slowly let go of my chapters and found the form in which these events are told. Still entirely responsible for the way this book is constructed, I hope also to have given the diverse actors some level of parity and independence. If I have made greater efforts with the voices of the guerrillas than with those of the government it is mainly because the guerrillas are larger actors in this story and because I feel that they are the more difficult ones to understand. Perhaps, also, I sympathize with them more, even to this day, than I do with the more mainstream actors in Colombia.

Letting go of parts of the emerging text, I found myself becoming immersed in the personal style that I had tried to avoid. My role at the beginning was to provide a historical context for the kidnapping and to round out the story by letting readers know about events that had transpired in the past and those that were taking place in Bogotá, Houston, and Charlottesville during the time that Jake Gambini was taken away. As the chapters fell away, my daily notes and the newspaper clippings came to the fore.

I have composed Jake's story and mine and perhaps provided an entry into the world of the guerrillas and into Colombia. Jake's voice and mine diverge strongly from those of others. I trust that we have not drowned them out, for if we have, I will simply have replicated the silences and the misunderstandings that Tirofijo bemoans in the epigraph with which this book begins.

I feel deeply and personally grateful to those who stood by me as I struggled with the many voices in this book. My friends will see their ideas and their suggestions peppered throughout these pages.

I asked Cecilia to read the manuscript more than one time too many. She was right about almost all that was wrong with it, even though it often took me months to agree with her. Fernando Operé and Carrie Douglass asked me one evening why I was trying to write chapters. Michael Leff offered all kinds of suggestions on how to tell the story while we rode our bicycles up and down the hills of Albermarle County, where I felt as far removed from the violence of Colombia. Walter Kelly's unabashed admiration for Jake Gambini's actions and beliefs forced me to keep going. Betsy Respess prodded me into expanding the sidewalks, into saying more about myself than I initially wanted to. William Taylor also did much to get me to place myself more thoroughly into the text. Tina Rosenberg forced me to say more about Colombia and its paths to death and destruction. Alexander Wilde's warm reception to these pages gave me more confidence than he can know. Melvyn Leffler offered me his continual personal support and encouragement from the moment I returned to Charlottesville from Colombia in November of 1988 to the day I finished writing. And the last to read this work before its publication is a sage at the University of Virginia. Bernard Mayes gave me the final go-ahead.

I am grateful to Bruce Fretts, Gene Bell-Villada, David Schnyer, Maria Doyle, Claude Dussaud, Relling Westfall, Marco Palacios, David Bushnell, Gary Allinson, Edward Ayers, Paul Gaston, Doug Day, Gordon Stewart, Davíd Carrasco, Jorge Secada, Mark Edmundson, Ben Bennett, and Hayley Froysland for reading all or parts of the text at various stages and offering telling comments. Fred Damon, George Mentore, and Susan McKinnon invited me to the Anthropology Department at the University of Virginia to talk about these events, obliging me to think in unaccustomed ways about them. And Carl Trindle and his undergraduate students in a reading seminar in our Monroe Hill Residential College told me where I was not making myself understood.

Two anonymous reviewers of this text offered valuable critical perspectives, which I have attempted to satisfy. Jan Kristiansson helped me with the informal language of the various voices in this book, and especially with my own. Luther Wilson, Jody Berman, Stephen Adams, and all the members of the fine staff at the University Press of Colorado took greater care with these pages than I could have hoped to expect.

We express our thanks once again to all those who helped us get through the events described in these pages.